something in the water

something in the water

HOW SKIBBEREEN ROWING CLUB CONQUERED THE WORLD

KIERAN McCARTHY

MERCIER PRESS

MERCIER PRESS

Cork

www.mercierpress.ie

ISBN: 978 1 78117 753 2

A CIP record for this title is available from the British Library.

Printed and bound in the EU.

contents

TO ALL THOSE ROWERS WHO HAVE PICKED UP AN OAR
FOR SKIBBEREEN ROWING CLUB AND WHO HAVE PROVED
THERE'S NO HARM IN BEING A LITTLE BIT CRAZY.

prologue

Paul O'Donovan couldn't see a clear path through the crowd. Everyone wanted a selfie or a handshake or a quick word. He needed to get from the far side of the banquet hall in the Celtic Ross Hotel in Rosscarbery to the Warren Suite on the opposite side of the building. He had to negotiate the hall, the bar, the reception and the stairs. It was a walk that should have only taken ninety seconds; instead, thirty minutes later, he was only halfway there.

Paul had tried to keep a low profile at the annual West Cork Sports Star Awards on Saturday night, 19 January 2019. He's not one to seek the light. But as soon as he got off his seat, fans were drawn to him. He is big news, after all. A genuine sports superstar. Internationally recognised. Incredibly talented and driven. One half of the O'Donovan brothers, who had won Ireland's first-ever Olympic Games rowing medal in 2016. The local lads who had transformed rowing in Ireland.

These two brothers from Lisheen, just outside the small town of Skibbereen in West Cork, caught the national spotlight in their heavily blistered hands and shone it directly onto one of the world's toughest and most demanding sports. They are the best thing that has ever happened to Irish rowing.

Paul's brother, Gary, had been forced to miss the local sports awards. He was training in New Zealand ahead of the 2019 season. So Paul flew their flag at the awards bash. Still, it had been a rush to get there. Earlier that day he had set a national record at the 2019 Irish Indoor Rowing

Championships in Limerick. Another medal for the collection of the twenty-four-year-old, a young man who is already a four-time world champion and is rightly hailed as Ireland's greatest-ever rower.

Before he left the banquet hall, the Drinagh Rangers soccer team, winners of the West Cork Sports Team of the Year Award, wanted a photo with Paul. Meeting him made their night. Fifty-two-year-old Drinagh goalkeeper Rob Oldham jumped in for a selfie to show his daughter at home, as she is a huge O'Donovan brothers' fan. A group of local road bowlers stopped in the middle of posing for a photo and insisted Paul join them. He did. Good man, Paul. Well done, Paul. Great stuff, Paul. Legend, Paul.

This is the life of Gary and Paul O'Donovan. Ireland's greatest rowers. West Cork's greatest-ever sportsmen. Skibbereen Rowing Club's best of all time. Lisheen's two boys who are the talk of world rowing.

But they are only two pieces of a bigger jigsaw.

***

A couple of years earlier, the evening after the Irish team finished sixth in the medals table at the 2017 European Rowing Championships in the Czech Republic, Paul grabbed the microphone at the homecoming event at Church Cross, a few miles outside of Skibbereen. He stood on a makeshift stage. Behind him hung a freshly printed twelve-foot-wide poster from the Ilen Rovers GAA clubhouse. In big, bold white letters, it shouted 'The Magnificent Seven'. On it was a photo snapped in the sweltering heat of Račice of the heroes and their medals.

Skibbereen Rowing Club had supplied the entire Rowing Ireland national team at the Europeans. All five medalled. Paul and Gary won silver in the lightweight men's double sculls. Mark O'Donovan and Shane O'Driscoll surged to gold in the lightweight men's pair. Denise Walsh rowed to silver in the lightweight women's single sculls.

Dominic Casey was their coach. The mastermind behind it all. He's one of this magnificent seven.

Only Italy, Romania, the Czech Republic, Germany and Poland won more medals than the Skibbereen team at those championships. Entire countries against a club with less than 100 members.

The poster also included a headshot of Aoife Casey, Dominic's daughter, who a week earlier had taken silver in the Ireland women's double at the European Junior Rowing Championships in Germany. It was the first time Ireland had ever medalled in this competition. More history.

Six of the seven were at Church Cross, Denise the only absentee. Paul, relaxed in a grey tracksuit and black top, took centre stage. Behind him Gary had a tricolour draped around his neck. Mark, Shane, Dominic and Aoife all stood in line. This was an intimate crowd. Paul knew them all. Family, friends, neighbours. Time to have some fun.

'It's fantastic to see the crowd out again tonight for this celebration of rowing in Lisheen and Aughadown and Skibbereen and Ireland, of course – but that's just Skibbereen again,' Paul quipped.

It drew a huge roar of approval from the home crowd under the dull grey sky.

This remarkable rowing club in a country town in West Cork, a club founded by a fisherman, a carpenter and a butcher in 1970, is tucked away from bright lights and fast cars in a small pocket of rural Ireland, but now punches well above its weight on the national and international stage.

This club creates Olympians, with five Olympic rowers since 2000.

It moulded Ireland's first-ever Olympic rowing medals at the 2016 Games in Rio. It shaped five world rowing champions inside four magnificent years between 2016 and 2019: Gary, Paul, Shane, Mark and Fintan McCarthy. Over 100 club members have represented Ireland on the international stage since 1976. The club has transformed Irish rowing, raising standards to new heights and making the world sit up and take notice.

Its clubhouse is built on the muddy banks of a farmer's field. It once used a dishwasher as a filing cabinet. Its main double door has splintered glass panels held together by strips of red insulation tape. Second-hand weights in a gym with no windows have been cut from sheets of metal. In other words, Skibbereen Rowing Club doesn't fit the normal profile of a rowing club. It's neither upper class nor snobbish. It's rough around the edges. This is a working-class club built on a foundation of simplicity, desire and, most importantly, its people. There's nothing fancy here. They rail against the rowing stereotype that the sport belongs to those up there who look down on the rest. This is a culture clash: the country folk against the privileged.

From rags have come magnificent riches. International winners. More national titles than any other club. Skibbereen is a town reborn because of its rowing club – a town which grasped the attention of a nation in the summer of 2016 and has held it ever since.

The club itself is shrouded in mystique and a secrecy that has never been about its physical structures but always about its people. Driven. Dedicated. Passionate. Half-mad.

They've broken down rowing, one of the toughest of all Olympic sports, to its basics. Get from A to B as fast as you can. Don't over-complicate it. Now they do it better than anyone else.

This is a country club from the back of beyond that has conquered the world, a club that defies logic and has changed an entire sport. It is the greatest Irish sports story of our time.

There really is something in the water in Skibbereen.

I
THE ROAD TO RIO

1

the ilen

John Whooley stood at the water's edge, where the land gave way to another world, a utopian existence where it was simply rower, boat and river. He had stood here before, thousands of times, and always followed the same ritual. He looked to the sky, where, in this case, the clouds sat sullen. There was a faint outline of the sun behind them, a lowering grey shadow waiting for its chance to shine. The seagulls were in, which meant it must be rough to his left, the west, where the Ilen River introduced itself to the Atlantic Ocean.

The Ilen is the playground for Skibbereen Rowing Club, its boat-house and clubhouse sitting behind John on the riverbank. Just metres separate these structures from the river.

The Ilen had been home to fishermen for generations before the rowing club was formed in 1970, but as the fishing died away it was the rowers who reinvented the Ilen. They have it to themselves now, a ten-kilometre stretch from the clubhouse without having to stop. It's the envy of every other rowing club in the country. Every year 7,000 boats are launched by the club onto the river.

John had it almost to himself on this October evening in 2007. There were four young bucks, early teens, getting ready to go out in a quad scull. They were busy doing their own thing.

The Ilen was in a good mood – not too choppy, not lazy either, but quite eager. The water rushed excitedly against his wellies, waiting to play. Its best time is an hour before high tide; that's when it's at its calmest as there's less current and flow on it.

The wind was in impish form too. It blew from the south-west, racing in off the Atlantic. On its worst days it bullied rowers, daring them to take it on. However, the rowers never shirk a challenge. The wind was simply another competitor to beat and it could be like this on race day. Saying that, when it's in a real mood, they know better. It's not worth the hassle on those days. But this evening, with the nights shortening and the temperature dropping, it was calm.

John knew the signs were good. Most of the time he rowed downriver towards Baltimore, going with the current. Other days, depending on the strength of the wind and its direction, the height of the waves, the tide, the weather and the sunlight, he would row upriver, towards Skibbereen town, for its calm and sheltered water. On those other days, when the weather gods played spoilsport, he would stay on land and take out his frustrations on the rowing machine. This evening, though, he would point his boat west.

He headed out on the water in his single scull, a boat designed for one person. This was his familiar Filippi, white with its distinctive blue stripe, which he had bought two years earlier for just under €5,000. It was good value. John and two other Skibb rowers, Richard Coakley and Kenneth McCarthy, bought one boat each in a package deal that Richard organised after competing internationally. This was the first single John had owned. His pride and joy.

A heron across the water stared straight at him, waiting to see what John did next. The bleating of the sheep in Carey's farm on the far side of the river didn't stir the heron. Neither did the odd car passing on the road behind it. Instead the heron eyeballed John. It wasn't keen on sharing the Ilen today. But it knew the signs, so it ultimately spread its wings and moved on.

John had been looking forward to getting back out on the water. By day he worked locally at O'Donovan's boatyard whenever they needed him – the recession had cost him his job as a CAD & Design Technician in Galway in early 2007 – and in years to come he'd retrain to be a maths and physical education teacher, but on the Ilen he was a rower. Even better, a Skibbereen rower. That's a badge of honour. It means something.

He lived on the opposite side of town, a short drive from the clubhouse, but for these next eighty minutes he would be in a different world. He quickly ran through his checklist: hat, leggings, enough layers of clothes to stay warm, shades, water bottle. He was good to go.

His bare hands felt the slightest chill in the air. It wouldn't be long before the fading sun set behind Mount Gabriel in the distance and took a large splash of what little heat there was with it. His right hand gripped both oars, locked into their gates, to keep him balanced as he set about launching his boat on the river. He sat on the sliding seat. His left hand steadied the boat. One leg in, the other out, coiled to push the boat away from the slipway. He was almost free from the land. He used his right oar, as well as his free leg, to gently push his boat into the water. It looked easy now, but had taken plenty of practice in the early days.

Soon he was in deep enough. He was free. It was just him, his boat and the water. Wellies off. Feet into their straps. All set. A quick look backwards opened up a view of the Ilen that stretched for 800 metres. There was no one else there. He was pointed in the right direction and he had it to himself – for now, at least.

The rowers' code says that your right blade should always be closest to the bank. That's the simple rule to remember. A handwritten sign on a door in the clubhouse carries other rules:

You must have lights at all times on your boat.
Do not launch without lights.
Always paddle in groups and not alone.
Down – clubhouse side. Back – Schull road side.
Always stay off the centre of the river.

John was experienced enough to go alone. Soon, he was warmed up, the half slide of his seat gone to full slide as his hands felt the oars connect with the Ilen. He pulled in, down and away, and slid his seat under him to take another stroke. In. Down. Away. Reach. Slide. This was repeated, stroke after stroke after stroke. It's a delicate balance of power and speed. He was in rhythm and conducting his own one-man orchestra. He would take over 1,600 strokes during this training piece. Practice makes perfect in rowing. It's all about mileage and building endurance.

He was in the zone now, fully concentrating. The boat glided along the water. From a distance, rowing looks deceptively effortless and elegantly beautiful, but life in the boat is different. It hurts and burns and hurts some more, pushing the body and mind to their limits. It's a life choice. You commit or you don't. John had committed long ago.

He manoeuvred through the dogleg corners of Newcourt and Oldcourt. The boatyards in Oldcourt were crowded with summer sailing boats, resting for the winter, their masts clanking in the wind.

He saw them first, in the distance. It was that Junior quad. Then he heard them, whooping and hollering, like Indians in a Western film. He was their cowboy. He shook his head. It was Gary, Paul, Shane and Diarmuid, four little terrors that were causing wreck on the river. He knew them all. They were four different bundles of energy, each more wired than the next, some cheeky, others quiet. But none of them ever rested. They were in secondary school now, in St Fachtna's de la Salle in town. Paul was thirteen, the youngest. The other three were fourteen years old and they were already fearless on the water.

John knew they wanted a race. That's what they did. It was time to teach these pups a lesson, again.

John was twenty-eight years old and one of the club's most experienced oarsmen, part of the Senior-level clan, along with Olympians Eugene Coakley and Timmy Harnedy, Richard Coakley (who was an Olympian in the making) and Kenneth McCarthy. Every weekend, when they were out in their singles, this Junior quad turned up and tried to beat them all. They trained all week for the weekend.

'Old man John,' broke the silence, carrying over the water. It was Gary.

It was time to race, to put them back in their box. All Skibbereen rowers are taught to race. Whether it's a training piece on the Ilen or an Olympic final, they all approach it in the same manner: first home, first past the finish line. First, first, first.

Concentration was key. He drove his legs down faster, keeping his balance, not letting his oars hit the water. One of the earliest lessons taught to him was that friction is wasted energy and leads to a slower boat. Those words came from Dominic Casey, who taught him everything he knew.

It was also Dominic who saw a rower in John when no one else did. This tall, gangly teenager was a late starter in rowing, almost seventeen years old when he was cajoled into a sport that he had no interest in whatsoever. But Dominic spotted that there was raw material to work with.

'One stroke at a time,' he told John, over and over again.

Always one stroke at a time. Stay in the present, John. If you pull a bad stroke, make sure the next one is better.

'You can't control what has happened but what you can control is what you do right now,' Dominic advised.

John took it one stroke at a time from the very start. And he got better and better. Faster than anyone could have ever imagined, apart from Dominic. His progress was startling.

But so too was that of the Junior quad, who at the time were coached by Gary and Paul's father, Teddy O'Donovan.

'Go get those old fellas,' he would tell the four boys, as they almost climbed over each other trying to get into the boat. 'Show them no respect.'

John had his game face on. This could be a race day. The quad was a good distance away still. He just wanted to make one burst, one lunatic minute. He made his move, pushing his burning legs, straining his body. It was the same stroke he had used to win his first National Championship title in the men's Novice coxed four in 1996, less than twelve months after he first picked up an oar. The same stroke that took him to the 1997 World Junior Rowing Championships in Belgium, where he represented Ireland in the Junior men's quad less than two years after he started rowing. The very same stroke earned him a scholarship to the University of California in Berkeley and saw him excel there. That stroke saw John finish fifth in the world in the single at the Under-23 World Rowing Championships in 2000. That stroke served him well.

After his manic minute, he could tell that they were not gaining. Point proven, for now. He moved down from top gear and the prize was a few moments taking in his surrounds. Creagh, Inishbeg, forgotten churches and old landlord houses, a glimpse into Ireland's past. This is a stunning backdrop for the rowers, a river with a variety of currents that prepare them for all conditions at regattas. It's a setting straight from a novel.

The river smelled different to John at this point, the earthy smell now salty. The Atlantic was closer. He heard it in the distance. The water looked and felt different. He was near the end of the river now, not too far from Sherkin Island, so it was time to turn around and head for home.

John took his time and let the quad catch up.

'Take it easy, lads,' he snapped, 'it's getting dark so quit the messing.'

They took absolutely no notice. Diarmuid just laughed.

'We'll race you back.'

He let them off, as the boats turned for home.

Soon, heading back up the river, he caught a glimpse of Dominic's house to his right. He was only in there a couple of years at this stage, but this beautiful, stone-clad, two-storey building perched on a hill in Ardralla that overlooked the Ilen from the north side was already the watchtower that cast its eye over the river. It has a magnificent view from Dominic's open-plan kitchen, sitting room and the glass-windowed conservatory that wraps around the far end of the house. They are all vantage points offering a different angle, upriver towards O'Donovan's boatyard at Oldcourt where he worked, downriver towards Inishbeg, an island, and directly across the river, where Lough Hyne hill rises in the distance. If a boat moves on the Ilen, Dominic knows who is in it, what they are doing and how well they are doing it.

He has binoculars upstairs and downstairs. And a megaphone too – his trusty messenger that has gotten wet more times than some boats. If he spots a boat on the wrong side of the river, they will hear about it. Or if he has advice, he will offer it too. He never switches off. Ever. He either stands on the picnic bench outside the front of the house or appears out through a gap in their hedge. Dominic, his megaphone and his words of wisdom.

There were plans to trim the hedge at one point but his wife, Eleanor, prefers nature's own look, no straight lines, so Dominic let it grow. It was over six-foot high now, as John passed it, the perfect camouflage to hide Dominic until rowers heard his voice bounce across the river.

Luck would have it, too, that his home is in line with 'the first slip', that is the starting point for Skibbereen rowers' 'pieces', which are training races. From this point the river runs straight for almost three kilometres down to Inishbeg.

But this evening there was no megaphone. There were lights on in the house, but there was no Dominic to be seen or heard. That meant he was at the clubhouse, making sure every boat that went out had come back in.

The wind was at John's stern now. This spin home would be faster, as he was on a speed-assisted tide. Daylight slowly fading, he rowed hard but steady, wanting to make sure that his time back to the clubhouse was minutes faster than the first half of the training spin. Stroke after stroke after stroke repeated. Before he knew it, and with a quick glance behind, he caught sight of the distant lights of the clubhouse as he rounded Newcourt corner. The Junior quad had already pulled in. Good, they're home, he thought. Not long for him to go now. A look at his watch showed his time was quick as he eased his way into the slip. Good job. Good row.

Gary, Paul, Diarmuid and Shane were cleaning the quad. Dominic was there, all right, checking in. So was Teddy, their coach, who sensed something about his two boys. They were catching up with the Seniors all the time. And they were always hungry for their next feed of rowing.

Finished, John lifted his boat out of the water and around to the side of the boathouse. Then he rested it upside down on waiting stands, washed it with soapy water and rinsed it off with the hose until it was sparkling again. Next he carried it over his head into the boathouse and perched it in its familiar spot, inside the door to his left, on the rack closest to the water. This is where the Senior rowers keep their boats, closest to the doors. Junior rowers' boats go to the back of the boathouse. You earn your spurs here, and the little perks that come with it.

'We got you this evening, John; we were in first,' Gary laughed, those wild eyes darting in John's direction.

He smiled back. Tomorrow was another day.

2

two boys

Gary O'Donovan announced to the room that he was going to get the hatchet. He was five years old. Paul was four and quite content on his bouncing hopper ball, holding it by the ears as he bounced away. But Gary wanted it. So the hatchet was required.

There was a usual sequence to their rows: Gary picked on Paul until Paul got cross enough to retaliate and then Gary would run.

Their second cousins from Dublin were visiting on this occasion, down in West Cork for the weekend. Two girls and a boy, a couple of years older than Gary and Paul. They didn't know their Lisheen relations too well. They were all in the sitting room when this fight broke out.

Gary shot out the door to hunt down the hatchet, but Paul stayed bouncing, while their mam, Trish, just shook her head. The cousins sat there, shocked, not knowing what was going to happen next. They didn't know if Gary was going to return with the hatchet in order to chase Paul, or to burst the bouncing ball.

Five minutes later, the brothers were both outside in the front garden, swinging off the palm trees to the side of the house. They had buried the hatchet, so to speak, and were best buddies again.

***

In the summer of 2002, with Gary and Paul now nine and eight, their father, Teddy, surrendered to their constant badgering to take them out on the Ilen for the first time. He waited until he was sure they were hardy and strong enough.

They'd already travelled throughout the country with him to regattas and so it was clear that they had the rowing bug. In those early days, when he headed off to Fermoy, Limerick, whatever destination held a regatta, he would only take one at a time, as the two live wires together were too much of a handful – barrels of endless energy needing four eyes on them at all times.

But the interest in rowing was undoubtedly there, passed down from Teddy. He is the reason they row. The water is in his blood. His home in Lisheen isn't far from the water. His mother's people were fishermen. His grandfather and grand-uncle had boats. Teddy worked in a boatyard, he rowed and he coached. So it was no surprise that his boys were drawn to the water.

That summer Teddy realised that, though they were young and mad, they were ready. Still, he had some concerns: 'If you take a young fella out in the middle of a football pitch and he gets a thump or a fall, you can pick him up in your arms. But when you are dealing with the water there is far more responsibility because if you go out, you have to get back,' Teddy says.

The Sunday after the Irish Rowing Championships in July was the big day. Teddy milked the cows on his small dairy farm in Lisheen, numbers usually in the mid-twenties, sometimes hitting fifty. He then made the short journey back home to the small, three-bedroom bungalow that he'd built and shouted down the hall to Gary and Paul to get up. Practically before he'd finished his sentence they were sitting in the car, beeping the horn.

Ten minutes later they arrived at the rowing club. They were going to use the cox training boat, stable and ideal for beginners. Teddy caught one end of it and most of the weight, though Gary and Paul did put their arms under the other end. Together, the three of them carried it to the water. It was pointed upriver. Teddy had always been taught to go against the flow with beginners. Keep them pounding away until they get tired, then turn around and they get home faster.

The tide was low. They hopped in. This was it, their first row. Competitive as always, they almost tried to race each other in the boat, but they settled down fast. They didn't need to be told how to row. They knew. They'd travelled enough with Teddy. After a small bit of nursing, soon they were rowing loops around the gravel bank that shows up at low tide right outside the clubhouse. Two natural-born rowers, Teddy thought.

Every Sunday morning from then on, for the rest of the summer and into the winter, the three of them went out on the Ilen. They got better and better and better.

Well before their first row, Gary and Paul already had their own rigger jiggers, the spanner that all rowers use. It is ten millimetres at one end, thirteen millimetres at the other, and it can look after every nut on a boat. Teddy had given them one each. Gary's was spray-painted red on the thirteen millimetre end, Paul's on the ten millimetres side, with Paul protesting that Gary got the bigger end painted because he was older. Already, he didn't like being second. But he wouldn't stay there for long.

Together they were a formidable team. They could rig a boat faster than any adult and there wouldn't be a nut or a washer lost. They had the knack.

They were new to rowing but already obsessive, and Teddy wanted them at the club when an Olympic gold medallist came calling in

October 2002. Great British rower Fred Scarlett was in West Cork for a private function, and was a friend of Arthur and Lydia Little, who knew him through their time at Oxford University in England. Arthur's family owned The Eldon Hotel in the middle of town. The Eldon was Skibbereen Rowing Club's sponsor at the time, so they organised for Fred to visit the club, have a chat with its members and bring the prized gold medal that he had won with the British Senior men's eight at the 2000 Olympic Games in Sydney. This was big news for the club. Fred's visit even made the local newspaper.

On a dull, grey day, that gold medal glistened. The contrast couldn't have been any greater: a prestigious Olympic gold at this small, rural club that begged, borrowed and stole (figuratively) in order to survive.

Teddy's two were mesmerised by the gold. Dressed in Republic of Ireland soccer gear – Gary in a grey Irish jersey and tracksuit, Paul in a white Irish polo shirt and matching white shorts – they stood either side of Fred at the entrance to the clubhouse and had their photo taken. Teddy stood beside Paul, his arm on his back. His sons, for once, looked shy. They were lost for words.

Paul wore Fred's gold medal around his neck. It was his first time touching an Olympic medal. It felt heavy. But he wanted one. Gary too.

'It shouldn't really have resonated with them so much, but it did,' Teddy says. 'From that day on, they always believed they were going to go to the Olympics. Nothing was going to stop them.'

The boys were convinced. They made no secret of their desire to win an Olympic rowing medal. They told whoever listened: family, friends, club members, even their teachers at Lisheen National School.

It was Teddy who saw their potential and drive first. He juggled being their coach with being their father. He lit the fuse and watched it explode as they developed on the Ilen. They were competitive on and off the water. At home, he put up goalposts in the garden, in front of which they would kick ten different shades of shite out of each other, then run into the kitchen – Gary straight to the fruit, Paul to the biscuits – scoff down the food and head off out again, running each other into the ground.

On the water they wanted to race. Everything was a race. They'd race Kenneth McCarthy and John Whooley, the club's Olympians Eugene and Richard Coakley and Timmy Harnedy, women's crews. The boat they were against didn't matter, but winning did. Others went for a paddle, they went for the challenge and to race.

Teddy has often wondered where that fiery competitive edge comes from. He never had that drive himself. He needed to be pushed. But his boys were different. Rowing suited them. They were built for endurance and power. They have Teddy's broad shoulders and narrow hips, big ribcages too. Their bodies responded to rowing.

Gary was a class ahead of Paul in school. There are sixteen months between them, but they have always been stuck together. They're two very different personalities. Gary's more forward and lively, and Paul's the quieter, reserved one, but they have each other's backs. Trish remembers trying to make them more independent of one another at a young age. But when Gary was sent to playschool, Paul was outside crying to go in to him and Gary was inside crying to come back out.

In later years, the gang did swell with the addition of two more boys from the parish. Diarmuid O'Driscoll, living a two-minute drive away, was in Gary's class and he was roped in. Soon Shane O'Driscoll, from just over the road and also in their class, joined their ranks. These were the four that formed the quad scull, four people with two oars each. That's sculling. They were like four brothers. They've always had a special bond. Still do.

It was a quad that gave Teddy his proudest moment. It was the 2008 Home Internationals at Cardiff Bay that July, an annual competition between Irish, English, Scottish and Welsh rowers that, for some, is the first step towards greater things on the international scene.

Gary, Shane and Paul were in the Irish quad with Waterford rower Barrick Parker. This was their first time representing Ireland. They were kids. Paul had just turned fourteen the previous April. Gary and Shane were only a year older. They were up against Under–18s. That was the challenge.

The course was shorter than the normal 2,000 metres. The water was choppy. Teddy's tactics were simple: fast start, settle down, then go hammer and tongs to the end line. It worked.

Gary and Paul's mother, Trish, was there too, roaring on her boys as they beat England into second. She was frightened they'd stop short of the finishing line, like other crews had accidentally done in some of the races beforehand. But they didn't. They won gold.

It was on the flight home from Cardiff that Trish realised she needed to start saving. For years, Gary and Paul had told her that they were going to go to the Olympics. What she saw in Cardiff made her a believer too. She went straight from the plane to Skibbereen Credit Union and started filling out cards with €2 saving stamps, planning for an Olympics.

Both Trish and Teddy, while separated for years, had the feeling that their two would achieve great things.

That Home International success sparked the first celebratory bonfire in their honour at Kilkilleen Cross, in between Gary and Paul's home and Shane's. It was soon to become something of a local tradition.

***

There's a field that separates Gary and Paul's home from Shane O'Driscoll's. It's the shortcut between their houses. But in rowing in September 2014 very little separated Gary and Shane in the trials to win a seat in the Irish men's lightweight double, while Paul was the fastest and led the way.

By now Paul stood out. He was in a different league to the rest. When he was fifteen years old he was Irish Junior single sculls champion – that's an Under–18 grade. That created a stir. He's a freak of nature. The exception to the rule who is better than everyone else. He proved it over and over again. He was always faster than Gary. And still is. There's no shame in that because he's faster than everyone else too.

On the way up Shane was also faster than Gary. But by 2014 their roles had reversed. Paul was fastest in the trial, as expected. Gary was second. Shane, third. Gary had stepped up, making the jump to elite level. Paul and Gary formed the Irish double because they were quicker than everyone else. It just so happens that they're brothers. It helps, of course, that they blend in nicely together, have similar styles and the same body composition. Also, having those years of rowing together means they both instinctively know what the other is thinking in the boat. It's telepathy. They complement each other too. Gary has the technique and Paul has the power.

As 2015 began, the world outside Lisheen and Skibbereen Rowing Club didn't know who Gary and Paul were. Slowly that changed. Fifth place at the European Rowing Championships was followed by fourteenth at World Rowing Cup I in Lucerne, before the 2015 World Rowing Championships at Aiguebelette-le-Lac in France. They needed a top-eleven finish there to qualify for the 2016 Olympics in Rio de Janeiro. They'd only started training together full-time in May, when they had both finished college exams. Paul was studying physiotherapy in University College Dublin and Gary was a marketing student at Cork Institute of Technology. It wasn't ideal. They were on their own a lot.

By now Dominic was their coach. Teddy had sunk deep foundations, but he had no choice but to pass the baton on to Dominic, with whom he had previously worked, rowed and coached. Gary and Paul wanted Dominic. He's the man behind the success of Skibbereen Rowing Club, after all. Gary and Paul wanted their freedom too. Like all teenagers growing up, they didn't want their dad around them all the time. So, having coached them up to Junior level, including Paul's bronze in the single scull at the 2013 World Under–23 Rowing Championships, Teddy had to step back.

'I'm happy being their father. It probably wouldn't have worked moving on to Senior level because they probably would have had doubts about me. It was getting difficult. It's like a teacher teaching their own,' Teddy admits.

Now Teddy had to shrug his shoulders and get on with it, just like he'd taught Gary and Paul how to act if they ever lost a race. He never really celebrated success or dwelled on a defeat, it was always about the next race.

Being a coach has never left Teddy. He has his own opinions on decisions made, but the fact remained – it was time for someone else to take them on.

Dominic was a part-time coach with Gary and Paul, juggling full-time work at O'Donovan's boatyard at Oldcourt, a few miles outside Skibbereen town, and another full-time job outside of that in running the rowing club. It wasn't ideal. But the early signs were encouraging.

At Aiguebelette, they clinched the eleventh and last Olympic qualification spot. In the B final on the Saturday morning they knew that if they didn't finish last of the six crews, then they were going to

Rio. They came fifth and beat Greece by 0.28 of a second – that was the minuscule difference between glory and failure. It was the big brother who made the difference that day. Gary got them over the line.

Paul was first to realise they'd qualified. Gary waited to see the result flash up on the big screen. When it did, they let rip. They were going to the Olympics, like they had always said they would.

There was another bonfire at Kilkilleen Cross the following Tuesday night. It was even better than the Monday night at Copper Face Jacks in Dublin, when their feet had touched down on Irish soil. There they mingled in the VIP section with the Republic of Ireland international soccer team who'd beaten Georgia 1–0 at the Aviva Stadium earlier.

But Tuesday meant more. They were home in Lisheen.

That week Trish cashed in her saving stamps. She booked nine nights in Rio for August 2016 with her partner, Mick McCabe, and Paul's godmother, Kathleen Kiely.

Her sons were going to be Olympians. She knew what it meant to them. She saw the lives they'd lived by choice in order to realise this dream they'd shared since they were kids. It's a monastic-like dedication, but one they don't look on as a sacrifice. This is a calling that they love. Some love going to the cinema, some love going to a pub on the weekend; Gary and Paul – like the rest of the Skibb rowers – love going training. That's where their friends are.

Trish understood this better than most. She used to ferry them to and from training in her small black Opel Corsa, packed with gear bags in the back and everyone squashed in like sardines in a can. When they got the Internet at home for the first time, Gary and Paul spent hours watching rowing videos from Olympics and World Championships on YouTube. Everything was rowing, rowing, rowing.

Trish had to drag them out to celebrate birthdays, sometimes almost against their will. Gary's twenty-first in late December 2013 had been a timid affair. He didn't want anything. Trish had to mark it somehow. She told him to call in to the West Cork Hotel in town after training for a quick bite to eat. He relented. Finishing up at the club, a session on the rowing machines, he dragged Paul with him. They met Trish and Mick. The four of them ate in the restaurant. As soon as it was over it was straight home and into bed for training in the morning. There wasn't even time for a Guinness in the Corner Bar in town or a stop-off at their local, Minihan's Bar in Lisheen.

Paul's twenty-first in April 2015 was an even smaller gathering. He was studying in Dublin. Trish and Mick drove up there to surprise him. He wasn't overly impressed and took some convincing to go for dinner. Training came first. Like Gary, he eventually relented. But it felt like a chore. The three went out and ate, then he went back to his place and into bed. It was just another day, nothing out of the ordinary.

The life of a rower is a quiet one, by choice and necessity. It is a lonely existence and, insists Dominic, you need three qualities to survive: you must be mentally strong, you must be physically strong and you must train hard.

Gary and Paul tick every box. And so does Dominic.

the secret is out

There's a canvas photo hanging on Dominic's kitchen wall that deserves a few minutes' attention. It was a Christmas gift one year from his wife, Eleanor. She bought it from Charlie Lee, who runs Skibbereen Garden Centre. That's where he also sells some of the photos he takes in his spare time. This particular photo is Charlie's bestseller. Sunday 10 November 2010 is the date it was captured. He didn't go looking for it. He left home that morning destined for Bantry, where his son was involved in a rally. Just on the Ballydehob road outside of town, heading west, he spotted a fleet of Skibb rowers making their way upriver, through the lightly hanging fog, like an armada.

They'll turn, he thought.

By then Charlie had pulled in to the side of the road, quickly changed the lens on the camera and jumped out, just in time to fire off three quick shots as they moved downriver and past where he stood.

Snap. Snap. Snap.

In the photo, the rowers, numbering into their teens, are emerging through the morning fog. Every rower is in sync. All the oars touch the water at the same time. The white house of Liam O'Regan, former editor of *The Southern Star*, the club's local newspaper, in the top left-hand corner adds a sense of location. It was a contemporary-looking house, ahead of its time when it was built in The Abbey. The location is unmistakeably the Ilen River, which has been a central character to Dominic's life from the very start.

His first home was Collatrum, down the river from where he now lives in Ardralla. His father, also Dominic, was a farmer and owned sand boats, first *St Anthony* and then the bigger *St Mary*. He moved all types of cargo from the islands to the mainland. Cattle. Sheep. Gravel. Lime. And lots of sand.

It was a hard slog. Dominic Junior grew up working hard. He knew no other way. Moving sand was particularly back-breaking. They'd set off at half tide in the morning, beach the boat on the island, shovel the sand onto it, wait for the tide to come in to lift the boat, drive upriver and drop the sand off at one of the piers.

That was work. But the water was also for pleasure. He'd watch the local Ardralla crew in the fixed-seat rowing. Regattas all across West Cork on Sundays were social events, family days out. He enjoyed those. At one stage it planted the thought of setting up a Lisheen crew using the Ardralla gig. It stayed an idea. Instead, sliding-seat rowing became his great love, as he set off on his own successful rowing career. Then Eleanor Lane came along.

She is the eldest of three girls, from Townshend Street in Skibbereen, a one-way route that has produced an above-average number of Skibb rowers. There were the MacEoins in No. 49, where Richard Roycroft, himself a rower in the early days, now lives. Of the six MacEoins, five rowed – Eddie, Mairead, Seamus, Gearoid and Rita. Across the way were the O'Briens, and Patricia, Barry and Ger were all involved too. Club Captain Seanie O'Brien was also born on Townshend Street and his father ran a filling station there. Seanie's children, David and Kate, went on to row with the club.

Next door to Seanie was T. J. Ryan, who joined the club in the 1980s as he chased the attention of a woman there. He lost that race but stayed rowing. These days T. J. is the club's secretary and the country's chief rowing umpire. Across from his house were the O'Donoghues, Triona, Kieran and Avril, all involved in the club at one stage. It was one street but many rowers.

Eleanor started with the club in 1985 and has been involved in rowing ever since. It's where she and Dominic met. Rowing brought them together. She understands him better than anyone else. That's why she didn't mind when a gang of guests went rowing the day after their wedding in 1990. The wedding was on Thursday, and on Friday afternoon celebrations had moved to Baby Hannahs bar on Bridge Street, continuing on from where they had finished at the West Cork Hotel. At Baby Hannahs a group decided to stretch their legs and arms, and clear their heads, on the Ilen. Eleanor saw that as normal. The biggest surprise was that Dominic didn't join them.

'Rowing is number one and that will never change. It's the biggest part of his life. It's in his veins,' she says.

Dominic struck gold with Eleanor. His wife and best friend also loves rowing. That's a huge piece of the jigsaw right there. It's why every summer since they moved to Ardralla in 2006, when Eleanor looks out the kitchen window at home and the lawn is approaching jungle status, she just smiles and accepts it. It's regatta season. The lawn probably won't be cut in the summer. Dominic's too busy.

It's also why, in the summer of 2016, she accepted the fact that he was practically a visitor in his own home. He was spending most of his time away with Gary and Paul ahead of the Olympics in Rio. That was tough because they have a young family. Even their energetic Golden Retriever, Tigger, noticed Dominic wasn't around.

It was more than forty years ago that Dominic started as a rower with the club and went on to become one of the best single scullers in the country. The next step had been to become 'Coach Casey', as he set about raising standards in the club. Then he was handed Gary and Paul at international level. After they qualified for Rio he backed them to come from nowhere and push for a medal. Everyone else found it hard to picture these two making up that many places in less than twelve months. They had qualified eleventh and scraped in, after all, though this meant that they at least had the element of surprise. Dominic spotted in them what Teddy always saw.

'The top half of the B final would be a good achievement,' club secretary T. J. Ryan said after the 2015 Worlds.

Dominic's response: 'A final. A final.'

The irony is that he had been at the club committee meeting a decade earlier that hummed and hawed over whether or not to kick two of that Junior quad out. Gary and Diarmuid faced the chop. The allegation was that they were 'disruptive influences in the club'. The committee debated the pros and cons. The consensus was that these two young lads needed to calm down. Gary and Diarmuid were banned from the club for one week. The punishment was being kept off the water.

Now one of those 'disruptive influences' was on his way to Rio.

***

'Fuck this, I'm out of here.' Gary was ready to jump out of the boat. 'It's not my fucking fault,' he roared.

Paul was even more stubborn. He wasn't taking a step backwards either.

'Get the fuck out so.'

Tired and cranky, they were both having a bad day. It was mid-June

2016 in Poznań and they were training just ahead of the final World Cup regatta of the season. Each year three World Cup regattas are held, all of which are linked, with an overall winner of each boat class crowned at the end of the run. In 2016 the regattas were ideal preparation for the Olympics Games in Rio, which on this day were less than two months away.

In Poznań, the freshly crowned European men's lightweight double sculls champions were halfway down the two-kilometre course and tearing strips off each other. It was windy. The boat wasn't balancing. Neither was it moving well. The more they rowed, the more frustrated they were getting. Gary was blaming Paul. Paul felt it was Gary's fault. The miserable dark clouds hanging overhead matched the mood in the boat.

'Shut the fuck up,' Gary shouted.

The hotel they were staying in was perched near the 1,000-metre mark of the course. Gary hatched a quick plan in the red mist: jump out, swim to the hotel and Paul could fucking row the rest himself.

He took a quick look around, but they were gone well past the halfway mark now. The hotel was shrinking further in the background. He had missed his chance. They stuck it out. The fight ended there. It stayed on the water. It wasn't even mentioned after.

They're two normal brothers. They fight, it's forgotten, they get on with it. And repeat. The difference is that they spend more time together than most brothers and it's in a high-intensity environment. Often just a few feet apart for weeks on end. In the boat. In the same hotel room. In the gym. Eating breakfast, lunch and dinner. They live in each other's pockets. They get frustrated. Fuck this and fuck that.

There was that time too when Gary swung a punch at Paul upstairs in the clubhouse as they jostled for position around a small rotating heater. That was their Junior–16 days. Diarmuid and Shane were there too. That Junior quad again. It was a cold, miserable morning, one of those where you'd roll over in bed and pull the duvet over your head, but they were already after a training spin on the Ilen. They were cold to the bone afterwards and shivering, and there wasn't enough warmth in that heater to share between the four. Gary and Paul got stuck into each other. Gary took a swing. Hit Paul. Hurt his hand. And missed a few days on the water. Gary learned his lesson and stuck to the verbals after that.

They need those outbursts too and being brothers there's no filtering or tip-toeing around feelings. That's not their style, anyway. There's a brutal honesty there that works.

***

The Tuesday after the World Rowing Cup regatta in Poznań, where they finished fourth in the A final on the Sunday, missing out on a medal in their last race before the Olympics, they stood outside the Celtic Ross Hotel in Rosscarbery. They were holding the West Cork Sports Star Monthly Award for May 2016. It was in recognition of their gold success at the European Rowing Championships in Brandenburg, the latest indication that these two were on an upward curve in an Olympic year. The signs were encouraging.

These two realistic Irish medal hopes for the summer's Olympics were now ranked fifth in the world in the men's lightweight double sculls, having been eleventh at the 2015 Worlds. They were freshly crowned European champions, but no one would pick them out in a line-up.

Soon, they'd fly off to Banyoles in northern Spain for a pre-Games training camp, but first they had made the short twenty-minute trip from home in Lisheen to pick up this local sports award.

Trish was there with Mick. Teddy was there too. And a couple of representatives from Skibbereen Rowing Club. It was informal and relaxing. It was time for the official photos that were taken outside, given that it was the summer and Rosscarbery Bay sat in the background. Heads turned and eyes peeked out from the hotel bar to see what the fuss was about. Just as fast, they tucked back into their food and drinks. Nothing, or no one, to see here.

Outside of the circles they moved in, nobody knew who Gary and Paul were. They looked like every other normal young fella their age, not very tall and just that bit leaner. Gary, at twenty-three years old, with the wild, darting eyes, fair hair and a mischievous smile. Paul, just twenty-two, with a darker head of hair. He is the more reserved of the pair, but his mind is always analysing every situation.

There was a shyness to them. A vulnerability that tip-toed on the right side of awkwardness. It was the way they moved when the photographer asked them to pose together on their own with the award. The spotlight was still new to them.

Future Republic of Ireland and Aston Villa midfielder Conor Hourihane, from Bandon, who was then captain of Barnsley FC, was accepting a similar monthly award on the same evening. Here was a professional footballer sharing the same stage with two students juggling college and training and living off funding from Sport Ireland's International Carding Scheme. The week after winning the Europeans, Gary sat his final exams in marketing at Cork IT. These were two different worlds of sporting fame. But within a few months that would all change.

***

'Don't come back in until it's sorted,' Dominic ordered.

They'd been in Rio for almost a week and the boat hadn't travelled well on any of their previous five days on the water at the Lagoa Stadium, home to the rowing regatta at the 2016 Olympics.

It was Saturday now. Their heat was the next day, but the double wasn't where all three of them wanted it to be, even after 8,000 kilometres of training behind them in their Olympic preparation. They checked the boat a few times in the days before. It was fine. But Gary and Paul felt a bit off on the water. It didn't feel right.

They told Dominic. He told them to fix it. They stayed out paddling that day. Eventually they came in and said nothing. Dominic didn't ask them either. He's the coach and one of his big strengths is that he encourages the rower to take control, to take ownership and responsibility. It's important to let the rowers learn how to solve problems on their own. In a race they are on their own, after all. He's on the bank. They need to be able to think for themselves and problem-solve on their own.

The next day was meant to be their Olympic debut, but the weather and wind acted up. The dirty clouds were a reminder of home as the day's action was postponed. They'd have to wait until Monday but took it in their stride. Grand job. Not a bother, they thought. Sure, regattas got cancelled in Ireland all the time.

It was back to the Olympic Village for the evening and Block No. 28, where Team Ireland was based. That was one of thirty-one high-rise buildings that housed over 10,000 athletes during the Games. The seventy-seven-strong Irish team took twenty apartments over the first five floors, with New Zealand above for company. Solid blocks of green, white and gold for the Irish tricolour on the front-facing glass balconies unmistakably marked this as Ireland's home. On the fifth floor, in one of the basic four-bedroom apartments, Gary and Paul shared one room. Filling the other three bedrooms were Dominic, Rowing Ireland High Performance Director Morten Espersen, Athletics Ireland High Performance Director Kevin Ankrom and Rowing Ireland Coach Don McLachlan.

The evening before the rearranged heat was spent in the company of some of the Irish boxers staying on the floor below. They'd a weighing scales Gary and Paul would use. Plus the banter was good. Paddy Barnes, Michael Conlon and Joe Ward were all there and the evening passed quickly.

Ireland's two other rowers at the Games, Claire Lambe and Sinead Jennings, were on the same floor as Gary and Paul. They had a weighing scales too, but the Skibb lads were drawn to the boxers. If there was craic to be had, they were there.

They didn't know it then, but the next day – Monday 8 August 2016 – their lives would change forever.

Back in Skibbereen, it wasn't a typical Monday afternoon in the Corner Bar on Bridge Street. The striking orange double doors of the main bar at the front and the matching orange side door of the back bar opened at 1 p.m. The rowing gang filed in, filling the front bar and the back area.

Owner William O'Brien was behind the bar, taking orders. This is home to a great pint of Carlsberg, with the Murphy's and Guinness also local favourites. A few half-empty pint glasses already dotted the bar's countertop, mostly to help calm the nerves. There was a glass of red wine sitting there too.

The crowd was building nicely. There were tricolour flags, hats and wigs. The local postman, Tony Walsh, was in an Ireland T-shirt, a bargain from Penneys. His day's work was already done. He was also chairman of Skibbereen Rowing Club. And it was the club that packed the bar.

For years this has been the rowing club's regular watering hole, not only because it's the closest bar in town to the rowing club, but also because William and Valerie O'Brien's son and daughter, Mike and Grace, rowed with the club for years, and won National Championship titles. And Mike coached too.

Richard Hosford was there, one of the three founding members of the club. His wife, Susan, was kitted out in her green Rowing Ireland top. The club's first international rower and first National Championship winner, Nuala Lupton, and her husband, Fintan, the club's former secretary, were there. So was Club Captain Seanie O'Brien, registrar Máire Keating, and coaches T. J. Ryan and Richie Keating. Club rowers swelled the numbers: the veteran Kenneth McCarthy, Irish international Denise Walsh, Shelly Dineen, Christine Fitzgerald and the experienced Orla Hayes. And more. And they were excited.

It was getting closer to 1.50 p.m., the start time of the heat, when the anticipation turned to anger: RTÉ weren't showing the heat live. Instead it was broadcasting Paddy Barnes' Olympic bout.

Quick thinking meant that an iPad was sourced. The heat was being streamed live online and so the crowd huddled around the main bar, hundreds of eyes fixed on this small screen propped up on the counter. All backs were turned to the thirty-two-inch TV hanging on the wall, showing Barnes' loss.

Now for the quietness. They knew Gary and Paul needed a top-two finish to go through to the A/B semi-final later in the week.

Slow to get going, they finished strong and pipped the Italians by 0.38 of a second to qualify.

It was their interview with RTÉ afterwards, however, that started a love affair that gripped the country. Skibb rowing's best-kept secret was out. It was time to share their Lisheen lads with the world.

When they were just out of the water and still in their green Ireland singlets, Paul quipped in his thick West Cork brogue that, 'We were almost disappointed we couldn't race yesterday, it would have been a bit of craic,' with Gary adding, 'We're well used to a bit of wind. That kind of thing wouldn't faze us at all.'

It was down to earth, quirky, refreshing and natural. The watching TV audience lapped it up. No clichés and boring run-of-the-mill answers; instead these two entertained by being Gary and Paul, the country boys from Skibbereen Rowing Club.

They thought little of the interview, more annoyed afterwards with themselves that they hadn't warmed down and gone through their recovery properly following the race. They made the decision then that when it came to the semi-final they would look after themselves first, take more control and let RTÉ wait.

Gary's phone started buzzing that night back at the Olympic Village, notification after notification. The more he flicked through Facebook and Twitter, the more posts of Paul and himself were popping up, and the hotter his phone became. They were aware something was going on back home, but in the Olympic bubble they were largely quarantined from the fever, away from TVs and newspapers.

In Skibbereen, Gary and Paul were the talk of the town. More tricolours sprang up. Bunting appeared in shops. The media interest was mushrooming. And the town's rowers were walking that little bit taller. Rowing was putting Skibb on the map.

***

With the typical Rio weather replaced by rain, mist and light winds, a second day's rowing at the Lagoa Stadium was postponed, pushing

Gary and Paul's semi-final back to Thursday. So what, they shrugged.

Six crews would line up in each semi-final. The top three from both races would advance to the A final and the battle for medals. The other six crews would go forward to the B final, where their final positions would be decided.

Gary and Paul's was a loaded semi-final. The French double of Jérémie Azou and Pierre Houin were reigning world champions and favourites for overall gold. The Great British duo of Richard Chambers and Will Fletcher had taken silver at the 2015 World Championships and the American boat was also dangerous. All four had been in the A final at World Rowing Cup II in Lucerne, but with only three to advance someone good was going to miss out. Germany and China were making up the numbers.

In the back of Gary and Paul's mind was the fact that the British boat had been misfiring a bit all year.

Halfway through the race the Skibb duo had moved from fourth, past Great Britain, into third. With their trademark fast finish, a trait in Skibbereen rowers, they stayed there until the end.

Even inside the last 200 metres, when Paul's energy levels dipped, they still had more than enough to hold off the British challenge. For a fleeting moment, Gary, full of energy behind Paul, thought they might even win, with the Americans in sight. Although they finished third in the end, they had the third fastest qualifying time of the six boats and the brothers took massive confidence from their performance because they were only one second off the French and still had more in the tank.

True to their word, they made RTÉ wait afterwards. But it was worth it. Their fan club numbers swelled as the sound bites kept coming.

'We'll get a bit of shteak, the food is fantastic, like you can have shteak for breakfast, lunch and dinner, and spuds if you like,' smiled

Gary in his green Team Ireland T-shirt, white cap and sunglasses, giving two thumbs up to the food at the Olympic Village.

'There's no Kerr pinks, Dominic's going mad,' joked Paul, a nod to Coach Casey's yearning for home delights.

'Strategy? It isn't too complex really, just A to B as fast as you can, close the eyes and pull like a dog,' Paul quipped, igniting a catchphrase that took Ireland by storm.

On the bus back to the Olympic Village, an hour's return journey through Rio, Gary and Paul sat together. They were tired and drained. It had been a long day. Both noticed the increase in media attention on them between their heat and the semi-final. From a few bodies in the mixed zone on Monday, there had been an influx of Irish journalists by Thursday, with even the BBC present.

Something's happening, they thought. Their post-race charm had seduced everyone, the two brothers who finished each other's sentences. But they were still unaware that they were now the Irish story of the Rio Olympics.

Back home the attention kept ratcheting up. The eyes of the nation were now fixed on Skibbereen, its rowing club and the Ilen.

4

rio grande

The view from Trish's kitchen at home in Lisheen, looking out to sea, is a knockout. Jeremy Irons' grand Kilcoe Castle is off in the distance. White Hall Castle is closer again. Horse Island is there too, sitting in the impressive Roaringwater Bay, where the Ilen meets the Atlantic.

Whoosh. Whoosh. Whoosh.

That was the noise coming from the attic.

The year was 2013 and Gary and Paul had recently brought a rowing machine from the club into the house and manoeuvred it up through the attic door that has since been replaced by a temporary wooden stairs. Back then they'd haul themselves up into the attic without a ladder and spend hours up there training.

Whoosh. Whoosh. Whoosh.

The noise reverberated throughout the house. This constant drone. Pull after pull after pull. Hour after hour.

Below the attic door, in the hall and just inside the front door of this pebble-dashed bungalow, one of the two would throw an old bedsheet used for painting on the ground, sit their training exercise bike on top of it, rest a laptop on a chair to watch a movie and pedal away for hours. The sheet soaked up the sweat.

Not one minute was spared. Everything was building towards a moment like Rio and a chance at the greatest prize in their sport.

***

'This is my last dinner before the Olympic final – what will I eat?' Gary asked Paul.

'Sure, whatever you want.'

'But it's my last meal before tomorrow …'

Before he had finished speaking, Gary was already heading towards the Asian section in the dining hall in the Olympic Village, which was the size of two football fields and a fifteen-minute walk from Team Ireland's HQ.

They had the choice of five different buffets: Brazilian, Asian, International, Pasta and Pizza, Halal and Kosher. The beef stir-fry noodles kept Gary coming back for more. The pasta was a let-down.

Gary and Paul had their preparation exact at this stage of the Games, learning each day. They went straight from the ice baths to the air-conditioned dining hall, so moving from the ice to the cold, they came prepared with extra layers. Back to Block No. 28 then and a stop-off at the boxers' apartment.

Rowing Ireland High Performance Director Morten Espersen called a meeting for later in the evening. Him, Gary, Paul and Dominic. Morten is a very straightforward guy. He calls it as he sees it. He knows the sport inside out and is incredibly knowledgeable. He's the man who first asked Dominic to coach Gary and Paul in 2015. It was a part-time role. Dominic was still working in O'Donovan's boatyard. He'd travel up to the National Rowing Centre in the afternoon and the weekends, though Gary and Paul were training a lot themselves too. The drive from Skibbereen to Inniscarra was doable, but it was the thought of the twelve-hour flight-time from Amsterdam to Rio that niggled at Dominic – who doesn't like flying – in the months leading up to the Games.

From the day they qualified to the day they boarded the flight he repeated the same few words: 'If we are going to travel this far away from Ireland then we are going to have to come back with something. I am not going all this way to come back with nothing.'

Now they had a chance to come back with something.

'Don't let them get away from you at the start,' Morten instructed in his Danish accent.

Advice that got Dominic's seal of approval. 'That's good, that's good. Don't let them get away from ye.'

They slept sound that night and were up at 5.20 a.m. the next morning for the bus to the Lagoa Stadium. They stopped in at the boxers' apartment on the way down to use their weighing scales. There was no one there. Everyone was already up and out. There was no time for breakfast at the Village. They wanted to get to the venue.

At the rowing course in the south of the city centre, overlooked by the famous Christ the Redeemer statue, Gary and Paul noticed the build-up was more serious than usual. In the weighing-room there was no chit-chat. The six finalists kept to themselves. There was an air of mutual respect. No one wanted to disrupt anyone else.

The two lads went to sweat down to make sure they were under the weight limit before the official weigh-in. Lightweight men's rowers must be below seventy-two-and-a-half kilogrammes or part of a seventy-kilogramme average.

By now Dominic was already down at the boat. He gave it a wash and a polish. 'Coach's therapy' is what Skibb rowers call Dominic's ritual. It's a superstition he repeats before every big international race and at the Irish Rowing Championships. While some feel polishing a boat causes friction between it and the water, Dominic is in the opposite camp. The boat is cleaner, it will run smoother and feel better.

Plus he likes to polish. Maybe it's his way of dealing with the nerves.

Everything was running bang on time to the timetable they had. It's the same at every regatta. They know who'll be where and at what time. It's the small details. Gary was first down to the boat. Paul was in the bathroom. Dominic spotted instantly that Gary was in the zone. It was the way he spoke and carried himself, the way he clapped his hands and rubbed them together. Gary was ready.

Half an hour before the A final, Gary and Paul sat in the boat, with Dominic beside them. They don't do pep talks. Dominic is a man of few words. He hates media interviews and avoids them when possible. Standing in the background is where he is most comfortable. When Gary and Paul picked up their West Cork Sports Star monthly award in June, he didn't attend the function, preferring to take club Juniors out on the Ilen instead. He speaks in a hurried West Cork accent, a Skibbereen rowing code locals understand but outsiders struggle to make out. It adds to the mystery of the club.

'As tough as nails,' were the last four words Dominic uttered to Gary and Paul, a nod to their upbringing in the rowing club on the Ilen. Only the tough survive there.

***

Trish and Mick were among the first to take their seats in the grandstand on Friday morning, 12 August. There's a picture of the two of them in that moment in their kitchen at home now: sitting in the front row with a sea of empty blue seats behind them. They weren't going to be late for the biggest day of Gary and Paul's lives. To be extra sure that they'd be at all the races on time, they had decided to stay in an apartment within walking distance of the Olympic rowing venue.

Dressed in a white T-shirt, wrapped in a Gary & Paul Ireland flag, with a tricolour hula necklace around her neck and two small tricolours painted on her cheeks, Trish stood out from the crowd. She is small in height but tall in personality, with a contagious smile. She was also the only fan in the entire stadium with a flag on a flag pole. Security was tight at Olympic venues in Rio and no flag poles were allowed. Trish had hatched a plan earlier that summer, however, to get a flag pole in without it being confiscated. In Heatons in Ballincollig, hometown to her mam, Mary Doab, Trish spotted extendable wool dusters. They were plastic and perfect. She bought two and a roll of masking tape. At home Mick sawed off one end on both of them and took the steel rods out. In Rio they fitted into her bag and went undetected when her bag was scanned on entry. Mick took them out once inside the venue, extended both and joined them together with masking tape. Ingenious.

Now, as the final neared, Trish was nervous. So was Teddy, who had come to Rio with his brother David. So was Paul and Gary's best friend, Diarmuid, who made the trip, and former Skibbereen Olympic rower Richard Coakley, who had travelled to Rio from his base in Sydney to support his clubmates. He had a feeling an historic first Irish Olympic rowing medal was coming. Dave O'Brien, another Skibb native, a former rower and son of Club Captain Seanie, had made the trip too. And the number of spectators was swelled by general Ireland fans at the Games.

Just minutes to go now.

***

Skibbereen had gone Olympic crazy by this point. The credit union – the main sponsors of the rowing club – on Main Street had become the unofficial Olympic HQ in town. Hundreds of people crammed in. The credit union branch manager is Donal O'Driscoll. His son, Diarmuid, was in Rio. His wife, Catriona, is principal of Lisheen National School, where Gary and Paul went to school. After internationals abroad they always visit the school with their medals to have a chat with the kids. They give back to their school and they give homework off too. When money was tight for Gary and Paul in the run-up to Rio, and the world didn't know them, it was Donal and Skibbereen Credit Union that presented the lads with a new set of oars – the town looking after their own.

There was a big screen in the banking hall and another in an upstairs room where the club members gathered.

Club secretary T. J. Ryan was one of the last in. That was one of his busier weeks. Between turning hay in his farm in Castlehaven and juggling media duties – he'd stop the tractor in the field and talk to any number of radio stations before getting back to work – he was flat out. Forty minutes before Gary and Paul's final, he'd dropped his last bail of hay into the shed. Wiping the sweat off his forehead, he went straight into Skibb and into the traffic jam clogging up the centre of town. But at least he'd made it in time for the race.

Former Skibb rower – and Olympian – Eugene Coakley was home from London and was upstairs in the credit union too. Another former rower, Ross O'Donovan, was holidaying in Barleycove with his wife and kids, forty-five minutes from town, and so they made the trip in to the credit union. Richard Hosford and his wife Susan, Nuala Lupton and her husband, Fintan, Tony and Mary Walsh, Kenneth McCarthy, Denise Walsh, Orla Hayes and her gang – basically all who rowed and were in Skibb that day were drawn together like magnets.

There was a carnival atmosphere. Skibbereen was alive. This once-proud town that had been the heartbeat of West Cork during the 1970s, the unofficial capital, but had now slipped down the pecking order, overtaken by neighbouring Clonakilty, had its mojo back. This was its own unofficial bank holiday.

Every second person was wearing a green and gold T-shirt emblazoned with some of the catchphrases Gary and Paul had made famous. Rowing club registrar Máire Keating had ordered ninety 'Gary & Paul's Crew' T-shirts on Thursday. They arrived at 1.30 p.m. on the day of the final. They were all gone by 2 p.m.

A samba band set up in the credit union. The atmosphere was building. Hundreds packed in. All around town, from the Corner Bar to Annie May's, locals were glued to the TV.

As an appetiser to the main course, Ireland's Claire Lambe and Sinead Jennings were in the A final of the women's lightweight double sculls, but there was disappointment when they finished sixth. When the TV showed a glimpse of Gary and Paul, the roof almost lifted off the credit union. They'd already attained cult status.

It was time.

Skibbereen held its breath.

***

It was an eerie silence in the dull Rio haze. The Irish double sat at the start line in lane one. The USA were next door in lane two, then it was South Africa, France, Norway, all the way over to Poland in lane six.

This was it. A lifetime of training coming down to the next six minutes.

The quietness was interrupted by a piercing, loud roar from a fan: 'COME ON IRELAND!'

Gary smiled. Not much point shouting now, he thought; we haven't even started.

All six crews waited for the signal to start.

Beep. Go.

Gary and Paul's first two strokes were wobbly. The naked eye wouldn't see that, but they felt it. Two bad strokes. But they settled quickly. 300 metres in, it was the start they'd wanted. They were sticking with the leading boats, doing what Morten had asked.

Gary uttered only two words during the Olympic final. The first was his comment on their start. They were reasonably comfortable and hadn't expended too much energy.

'Good.'

They were in fifth place after 500 metres of the two-kilometre track. At the halfway mark they were still fifth, but the five boats were separated by only one second, with the French ahead.

Now the Skibbereen men started to motor. That raw, agricultural power moulded in Lisheen helping their dad on the farm and strengthened on the Ilen was starting to count. They helped Teddy turn cattle. They picked stones. They fetched shovels and pikes. They rode in his tractor. They were used to grafting. It was time to go to work again.

Paul had his eye on the American double in the next lane. It was the only yellow boat in the final so it stood out. Out in lane one, that was Paul's point of reference. He wanted to be just ahead of the Americans, so that when they came through down the middle, like their form suggested they would, then the Irish double could use them to bring them up onto France. That is what happened.

With 500 metres of the 2,000 remaining, Gary and Paul had surged into second place, though the race was still bunched, with France ahead, Norway in third, then South Africa, the USA and Poland. The race for a medal was on.

In Banyoles, on the pre-Olympic training camp, Gary and Paul would row 1,500-metre pieces. With 200 metres left, Gary would call 'Up' and they would give absolutely everything to the finish line. Up the rate. Up the power. Up the technique. The boat would rise out of the water and the speed would rocket for those last twenty strokes.

In Rio they hadn't used this in practice or in the races, but Gary felt strong. He knew they could win.

'UP.'

He called it a lot earlier than usual. There was still 400 metres to go. Don't ever regret anything, Gary thought, it's time to empty the tank. The boat lifted. Incredibly, they closed up on France. The favourites were clinging onto their lead.

Coming to the line, in those last 100 metres, Gary and Paul's vision and hearing were gone. Holy fuck, they were both feeling it. It was just muscle memory now. Their bodies knew what to do. Keep going. Those strokes they'd pulled millions of times before. They may as well have been on the Ilen in Skibbereen. Two ordinary men in a boat on water doing the extraordinary.

For one brilliant moment gold was a possibility. But the French started to pull away slightly and now Norway were closing in on Ireland. In a desperate final surge, Gary and Paul hit the last two buoys before crossing the line in second place in 6:31.23, 0.53 of a second behind the French and 0.16 of a second ahead of Norway. The tiniest of margins separated gold from bronze.

Everything changed in that moment. Their lives, their legacy and Irish rowing.

The big screen confirmed the news that saw Skibbereen explode: Gary and Paul had won an Olympic silver medal.

It was the country's first-ever Olympic rowing medal. After years of near misses and pain, Ireland had that first rowing medal, and their first of these Games too.

In the middle of the controversy surrounding Olympic Council of Ireland President Pat Hickey, who was knee-deep in an Olympic ticket scandal that cast a dark shadow over Ireland at the Games, two Lisheen boys put sport on the front pages for the right reasons, with the most important result in the history of Irish rowing.

Gary leaned forward out of his seat and wrapped an arm around Paul. No one else mattered right now. It was a reminder of the embrace they shared less than twelve months earlier in Aiguebelette when they qualified for the Olympics by the skin of their teeth, again by just a fraction of a second. Just out of the boat, then, like now, Gary swung his arms around Paul and rested his head on his younger brother's chest. And they stayed there. Brothers.

Back in the boat park Dominic had watched it all unfold on a TV screen. Afterwards, he didn't go down to the presentation or the grandstand to celebrate. His work was done. He preferred it where he was. But he was undoubtedly the third man in the double that day.

In off the water there were immediate media interviews and the medals ceremony, before they finally met their parents, Trish and Teddy, and the rest of their growing support. Hugs, kisses, tears and back-slaps.

Gary wanted the spare Irish flag Trish had brought with her to Brazil. Mother's intuition, she had been convinced they'd medal and so came prepared. It was her flag that they hoisted proudly on top of one of Paul's oars as they performed a lap of honour in front of the grandstand.

'Olé, Olé, Olé.'

'Ireland, Ireland, Ireland.'

The party was just getting started in Rio and at home in Skibbereen.

The credit union had erupted and the entire town shook when Gary and Paul crossed the line in second. The streets flooded with locals celebrating. Champagne flowed upstairs in the credit union. Tears flowed too. T. J. Ryan was sobbing with joy moments before he went on RTÉ's *Liveline* with Joe Duffy. It was pure euphoria, shared across the country, but felt most keenly in Skibbereen.

***

Back at the Olympic Village with their silver medals, and all the interviews finished, including for RTÉ and the *Six One News*, the shattered and worn Gary and Paul showered, changed and headed to the usual Irish meeting point in the dining hall for food. Cork marathon runner Lizzie Lee and the gang around her, mostly athletes, stood up and clapped.

A bunch of Irish athletes had packed into the Irish common room to watch the final earlier. It had been standing room only. A huge cheer erupted when the silver medal was confirmed. Some New Zealand athletes, who shared the same apartment block, rushed in to offer their congratulations at Ireland's first medal of these Olympics.

You guys finally won a medal!

Now the heroes were back from war with their spoils. Gary and Paul sat down and ate dinner as normal. Pizza, steak and spuds were all on the menu. But the other Irish athletes noticed that the Skibb brothers seemed a little flat.

'Why aren't ye out celebrating?' they were asked.

'Ya. Silver,' Gary replied. It was almost a sigh.

That's when the penny dropped with everyone else around the table. Gary and Paul weren't happy with silver. That's not what they had wanted.

Oh.

'We thought we had the beating of the French today,' Paul added.

Afterwards, another Cork Olympian, race walker Rob Heffernan, hinted at the changes ahead. 'Yer lives will never be the same lads, I can tell ye that now.'

Gary didn't know what he meant, but it would make sense in the weeks and months to come.

Back at the apartment, Gary, Paul and Dominic sat on the couch. Any plans for a night of celebrations in downtown Rio were shelved. They were drained. Panned out. Gary's phone had taken on a life of its own. Earlier, in the dining hall, when he'd left the table for three minutes to get some more pizza, he'd returned to find over 500 notifications waiting. It was hopping off the table. Gary put the phone away that night. He hid his medal in a sock too. He had heard stories of cleaners stealing from athletes' rooms, so he took the silver from the box it had come in and stuffed it into a white sock.

Paddy Barnes, Team Ireland boxing captain, popped up to offer his congratulations and take a photo with the men of the hour.

'I think this is big, bigger than we think,' Dominic suggested.

It was bigger than they could have ever imagined.

And there were still the 2016 World Rowing Championships in Rotterdam to come the following week.

5

best in the world

Paul and Dominic flew out to Rotterdam the Monday after the Olympic final because Paul was gunning for glory in the lightweight single sculls at the 2016 World Rowing Championships. Gary, on the other hand, stayed in Rio to celebrate that week. The party followed him. An entire WhatsApp group of Irish in the Brazilian city waited to see where he would pop up and would then follow him. However, after being the Irish flag-bearer at the Olympic Games' closing ceremony at the famed Maracanã stadium, Gary knew that it was time to go and support Paul and all the other Skibbereen athletes at the 2016 Worlds.

The World Championships that year combined the Seniors, Under–23s and Juniors. Skibbereen Rowing Club was well represented. There was Paul at Senior level, along with Shane O'Driscoll and Mark O'Donovan in the lightweight men's pair. (The difference between the double sculls and the pair is that Gary and Paul have two oars each, sculling, while Shane and Mark have one each, sweeping.) At Under–23 level, Fintan McCarthy was in a lightweight men's quad (four rowers with two oars each). Aoife Casey, Dominic's second oldest, and Emily Hegarty were in the Junior women's double scull.

Padraig Murphy was waiting by the tourist information box across the way from the Centraal Station in Amsterdam, just like Gary hoped he would be. Padraig had been there since early morning. The last text message that Gary sent using his Brazilian SIM card in Rio was to ask Padraig to wait for him at that exact spot. He had calculated roughly what time he would land in Amsterdam via a few airports en route. The hard-earned blow-out was moving from Brazil straight to The Netherlands.

Gary and Padraig have been friends since they were in the same class in secondary school at St Fachtna's. Padraig is also one of the best coxes at the rowing club.

After meeting up, they got the next train to Rotterdam and checked in to their hotel. A quick shower and shave later and they were walking into the Irish pub Paddy Murphy's. Taking centre stage on the window facing the street was the large glossy poster of Gary and Paul with their Olympic medals and Trish's tricolour that had been in the previous week's edition of *The Southern Star* at home in West Cork.

It was the first time Gary saw it. 'A pub in Rotterdam with my photo in the window. Mad stuff.'

Gary and Padraig walked in. Casual as you like, they strolled up to the bar where Gary called for two pints of Guinness. A few minutes later the barman propped their drinks up in front of them. No charge, lads. He moved on to the next customer.

Gary played it cool. Thanks. Free pints. Nice.

The celebrations continued for one half of the Olympic silver-medal-winning team with a big gang from Skibbereen joining in.

It was Skibb on tour.

Paul, however, was still focused on winning another medal.

***

Paul is wired differently to Gary. Their personalities are at opposite ends of the scale. Gary is gregarious and colourful, with an infectious enthusiasm, and he always seems on the verge of mischief. His head is screwed on too, to be fair; he's media savvy and well able to talk, with a marketing degree from Cork Institute of Technology in his back pocket. He's as quick with his wit as he is on the water.

While looks-wise Gary is more like his dad, Teddy, than Paul, it's Paul who shares a lot of Teddy's characteristics. He's not as shy as Teddy, but he is quite comfortable in silence. He'll sit back and listen. Paul doesn't talk as much as Gary but still stands out in a room. He has presence. He's more self-aware, more clinical and more ruthless.

Paul is the stronger rower too. Fiercely powerful. He moves the boat faster than any other lightweight rower in the world. Gary's constantly chasing him. He knows he'll likely never catch Paul, but he won't stop trying either. It gives them an edge. Paul wants to stay number one. Gary wants to catch the number one. That's the dynamic.

Paul is also the more confident of the two. He knows he's the best, although he doesn't carry the crown arrogantly. That's why, in the double, Paul sits in the stroke seat and Gary in the bow. When they were first paired together in the double after coming out on top in trials in 2014, Gary was stroke and Paul was bow. At the 2015 European Rowing Championships in Poznań, they finished fifth in the A final but, by the next event, World Rowing Cup III in Lucerne, they had swapped seats. That was their preference in their younger days and it always worked. It means Gary in bow can see what Paul is doing in stroke, where you need to be a little bit more confident in what you are doing. Paul being so good in the single means he has that confidence and consistency, so Gary found it easier to follow his stroke length and rhythm, replicating from behind. The proof is in the result: Olympic silver.

Physically, Paul is a beast. He always was. He has raw power. When they were at Lisheen National School, they'd travel with Teddy to the local Co-op when he collected rations for the farm, things like dairy nuts and calf nuts. He would back his trailer into where the dairy nuts were stockpiled. However, Paul had no interest in lifting bags of dairy nuts a short distance. Instead he'd walk to the opposite end of the store, wrap his little arms around a twenty-five-kilogramme bag of calf nuts and do whatever it took to carry it to the trailer. Bull-headed and stubborn, he'd get the bag there on his own.

Now, in Rotterdam, Paul was on his own again. He was in a single scull and determined to show that he was the best lightweight rower in the world. He didn't doubt for one moment that he'd peak again so soon after Rio. That was his confidence.

Swapping the double for the single wasn't a problem. In Banyoles before Rio, Gary and himself spent time in the singles too, to mix up training. Paul was also a bronze medallist in the single sculls from the 2013 World Under–23 Rowing Championships when he was nineteen, and finished fourth one year later. He was also fourth in the single at the Junior Worlds in 2011, where there's no distinction between lightweights and heavyweights. That was the last time he cried after a race, gutted at missing out on a medal. There was also the fourth at the 2014 Senior World Rowing Championships. The single comes naturally to him.

On 22 August, ten days after winning Olympic silver, Paul romped to success in his heat in Rotterdam, with five seconds to spare over Japan in second. On to the quarter-final two days later and another win, this time with over two seconds to spare.

Paul was winning, but he wasn't happy. He felt he was rowing like, in his words, a bit of a gobshite. The transition into the single wasn't going as smoothly as he'd like, so, much like with Gary and himself in the double in Rio, he went out for a paddle on his day off between the quarter-final and semi-final to sort it out and work on a few technical aspects. He knew he was in good shape. He felt fit and strong. But it took a few days to find a routine after the jet-lag and what had gone on before.

The semi-final the following day, Thursday, was close: he won by just over half a second from Slovenia. Back in the hotel that night, Diarmuid, still living it up in Rio, rang. He reminded Paul of the conversation they had at a Red Bull party on the Saturday night after the Olympic final.

Diarmuid, Paul, Richard Coakley, Dave O'Brien, all Skibb rowers present and past, were programmed the same from years under Dominic and they were already looking to the next race and medal opportunity: Paul in Rotterdam.

Paul was confident. He has that belief. So when Diarmuid had suggested at the party that he should win the single by open water, Paul took on the challenge. No bother.

There's no filter with these two, great friends since school. As much as Paul is brutal and honest with people, so too is Diarmuid. They're always a few words away from bringing someone back down to earth. And now, on the phone, Diarmuid was quizzing Paul about the deal they'd struck in Rio.

'What happened about winning by open water?'

'I'll make an effort so for the final.'

Time to prove a point.

In the warm-up for the A final at the 2016 Worlds Paul knew he was in good shape. He kept one eye on the B final beforehand. The conditions were similar to how they'd be for his race and so he wanted to see the times for the top three. He worked out how close they were to him in the semi-finals. Everything pointed to something special.

In sixth place after 500 metres he was rowing within himself, almost toying with the rest. His surge was inevitable. It was magnificent to watch, like a warrior slaying his enemies all at once with one swing of his giant sword. Paul put in a huge effort in the middle section and blew the rest away. Nobody could live with his pace. Not even 2015 World Champion Lukas Babac. It was an awesome performance as he powered to glory in 7:32.840, over four seconds ahead of Peter Galambos of Hungary in second, Babac following in third.

As promised, it was by clear water. Back in your box, Diarmuid.

'I was looking around and saying to myself, "Come on lads, are ye going to sit there or what?" I was a bit shocked. If I had gone earlier I think I could have won by more but there was no need,' Paul later said.

He made it sound easy. It wasn't. There was no need to go into the lunatic zone for this win. Gary celebrated in the grandstand. Shane and Mark too, having come fourth themselves in the A final of the lightweight pair, an improvement on seventh from the 2015 Worlds. Aoife and Emily finished sixth in the B final of the Junior women double sculls, Fintan and the Under–23 quad came fifth in the A final. They were impressive results on the world stage, but overshadowed by Paul's heroics.

'The greatest Irish rower ever,' tweeted Niall O'Toole, former Olympic rower and Ireland's first world champion rower when he won gold in the lightweight single scull in 1991. Another former Olympian, Skibbereen Rowing Club's Timmy Harnedy, who had watched Paul develop on the Ilen, described him as phenomenal: 'To be a world champion, European champion and Olympic silver medallist in the one year, that's unheard of.'

The next stop for those medals and the O'Donovan brothers was the homecoming in Skibbereen on Monday night. Plans were in full swing back home.

***

The walls are cold at Skibbereen Rowing Club. The concrete floors are even colder. It's a building that depends on body heat for warmth. It's basic and primitive. It's battered in places. It's certainly not perfect. The glass windows on the main door are cracked and are held together by strips of tape. That door has been kicked in several times over the years and looks the worse for wear. The roof is leaking. Some of the rowing machines in the long room at the back, the old boathouse, have wires and batteries missing. Computers hooked up to some rowing machines are relics that belong in a museum, not a functioning club. There are torn seats on chairs. Filing cabinets are kept on top of an old dishwasher.

Thrown on the ground of the narrow hall leading to the gym is all sorts of equipment. An old weights machine, a leg press, is lying in a heap, all chopped up, waiting to be put back together sometime. Dominic spotted it in Seville on a training camp, took out an angle grinder and made it easier to bring home. It's a jigsaw he'll put together at some stage when he has the time.

But this is home. It's the playground for Olympians and world champions. It's base camp for the most successful rowing club in the country. The facilities are what they are. The club has always been poor. Money has always been hard to come by. But no one gets bogged down by that. They drive on.

In the small gym with no windows sit a varied collection of weights. Some are borrowed. Some are hand-made by Dominic from sheets of metal. Some are second-hand parts off trawlers. None are new. Dominic's handwritten weights programmes from different years are taped to the walls, reminding athletes how many squats, chin-ups, bench presses, leg presses, crunches, twist sit-ups they should be doing.

The club never had the money to invest. But it always survived, always kept going, driven by the community and volunteers.

And ahead of Gary and Paul's homecoming it was all hands on deck at the clubhouse to paint it and give it a facelift before its moment in the spotlight. A press conference with the national media and the watching world was to take place there the following Monday afternoon.

***

The first inkling Trish had that life had changed was when she landed home from Rio the Monday after the Olympic final. After nine days away, the fridge was empty. They needed supplies for the week before flying out to Rotterdam. She went into Field's SuperValu in Skibbereen, walked in the back entrance at 10.30 a.m. and only got back out to the car at 4.30 p.m. Well-wishers, friends, strangers, everyone passed on their congratulations. That was her last time shopping for three months. Mick took over those duties then. She messaged Gary and Paul to say they had no idea what was waiting for them. But soon they would see it for themselves.

6

the homecoming

The club's senior rowers had been a good influence on Gary and Paul from the start. Their success in Rio was built during the previous twenty years in Skibbereen, where that winning culture was instilled, nurtured and grown. It can be traced right back to the 1996 men's Novice coxed four who won a national title. That was the boat with Eugene Coakley, James Lupton, John Whooley and Paul O'Sullivan. That boat had spirit. It was also competitive. All four wanted to beat each other too. That drove it on.

When those four started they had very few peers to look up to. They carved out their own path. Three of that quad – Eugene, James and John – raced for Ireland at the 1997 World Junior Championships. The spark was lit. Championship after championship, titles followed. Numbers swelled. Success followed. World level became the norm. Olympians were honed. Others followed. Mistakes were made, but they were learned from.

Kenneth McCarthy was another of the gang that was part of the club's success from the mid-1990s on. In 2003 he came third with the Irish men's heavyweight four at the World Under-23 Championships in Belgrade.

That July he also unleashed 'schnitzel' on the world-famous Henley Regatta. Schnitzel is a German word for meat, but it was also Skibb's secret code word at the time to unleash the beast in the last twenty strokes. It only existed in Skibbereen. When 'schnitzel' was called, they shortened their stroke and pulled harder and faster. Kenneth was the only Skibb man in a four at Henley – the rest were from NUI Galway. Before the semi-final of the Visitors Challenge Cup he shared 'schnitzel' with Alan Martin, Marc Stevens and Paul Giblin. He called it in the race. They won. Then they took gold in the final, beating Cambridge University.

Schnitzel worked.

As that Junior quad of Gary, Paul, Shane and Diarmuid developed on the Ilen, racing anything that moved, Kenneth and John Whooley were two of the club's top rowers. On the next level up were Olympians Eugene Coakley, Timmy Harnedy and Richard Coakley, though they weren't around as often because they were involved with the national team.

The four youngsters looked up to the older group. There was a strong rapport and the banter was good. These up-and-comers caused war at the time, getting in the way of training pieces between Kenneth, John and Richard, who was the top sculler in the country. But having an Olympian and international-class rowers in the club made reaching the top more tangible for the young guns. The attitude was, if they could do it, then so can we. The Seniors' experience was passed down the line too and that helped to fast-track Gary and Paul. They watched, listened and learned.

Kenneth knew the discipline it took to row at a high level and compete regularly for national titles. Like them all, he questioned it at times. But he was drawn back to it. Dominic saw a rower in Kenneth's long, six-foot-two-inch frame and got the best out of him.

On a typical day in his teens, he was up at 7.30 a.m., had breakfast, cycled the few minutes into town for his newspaper delivery run, into school at St Fachtna's for 9 a.m. and was there until 4 p.m. After that he cycled out to the rowing club, was on the water for 4.30 p.m., back onto land, ran into town and back out again, cycled the ten minutes home afterwards, had dinner and started into homework. That routine was repeated from Monday through to Friday. On Saturdays he had two training sessions: morning and evening. It was physically and mentally demanding. Every move was made in order to be ready to race.

Not that things always ran smoothly. Kenneth was in the Skibb Junior eight the day that Dominic turned up with an old Aer Lingus headpiece for Richard Coakley, who was the cox. No one asked where he got it from. It was hooked up to the cox box they had, which helped the cox relay orders to the boat. (There were speakers dotted all through the boat so all the crew could hear what Richard was saying.)

Dominic warned him not to turn on the cox box beforehand because there was only enough battery left in it for the race. When the race started, Richard pressed the on button on the cox box. But it wasn't his voice the crew heard thunder through the speakers. It was a local radio station. Richard couldn't turn it off. Traditional Irish music boomed out of the Skibb boat as they sped down the course. They rowed harder than ever to get to the finish to escape the music.

That was one of the stories that Gary and Paul loved to listen to from the older lads in the club.

A lot of Kenneth's friends from the club, the guys he called his brothers, had to leave Skibb for work. There's not enough industry in the town to keep people. Ciarán Hayes and Eugene Coakley moved to London, James Barry and Richard Coakley went to Australia, John Whooley set up roots in Carlow, Dave O'Brien switched to Saudi Arabia. Christmas is the only time the gang gets back together. They shuffle up to the Corner Bar, take over seats at the back and talk about their rowing days deep into the night.

Like Kenneth's tale of when he was involved in an Irish heavyweight four in the run-up to the 2004 Olympic Games that rolled up at Leander Rowing Club on the Thames with no boat and no coach. Leander has produced more world and European champions than any other club in the world and the Irish boys stuck out like a sore thumb. They had notions of qualifying for the Olympics, but they had no one to help them train at Leander. They eventually persuaded a man who used to walk his dog up and down the banks to be their temporary coach. It reminded Kenneth of the movie *Cool Runnings*, about the Jamaican bobsleigh that, despite never seeing snow before, qualified for and competed at the 1988 Winter Olympics. The difference is the Irish heavyweight four didn't qualify for the Athens Games in 2004.

The clubhouse at Leander stuck with Kenneth. Marble counter tops in the toilets. A club with its own chef. The best of everything. A different world to Skibbereen.

***

Gary and Paul needed a favour from Kenneth. He obliged.

He was part of the Skibbereen supporting contingent in Rotterdam at the World Championships and, given his car was at Cork Airport, he was the obvious route home for the returning Olympic heroes, who needed a lift.

Both in Team Ireland Olympic T-shirts and shorts, with backpacks, and wearing their Olympic silver medals, the O'Donovan brothers walked down the exit stairway off the Aer Lingus flight and onto the runway. A row of people lined up to welcome them home. The third and fourth people they met, and hugged, were Skibbereen Rowing Club President Nuala Lupton and founding member Richard Hosford. Familiar faces from home. Those hugs lasted that bit longer and were much tighter.

Kenneth didn't hang around for the official greeting inside the airport. He missed the mayhem as Gary and Paul were mobbed in the arrivals hall. Chants of 'Olé, Olé, Olé' broke out as the two men of the moment, now wrapped in a tricolour, were interviewed by the media, all clamouring around them. There were selfies with fans. Cork boxer Gary 'Spike' O'Sullivan presented them with steak and spuds. Gary and Paul never imagined, when leaving Skibbereen, that they'd come home to a heroes' reception like this.

Outside the arrivals hall Kenneth sat in his black Honda Accord, which had been driven around to the airport entrance by security. He waited. He could hear the cheers and roars inside. An exit door opened, Gary and Paul were ushered out and quickly rushed into the back seat of Kenneth's car. They were given a garda escort for ten minutes until the coast was clear and the three were on their own then, heading west, homeward-bound.

Innishannon was quiet. So too were Bandon and Ballinascarthy. They drove through Clonakilty around 10.30 p.m., windows down, with Gary and Paul urging Kenneth to beep the horn. It was still quiet. But that soon changed.

As they drove down the sweeping hill onto the causeway at Rosscarbery, the huge bonfire outside the Celtic Ross Hotel lit up the night's sky. Guests and staff were out in force. The car had to stop. Hotel general manager Neil Grant handed a bag of sandwiches through the window. Perfect. They were hungry.

The next village on was Leap, halfway between Rosscarbery and

Skibbereen. They'd expected to drive straight through, but Leap was out in force. At the far end of the village, the road was full of bodies from The Harbour Bar right across to the Leap Inn. Gary and Paul put the windows down in the back, climbed outside the car and sat on the edge. They were living it up. If they stopped in Leap, though, they wouldn't see Skibbereen for a week, so they ploughed on.

It was almost midnight when they hit Skibb. The lads wanted to drive past the Corner Bar, to see if anyone was around. It was past serving hours. The doors were shut but the lights were on. Gary and Paul hopped out. They peeked in through the windows and knocked on the main door, stood back and waited to see who would emerge. One by one, the last few survivors trickled out, all shaking the hands of the two young men. Albert Swanton was there, a former Skibb rower in the 1970s who had emigrated to the USA. He had flown back to Skibb especially for the homecoming, and now met Gary and Paul on his first night on West Cork soil.

Next stop was home. Lisheen. The roads were fierce dark and quiet. Not a sinner was about. Pulling up outside their house, Kenneth heard the debate in the back.

'Will we go up?'

'Will we?'

'Ya, we'll go up.'

That meant slipping back into second gear and moving the half mile straight on to Minihan's pub a bit after midnight. There was a man standing outside smoking a cigarette. The car stopped. He peered over. He took one more drag and wandered towards the late-night visitors. 'The boys are back, the boys are back!' he shouted when he saw who it was.

He got emotional. Their boys were back. The two O'Donovan boys.

Still outside Minihan's, the man told Kenneth to drive down the road, turn the car, come back up slowly and he'd have a gang out to welcome them. Kenneth did as instructed.

Slowly, he inched back towards Minihan's. But nothing. He stopped the car outside. Still nothing. No one to be seen. It was eerily quiet. Then a man walked out of a ditch and another from a bush. More people started to appear out of the blackness of the night. It turns out that when the man had gone back into Minihan's, shouting 'they're outside, they're outside', whoever was left thought he'd meant the gardaí were outside, so they had taken off out the back door.

Gary and Paul didn't stay long. A few minutes later they were home. Trish and Mick were there. Nana was there too and some more family and friends, as well as Adrian McCarthy, a local producer and director with Wildfire Films, who had begun filming a documentary, *Pull Like A Dog*, as soon as Gary and Paul's feet touched down at Cork Airport. Trish's brother Mike had stayed in Lisheen to mind the house in case well-wishers started to descend. All the curtains were closed on the front of the house, facing the road, and the lights were turned off. Everyone was camped out in the sitting room on the far side. From the outside the house looked asleep.

Dominic was home now too. Coach Casey had been third off the flight at Cork Airport. As he worked his way down the line of dignitaries, shaking hands and exchanging pleasantries, his eyes were already on his wife, Eleanor, and three of their kids, Niamh, Caoimhe and Dominic, the two youngest wrapped in tricolours jumping in to hug their dad, who had been away for months. He finds being away from his family difficult; it's the hardest part of the job. But now he was home as the reluctant hero who was already dreading the planned press conference the following afternoon.

He won't kill you with conversation, Dominic. He keeps his answers brief. He has his faults too. One that irks athletes away on training camps is his dislike for warm butter. It has to go in the fridge, even though then it's rock solid and too hard to spread on toast and bread. Another fault is he cuts people off. He doesn't have time for idle chit-chat. One minute you're talking to him, the next he's gone. That's the price to pay for a man with 20,000 thoughts about rowing racing through his head.

However, on the Monday afternoon of the homecoming, he had no choice but to sit down and talk. He was in front of the media, sitting to the left of Paul and Gary, Morten Espersen on the far right, the interview taking place upstairs in the rowing club.

Beforehand, he walked outside the front door of the clubhouse for fresh air and some quietness. The media hunted in packs inside, searching for new angles to the biggest sports story of the year. Dominic would rather have been anywhere else. But soon there was nowhere to go. The press conference was up and running. There wasn't a spare seat to be found.

Thankfully, from Dominic's point of view, the bulk of the questions fell to the two men of the moment, and he got off fairly lightly on his first visit back to the club since before the Olympics. It wasn't as bad as he had feared. All that was left was the homecoming parade that night.

***

Brian Hennessy, the owner of Hennessy's Londis on Bridge Street, maintains that he never saw a crowd like it in Skibbereen before. From mid-afternoon through to closing time, his wife, Kathleen, and himself were serving the queues that stretched from the counter to the back of the shop. The drinks and bars shelves were almost bare by closing time.

It was the busiest night ever too for William O'Brien in the Corner Bar. The second busiest had been after Gary and Paul won silver. On both nights the crowds spilled out the doors.

On that same artery into the town centre, the Busy Bee Fast Food Restaurant recorded their busiest night since the Welcome Home Week Festival had been in full flight decades before. It was the same story all over town. Business was booming.

The Southern Star newspaper produced a special souvenir publication on Gary and Paul that week. It was called 'Lisheen Legends'. Twenty pages dedicated to rowing. That was unheard of, but this was the Gary and Paul effect. Posters of them were plastered on every window. Tricolour bunting stretched across the streets. Ireland and Brazil flags popped up everywhere. 'Gary & Paul's Crew' T-shirts were the must-have fashion accessory.

The narrow streets were flooded with locals and outsiders bringing Skibbereen to a standstill for one magical night. The population of the town is 2,500. There was four or five times that number packed in as Gary and Paul shut down their hometown.

It was the biggest gathering in Skibbereen in modern times. When the local GAA club, O'Donovan Rossa, captured the All-Ireland club Senior football title in 1993, a large crowd had welcomed them home. But this was on a different level.

Skibb mattered again. For too long it had been a forgotten town. The recessions of the 1980s and 2000s hit this market town hard. Businesses shut. Big employers such as Erin's Food closed up. Buildings along the main streets sat empty. Locals emigrated. Every year young people left in search of the opportunities that Skibb and West Cork didn't provide. They wanted to stay. It's a special place. Artistic. Eclectic. Diverse. Inviting. Colourful. Beautiful. But the opportunities weren't available.

So instead the town stagnated and suffered. It's a story echoed all over rural Ireland.

The homecoming injected new life into Skibb. Another positive national headline. The year before, Skibbereen had become the country's first gigabyte town with the opening of the Ludgate Hub on Townshend Street, a shared office space designed to attract and keep more entrepreneurs and young families in the town by offering a place to work at the highest possible broadband speed. Proper broadband speed in Skibb at last. That was a good-news story. But Gary and Paul's story was better again.

The organising committee for the homecoming left nothing to chance. At one stage, and with concerns over the huge numbers expected to attend, the suggestion was put forward to host the homecoming in the new mart grounds on the edge of the town, but alarm bells went off regarding safety concerns, so that idea was quashed quickly. The Fairfield car park, the old mart in the centre of town, was the preferred option for the organising committee.

Everyone in town helped with the preparations: the Skibbereen District Chamber of Commerce, the gardaí, the coastguard, civil defence, volunteers. Skibbereen Rowing Club Captain Seanie O'Brien stayed camped in the Fairfield car park that Monday, keeping an eye on proceedings and hunting away out-of-town chip vans that spotted an opportunity to pull up the handbrake.

From early afternoon the carnival atmosphere built. Shops closed early. The air was buzzing. Constant noise. By evening time excitement had reached fever pitch. The Fairfield car park was already crammed, thousands watching the big screen that had been erected to show replays of the Olympic final, while the stage sat empty, waiting for the men of the moment. The boys would soon be back in town.

Just outside town, near the Spar shop on the Cork road, Shane O'Driscoll rolled up in his Volkswagen Golf with Gary and Paul in the back. A red double-decker bus was waiting there. Its first floor was packed. Gary and Paul took their places, dressed in their official Team Ireland white and green tops, light grey tracksuits, with their medals around their necks.

Dominic was there too, swapping his shirt and pants from earlier in the day for a suit with a patriotic dark-green tie. Any Skibb rower that competed internationally for Ireland that year took their place on the bus, as well as committee members and family. Denise Walsh. Shane O'Driscoll. Aoife Casey. The twins, Jake and Fintan McCarthy. Emily Hegarty. Lydia Heaphy. T. J. Ryan. Tony Walsh. Kenneth McCarthy. Up the front sat Trish with Nana Mary Doab, Mick, Teddy and Jackie Neville, Gary and Paul's aunt.

At 7.06 p.m. the bus bearing the words 'Home are the Heroes' left the Cork road, turned left at the first roundabout and inched down North Street. The St Facthna's Silver Band marched in front of it. The closer it nudged towards Main Street and then the Fairfield, the more the crowd swelled. Hand-made posters were waved. Fans hung out of first-floor windows. They stood on cars. Kids waved from their parents' shoulders. Every vantage point was taken.

Gary and Paul waved to their fans. They were like rock stars. The noise was deafening. The Pope would struggle to gather such a crowd if he came to Skibb.

Eventually, the bus stopped outside the Fairfield and Gary and Paul were ushered through Abbeystrewry Hall and then onto the big stage, where RTÉ's Jacqui Hurley was the emcee for the night. The crowd went wild.

Paul announced it was 'just a standard Monday night in Skibbereen'.

'It is hard to take it all in,' he told the thousands and thousands. 'The scale of this is giving us a shock. Events like this make us proud to say that we are from Cork, we are from West Cork, but most importantly, we are from Skibbereen.'

Standing to the side was Trish, wrapped in a tricolour, her hands joined in the prayer position, trying to take it all in. Not long after, when festivities at the Fairfield were over, she used Mick as a shield to negotiate her way through the crowds and get to the West Cork Hotel. Gary and Paul were already there, live on *The Nine O'Clock News* on RTÉ. Such were the numbers at the hotel, Trish and Mick couldn't get through to the function room that was closed off for just family, friends and the club. Barry Looney, son of hotel owner Tim, had to lead them through the kitchen.

Later, Gary and Paul escaped to the Corner Bar, less than a minute's walk away. They went in through the side door and sat at the back for a chat with friends. They were still naïve enough to think they might be left alone. Shane, Diarmuid, Denise Walsh, they were all there. But word soon got out where Gary and Paul were. It was already like their wedding day, but this was too much. They had no time to themselves. Grown men and women were pulling at them. The onslaught of attention was ferocious. All they wanted was a quiet pint. William's son, Mike, took the two lads upstairs. That's where they stayed for most of the night of their homecoming, away from the crowd.

Life had changed, they were quickly realising.

Down below, the party lasted into the bright hours. Skibbereen was rejuvenated. It was one of the best nights ever in the history of this town, thanks to the rowing club.

Kenneth got a taxi late that night. Des Quinn was the driver. He was all chat about rowing. The Olympics. Gary and Paul. Their races.

Paul's gold in Rotterdam. He knew it all. That conversation stayed with Kenneth for a long time after.

After all, there had been a time when some in the town didn't even know where the rowing club was. Before Eugene Coakley travelled as a sub to the Sydney Olympics in 2000, the club hung up posters around town to let people know the news, but they hadn't paid too much attention. The rowing club is smack in the middle of a powerful GAA stronghold, surrounded by the O'Donovan Rossa, Castlehaven and Ilen Rovers senior football teams. They've always taken precedence. Men like Don and Anthony Davis and 'Small' Mick McCarthy are three of the town's finest-ever footballers, all inter-county players. Fachtna Collins of Ilen Rovers. John Cleary and Niall Cahalane of Castlehaven. All men with a status locally. Known throughout. All respected.

There's the rugby and soccer clubs in Skibb as well. The rowing club wasn't even an option for most. It took in cast-offs from other clubs, youngsters who couldn't kick a ball straight or had no co-ordination, and then moulded and turned them into national champions, and then international champions. It survived on a shoestring and hard work. And now, after years of pulling at peoples' coats and asking for money to keep the club afloat, they were the pride of the town and the rowing club was the reason Skibbereen was plastered all over every national newspaper and TV station in the country.

***

The evening after the homecoming, the party moved out the Schull road to Church Cross in Gary and Paul's home parish of Aughadown for a more intimate welcome home.

This parish is a bit special for producing rowers. It has its Olympians with Gary and Paul in Lisheen, and Timmy Harnedy and his sister Áine from Cloghboola. Former world champion Shane O'Driscoll is from Kilkilleen. So is Teddy O'Donovan. The same for Dominic and his gang. Kilkilleen is home too to the Leonard sisters, Caroline and Aileen, who have won multiple national rowing titles. Diarmuid O'Driscoll is from Church Cross. Jake and Fintan McCarthy, who have rowed for Ireland at Under–23 and Senior international level, are from Foherlagh in Aughadown. Fintan won senior world gold with Paul O'Donovan in 2019. Lar Collins, who rowed with Dominic in the 1980s, is from the parish – Big Marsh to be exact. Emily Dulohery and her sister Kate, from Holyhill, have shared seven national rowing titles between them. Irish international Emily Hegarty is from Moonagh, as is Brid O'Driscoll, both of whom have won their share of national titles. Former National Championship winner and coach Mike Cotter is from Lisaree. For many years, Aughadown has been a fertile breeding ground for the rowing club.

Organised by Aughadown Community Council, the crowd was in its hundreds, with many of the elderly in the parish who couldn't make it into the town the evening before having the opportunity to meet their two boys. The light rain that fell didn't dampen the mood, but Paul quipped, as Gary and himself took part in a questions and answers session on stage, that a lot of people were glad that the rain was coming down so as to hide the tears.

After the mayhem of the night before, this was a lighter pace, and Gary and Paul were more relaxed.

'Whatever about Ireland, in fairness to this community, to Lisheen and Aughadown, everyone knew in their hearts before we went out that we were heroes and we were treated like that before we left. It's no different now because we are here with two medals. They have been so supportive since we were growing up really,' Paul said, before passing the microphone to a croaky Gary, who added, 'We said to each other that the further west we came and closer we got to home, the less people cared about seeing the medals and the more they cared about seeing us.'

Later that week, Gary and Paul appeared on *The Late Late Show* and in early December they flew across to London to record *The Graham Norton Show*'s New Year's Eve special. The two Skibbereen rowers shared the couch with Hollywood actress Marion Cotillard, A-list actors Michael Fassbender and James McAvoy, and comedian Frank Skinner. The awards flowed too, including the RTÉ Sports Team of the Year gong.

At Christmas 2016, Kenneth McCarthy and his wife, Christine, took their kids, Micheál and Nell, to visit Santa Claus in Blarney. Santa asked where they were from. They answered Skibbereen. Oh yes, Santa replied, that's where Gary and Paul are from. They were on his naughty list for a few years, he told the amazed children, but they're firmly on the nice list now after Rio.

From nobody knowing who they were six months earlier, they were now the most famous brothers in Irish sport. They'd gone global. And they had achieved all this while coming from a club that had the most humble of beginnings.

II
BEGINNINGS

founders

Richard Hosford is the reason that Gary and Paul won Olympic medals. He is the reason that Dominic was named World Rowing Coach of the Year in 2018. He is the reason that Eugene Coakley, Timmy Harnedy and Richard Coakley are all Olympians. He is the reason the club is the best in the country. Long before Gary and Paul were born, and for years before Dominic became involved, Richard was the man who kept the rowing club afloat.

He is one of the three founding members. It wasn't him who thought of the idea, but Richard was there the moment the rowing club was conceived. He soon became the driving force on and off the water.

That first summer in the 1970s was a good one in Skibb. The annual Maid of the Isles Festival packed the town again with something for everyone. The roads were busy, pubs and restaurants were booming and tourism was strong.

The Erin Foods factory on Marsh Road, on the edge of the town, was a major local employer, with hundreds working there. Mart days in the middle of town brought big crowds too. Skibbereen was number one in West Cork, the capital. It had mid-week discos in The Eldon Hotel, there was the cinema on Townshend Street and there was Tops of the Town, regular pantomimes and plenty of pubs too.

Skibb also had Hosford's store on Bridge Street, run by Richard's brother John. This was a grocery store that would go on to become the first supermarket to open its doors in Skibbereen. It was a novelty at the time. It was a shop without a main counter.

Richard trained as a butcher and was a jack-of-all-trades around the store. He was the youngest of five and slight at five foot two inches tall. The initial plan was for him to work in the millers behind the store, but asthma put an end to that. Then a back injury suffered when he crashed against the base of a post while playing for Skibbereen Rugby Club slowed him down too and kept him sidelined for a spell. But he had other interests, like fishing on the Ilen.

So did Danny Murphy. The day after they met for the first time, when Danny was gardening at Richard's brother's house – a six-bedroom Victorian manor, Rosebank, two miles outside town – the two went fishing.

Danny's an islander and was a lot more used to the water than Richard. Danny grew up yards from the water on the west side of Heir Island, which is nestled midway between Baltimore and Schull in Roaringwater Bay. It's tucked away from the masses. His family's link to the island and the water stretches back generations. The first view out his small bedroom window was the Atlantic Ocean stretching off into the distance. To be christened, he and his family had been forced to travel to the mainland, a trip that takes five minutes by boat and connects two very different worlds.

In those days he couldn't swim, but that wasn't unusual for an islander. Surrounded on all sides, he was taught to never fear the water but to respect it. As an only child, he'd wander down to the sandy beach to where the ocean touched the island, walk in ankle deep and feel the cold water lap against him. Curiosity always encouraged one more step, up to his knees at least, only for his parents, watching on, to bark after him, 'Come up out of that, Danny, you'll drown.'

He lost count of how many times he heard those words. He stopped inching forward. Superstition is one of the reasons he never learned, or was taught, to swim. There were islanders and fishermen who believed that being able to swim was inviting trouble. Also if your boat sank out at sea, not being able to swim meant a swifter death. Danny did learn to swim years later, however.

That summer of 1970, he was twenty-eight years old and life revolved around the water. It gave him work too, on fishing boats and tugs. Living in Skibb with his wife, Triona, and two kids, Karen and Patrick (Sonia and Daniel followed in later years), Danny worked on the tugs with Bantry Bay Towing Company, guiding tankers in and out to the jetty at Whiddy Island Oil Terminal.

He worked there until the Whiddy Island disaster on 8 January 1979, when an oil tanker, *Betelgeuse*, exploded at the offshore jetty on Whiddy Island killing fifty people. Danny was working on the tugs that night and he saw too much. It's a nightmare that never leaves. Even now he doesn't like talking about it.

But in that first summer in the 1970s, Danny had moved out of his rented apartment on Main Street and bought his first house on the mainland: 61 Mardyke Street in Skibb town. A local carpenter, Donie Fitzgerald, the boyfriend of Danny's cousin Eileen Collins, looked after the renovations. As it turned out, he was the final piece of the puzzle.

One Sunday afternoon that June, Donie walked into town from his home, which was one mile outside on the western side. He came in search of a road bowl, a twenty-four-ounce steel ball, to go bowling with his friends later that evening. John O'Donovan's pub on Lower Bridge Street, which was right beside Hosford's yard and Richard's home, was a local supplier. John O'Donovan also owned a taxi and so, when Donie turned up, he happened to be out on a job. The pub was shut. (If John had been in his pub that day and sold Donie the bowl, Skibbereen Rowing Club might never have existed.)

Donie couldn't buy the bowl. But it wasn't a wasted trip. He saw Richard and Danny, next door in Hosford's yard, plotting plans for the evening. Donie joined them.

The three jumped into Richard's dark-red Renault Four. It was a car well known about town. Immaculately kept and in mint condition. Richard had owned an Austin A40 before this, but his Renault Four hatchback was different. He had bought it from O'Brien's car dealership on Townshend Street. He loved that car. It had its own personality. It would go on to become a character in the rowing club's early days, ferrying as many as could fit into it, and boats on top, to and from training and regattas. It would lose its driver door at a regatta in later life, coming off worse when a bottle was wedged in the opening and the door was banged shut.

This particular evening, Danny sat in the back with his head between the two front seats. The conversation drifted to a recent rowing regatta that had been held locally. Danny knew his stuff when it came to rowing and he could row. He needed to, after all, to leave Heir Island. Of the three twenty-somethings, he was the only one who had rowed competitively before, in coastal regattas between the islands.

Now an idea struck him.

'Let's start our own rowing club here in Skibbereen,' Danny blurted out. It had crossed his mind before, but he had never shared the thought.

Danny has always held a soft spot for the Ilen. It's everything a river should be and more. On calm days it's the perfect mirror to the sky, so still it looks like it's posing for a photo. It has its touch-and-go days too, of course, but the good far outweighs the bad.

Danny's idea wasn't dismissed. Instead, it quickly grew legs, oars and a boat. The fact that none of the three could swim didn't dampen their enthusiasm. Danny had heard of a boat for sale in Union Hall, a fishing village on the coast a few miles outside of town. They adjourned for Sunday dinner, Danny made a call and they all met back in the yard later that evening.

Later on, as they drove down to Union Hall, they were convinced they'd spotted a gap in the market. Skibbereen Rowing Club. The name made sense. It was simple and to the point.

Waiting by the small quay in Union Hall were Pat Joe Hayes, Bobby Limerick and Diarmuid O'Donovan, all three locals involved with Myross Rowing Club, one of many coastal rowing clubs in West Cork. River rowing in Olympic-class boats, what the club is now famous for, had not arrived yet. So Skibbereen Rowing Club began life as a coastal rowing club. The boats were wider, heavier and sturdier, to handle what the sea could throw at them. Regattas took place in various towns and villages along the coast from August through to October.

Danny knew Myross had a second-hand four-oar gig for sale. That was a traditional open-water boat with fixed seats. It was the *Myross Brown*, built by Kilderry, a well-known local builder from near Bantry. Made of timber, it wasn't in the best of health, all thirty-two feet of it showing its age. It needed to be kept in the shed for the winter, out of the rain and cold, but it was a start. The deal was struck. The *Myross Brown* would be Skibbereen's first boat. It cost £200.

Richard, Danny and Donie each searched in their pockets in order to make up the deposit of £3. The boat was theirs.

'They told us to take it away up to Skibbereen with us,' Richard recalls, 'but we said no, it wasn't moving out of the parish until we had it all paid for. Even from the start we wanted to make sure the club didn't carry any debt for too long.'

A few days later, after a business meeting in town, Richard started chatting to John O'Neill, manager in the local Bank of Ireland branch. Richard filled him in on the recent developments. O'Neill saw the chance to help. A meeting was arranged. It didn't last long. O'Neill heard enough to loosen the purse strings and told Richard they could pay the money back when they were able.

They paid off the loan that summer. They fundraised around town and used a community hall in Lisheen to hold dances in those very early days. Richard borrowed a speaker from Thornhill's electrical shop, tied it to the top of his car, and drove laps of Skibbereen announcing the Friday night dances. He would pick people up in town, drop them to the dance and spin them back in afterwards, almost spending more of his own money in petrol than they made.

Off the water, word of this new rowing club in Skibbereen was spreading and more locals were getting involved. On the water, they trained in Union Hall in the *Myross Brown*, learning as much as they could from Myross Rowing Club and anyone else who knew how to row. In those early weeks the crew was mixed between Skibbereen and Union Hall rowers as they travelled to a few coastal regattas locally, in Baltimore in mid-August and Bantry.

Then came the Glandore Regatta in early September 1970. This six-oar challenge was advertised in *The Southern Star* and Skibb interpreted it as meaning that anyone could enter the race. But it wasn't that straightforward. Rosscarbery and Glandore were both entered but didn't want Skibbereen involved. However, Skibb maintained they should be allowed to race, and did, though they had to borrow a six-oar gig off Donie's cousin, Jackie Crowley in Ardralla, to do so.

On the day of the regatta, the three crews lined up at the starting line and even then the Skibb crew of Jim Shanahan, who was the cox, Pat

Joe Hayes, Donal Finn, John O'Leary, Donie Fitzgerald, Danny Murphy and Bobbie Draper didn't know the course of the race. They hadn't been told. They clearly still weren't welcome.

Richard was on the bank, watching the drama unfold. He lived and pulled every stroke as Skibb shadowed the Rosscarbery and Glandore boats. Once they turned the third buoy they knew it was a straight race for home. There was no stopping Skibbereen. They took control and powered past the finish line.

It was the club's first-ever win in their first-ever six-oar race. The six oarsmen held their oars in the air in celebration as they came back towards the pier. Jim Shanahan lifted his two arms aloft in triumph.

It was a moment in history that wasn't recognised, however, as they weren't announced as the winners. Glandore were. But Skibb weren't too bothered. They'd won. They'd arrived.

***

Denis McCarthy had a lot in common with Danny Murphy – he was another islander who couldn't swim. Ringarogy Island, near Baltimore, is joined to the mainland by a long narrow causeway, but it's still an island and still Denis' home.

He was the eldest of six siblings, including four girls. There was a tradition of fishing in his family and during the 1960s he found himself spending his summer months fishing for salmon on the Ilen. All the houses on Ringarogy – and there were seventy-five people living on the island in the early 1970s – had someone fishing on the river for those three, four months of bright mornings, long evenings and sensational sunsets.

If you were lucky and hit a good run of fish, there was money to be made. The Ilen was a good river for salmon. Denis would come across the odd trout as well and a bit of mullet, but they weren't great sellers so he could use them for himself.

He had finished school by now. Salmon fishing was the obvious next step and it was, until drift netting began further down the river. That was the beginning of the end for fishermen like him. Denis reinvented himself on the land, working in agriculture and driving tractors, diggers and whatever else was needed. The hours were long and they weren't suited to rowing, but after the pubs had shut one Sunday night in town he met Danny, who filled him in on the new rowing club. Denis' interest was piqued.

He had never rowed for Ringarogy in the six-oar gigs, but he had gone to watch regattas as a young lad, travelling by boat from his home and into Schull. They were magical days, those fearless men battling stroke for stroke for local bragging rights. Those images stayed in his head.

In 1970 he had the chance to create his own memories. He knew how to row. The twenty-two-foot boats used for salmon fishing had no engines. He had the power. He was almost six feet tall and a man used to nothing except hard work. His hands were his CV. Danny knew this. He knew Denis and what he could bring to the club, including his younger brother Jack, who soon followed.

The rowing appealed to Denis, but more than anything else it was a social outlet. He didn't play Gaelic football. He didn't start going to town on Sundays, the busy night, until he was in his twenties.

'There was nothing much out our way at the time,' Denis says. 'Rowing meant that there was somewhere to go on a Sunday. I was working for an agricultural contractor and the hours were long, so I'd look forward to whenever there was a regatta somewhere. The racing was good and the craic after was even better.'

The number of recruits was swelling. Interest was picking up as the 1970 gig-racing season came to an end. The four-oar gig from Union Hall was now paid for and it was transported into Skibb to its new home, a field in Oldcourt, Baltimore, nestled under bushes for protection. Winter was coming, but there was a feeling that next year, 1971, would be a big one.

***

Richard Hosford had to steady himself. Deep breath. Shoulders back. He stood up, hands on the table as his seat creaked backwards on the wooden floor upstairs at O'Donovan's pub on Main Street. It was a run-of-the-mill club meeting and it was ambling along at its usual pace. But Richard was about to suggest a monumental change to this club that was less than one year old.

His hands were sweaty. He was fearful that the committee would reject his idea. A quick sip of water later, and he was up and running. Richard told the room that the club needed to move from fixed-seat rowing to sliding seats. These were the Olympic-class boats. He had the attention of the room now, as he filled them in on his recent trip to the Lee Rowing Club in Cork city.

It had all started with broken oars. There was a shortage of oars in the club. Richard had been saying this to Len O'Flaherty, a Lyons Tea salesman whose route included Hosford's store.

Once a fortnight, Len, from Glasheen in Cork city, would point his work van west. It was a salesman's journey he always enjoyed. There was a purity and sincerity about this part of the country. Len liked the people here. Normal, honest-to-goodness country folk. No bullshit.

They were always willing to help out where they could, like in the late 1960s when Denis McCarthy came across Len for the first time. Len's van had run out of petrol. He was stranded, miles from Skibbereen. Denis picked him up and took him to town; they got petrol and he drove back out to his car again and waited until Len was up and running before moving on himself. That's the Skibbereen Len knew.

Len was heavily involved with Lee Rowing Club. They had oars to sell. Richard drove up to the city that week, ready to strap as many as he could to the roof of his Renault Four. There, Len showed him Lee's fleet of boats. Richard was gobsmacked. There were singles, doubles, fours, eights, all sliding seats. Richard wanted to know more. Len filled him in. Lee even had special trailers to transport their rowing boats, in contrast to the Skibb approach, which was to put them on top of cattle lorries with the rowers often standing in underneath.

It was a whole new world of rowing. The committee liked what they heard. Richard explained what the move to sliding-seat boats involved, that the club could then join the Irish Amateur Rowing Association, and how that would be a positive. But they would have to give up the gig racing because there was money swapping hands.

The move to sliding seats was ultimately given the thumbs up. This would turn out to be one of the most important moments in the club's history. If the club had decided to stay with the gigs and coastal regattas, there's a strong chance it wouldn't have survived beyond the 1970s.

At the next Irish Amateur Rowing Association meeting, Skibbereen Rowing Club joined. Now a familiar problem appeared. They needed new boats with sliding seats instead of fixed seats.

Again Lee Rowing Club and Len came up trumps. There was an old four with sliding seats rested outside their clubhouse that had seen better days. There was a hole in it, but it was Skibb's if they wanted it. Done deal.

The club was taking a new course. For one of the founding trio, however, life was about to change.

***

It was the day before a Skibbereen contingent travelled to Carlow Rowing Club to look at a boat, but Donie was standing in the middle of London, his brown suitcase by his side, staring at this new world.

There were buildings that reached for the sky. There were double-decker buses. There was more traffic on one street than Skibbereen would see in a day. People passed him without saying hello or flashing a friendly salute. Then there was the noise. Constant noise. This country man, the second oldest of eight siblings, was dazzled by the bright city lights.

On the way into the city from Heathrow Airport he was doubting his decision. Skibbereen and its familiarity and its openness and its greenness and its fresh air and its friendliness seemed more than an airplane journey away. This wasn't home. It definitely wasn't Skibb.

Donie had braced himself for this. He knew when he made the decision to move to London for work that he was giving up a lot. His fiancée, Eileen, was still at home, working in the Erin's Food factory, but the chance to earn more money in London was too good to turn down. There was a wedding to pay for, after all.

Donie was a carpenter by trade. He had trained as an apprentice under Paddy Murphy in Townshend Street and then Coffeys in Bally-dehob, before working for Sean Browne, a local builder in Skibbereen. By then he had already heard tales of London and its riches from his uncle Paddy Finn, who was regularly back and over between the two. After Donie's grandmother passed away, he made the decision to move to London. And now he was in the middle of it.

Home became Cricklewood and its strong Irish community, as he worked for his uncle Paddy. Travelling to work on the tube with his box of tools offered him lots of time to think of home, of Eileen, who followed him out the following February, and the rowing club he missed.

He'd eventually spend a few years rowing with a club in Northampton and have seven kids – Mark, David, Claire, Brian, Christopher, Anna and James – with Eileen as England became home, while life back home in Skibb continued without him. Donie has lived in England ever since.

***

A gang left Skibb on a boat-finding mission to Carlow Rowing Club in 1971. Richard, Danny and a local shipwright called Paddy Hurley, who had joined the club in its first year, were all there. They needed a boat. They didn't have a racing four or eight at this stage. Word of mouth had led them to Carlow for an eight, a sliding-seat racing boat that would hold eight rowers and a cox.

They were taken out on the River Barrow in the eight that they were interested in. It was the Skibb men's first time in a sliding-seat eight and it was much narrower than the wider gigs they were used to. Richard sat in the cox's seat near the stern of the boat, facing the rowers. They control the steering and the rhythm of the boat. This was a new experience for Richard at the time.

Back on land, the deal was struck. Skibb had an eight to bring home. But they weren't finished yet. Over a pint Danny got talking in the club-house, explaining Skibb's story, and a Carlow man pointed to an old, battered wooden four hiding in the rafters. It had a hole in it the size of a man's head. Take it away, Danny was told. The same four, after a bit of patchwork, was as good as new, and was rolled out to race soon afterwards.

Money was tight, so they were inventive and worked with what they had. The bottom floor in the two-storey store in Hosford's yard became the club's first gym. It was filled with basic weights bought cheaply, or makeshift weights fashioned from whatever was closest to hand. This was training headquarters. It wasn't plush or shiny. Far from it. But these were the rags that eventually led to riches.

The club began entering regattas in Carlow, Cork, Dungarvan and New Ross, even winning at the Head of the River in Fermoy. By now the boats, rarely covered to protect them from the elements, were being kept in a field at Deelish pier owned by Joe Connolly, a short distance from where the clubhouse now is, and this was home for a few years. The only problem was the tide. When there were spring tides the boats were kept on the other side of the road, as otherwise they'd be carried away. When the tide was out and the water was low it wasn't ideal to launch, either, as it meant dragging boats through the mud, so they also used to train on Lough Hyne, a seawater lake that was a few minutes outside town.

***

Donal O'Sullivan can strip a car and put it back together as easily as a kid could finish a twelve-piece jigsaw. He was brought up on a farm full of machinery, including a tractor, and was introduced to the mechanics of an engine at an early age.

Even the basic electrics – the lights and the ignition – didn't bother him. They were another puzzle to solve, and the odds were always in his favour. To top up his knowledge he took a night course in electronics in Cork city.

Fords were popular in Skibbereen in the early 1970s. Skibbereen Motor Works was the local Ford dealer. When Donal decided to take over Charlie McCarthy's garage on Bridge Street in 1971, Opels were his speciality. The Opel Cadet struck the right note locally.

'What we were doing was helping people to keep their cars going, patching them up, welding floors,' he says.

Donal had worked in a few local garages before, in Dunmanway and Bantry, before coming back to Charlie McCarthy's, where he had served his apprenticeship years before. The difference now was that he was going to run the garage. Charlie wanted out. Donal wanted in.

Now in his mid-twenties, he saw an opportunity to go into the motor business on his own and took it. He grasped it with those giant hands that would soon make oars look like lollipop sticks in his grip. Naturally strong, with wide shoulders and a chest you'd bounce a car engine off, Donal worked hard. That was his mindset, coming from a farming background at home in Milleenahorna in Caheragh, a few miles outside Skibbereen.

He was a powerful man built for coastal rowing. He was also a man built for the boardroom. Clever, reasoned, unruffled and intelligent, he chooses his words very carefully, with long pauses for thought in mid-sentence. What's worth saying is worth saying right.

Donal was just the man that Skibbereen Rowing Club needed on-board and luckily for them he saw the light, literally.

Long hours were the norm for him and it was during one of these work days that hurried into the night, while working on a car at the very back of the garage, that he noticed a light out a back window coming from the store at the rear of Hosford's yard. He rested his tools and his inquisitive mind soon saw him standing in the store, chatting to Richard and a few more who were working on a boat.

Donal had never rowed before. But he was interested, so he helped to fill the eight the club now had. However, for all that Donal achieved on the water, it's his impact off the water that leaves a legacy. He went on to become club chairman in 1973 and held that position for thirty-five years. He was the rock that steadied the club. His judgement was never questioned.

Donal is one of the most influential and respected figures the club has ever had. So too is Nuala Lupton, who was soon to make everyone sit up and take notice of this country rowing club in West Cork.

here come the girls

Nuala Lupton was twenty-four years old with three young kids and her hands full, but she was looking for something to do. It was the winter of 1971. The evenings were shortening. The nights were lengthening. The air was growing damp and cold. This stay-at-home mother wanted an outlet.

She spotted a notice from Richard in the 'Seen and Heard', the Skibbereen notes section of *The Southern Star*, calling out for new club members for the rowing club, both men and women. There were few sporting options for women locally at the time, apart from athletics, badminton and golf, and none of those appealed to Nuala. Rowing did.

Back home in Durrus near Bantry, from a farming background, her family always had a boat. They loved the water and being on it. The timing felt right for Nuala.

Liam, Caroline and Fionn were five, four and three years old respectively. With the full support of her husband, Fintan, a garda in town, the next day Nuala made it her business to track down Richard in Hosford's store.

She signed up and became part of the club's first women's crew, which would be the first crew to really put the Skibbereen Rowing Club on the map. This was the first crew that made winning a habit. They set the highest standards and made people take notice.

Mairead MacEoin, who babysat for Nuala, was the daughter of

Inspector MacEoin, who worked in town with Fintan. Mairead was in her early teens, going to secondary school at Mercy Heights, an all-girls school. She was a live wire. The oldest girl with four brothers and a younger sister, most of whom rowed. She wanted in too.

Across the road on Townshend Street lived one of her best friends, Patricia O'Brien. They were in the same class at school. Mairead persuaded Patricia to join the rowing club and they roped in another school friend, Deirdre O'Byrne, daughter of a local pharmacist.

Ladies' numbers were swelling. This meant that Richard Hosford was a busy man. He encouraged, coached and coxed, and did a lot more. It followed a familiar routine. He'd rustle the troops before the dawn chorus for training. At 5.30 in the morning he'd hop into his Renault Four and circle the town twice, first to wake his rowers up with a short beep of his car horn, second to collect them.

Martina O'Regan and Deirdre lived out the Baltimore road. He'd then circle back towards Townshend Street and throw pebbles at Mairead's window. She was a light sleeper and would spring out of bed, pop across the road and throw pebbles at Patricia's window. Patricia's father, Denis, without fail, would shout down the hall for her to get up because Mairead is outside. The light thud followed as Patricia jumped off her bunk bed onto the wooden floor.

One by one Richard would collect them all. Nuala would clutch her cup of coffee to wake up and keep warm. They'd head to Deelish pier and whatever combination of four he had would fill the old four the club had bought from Lee Rowing Club.

Those early morning training sessions on the Ilen became the norm. A local farmer, Jim Shanahan, always knew it was time to get up, 6.30 in the morning, and milk his cows when he heard Richard's words of encouragement drift across the Ilen.

Nuala was enjoying it. She rowed to keep fit. They trained that winter and into 1972 and it soon got to the point where there was talk of regattas, but Nuala quashed that. She had convinced herself that she was never going to row in public. But the boat couldn't race without her. So Nuala ultimately gave in.

There were already signs that she was different to the rest. She was strong and athletic, a natural rower. But before she dipped her oar in the water for the first time competitively, she'd already made her presence felt off the water.

***

Richard Hosford was working hard on and off the water, but he wasn't an expert and he needed help. He was travelling to coaching seminars and bolstering his own knowledge, but he knew it wasn't enough.

It was a visit from Irish Amateur Rowing Association President Wally Stevens to Skibbereen that joined the dots between the club and Frank Durkin, who had just started work as a junior doctor at Bantry Hospital. Stevens saw the club's set-up at Deelish pier and suggested that the new doctor, who had rowed for University College Dublin (UCD), would be the ideal fit.

So Richard and Nuala joined forces and made the short half-hour trip to Bantry. Unannounced, they surprised Frank at the hospital as he walked out of a ward. They explained the situation. This new club was eager to grow but was lacking in expertise and that's where they envisaged Frank coming in.

Here was a man who, while at UCD, was part of the Senior men's eight crew that won the national title in 1969, the premier event in Irish rowing. Not bad for someone who had only started rowing the previous year. He was hooked from day one and became a fanatic. Frank would talk rowing all day every day. He'd go on to become president of the Irish Amateur Rowing Union later in life, but in 1972, at twenty-seven years of age, the student was already set to become the teacher.

Out of courtesy, Frank made the trip to Skibbereen to view the rowing club after work. He was intrigued to see how this new club with a coastal rowing background was adapting to river rowing. His experience in gigs was non-existent, but he had rowed internationally at the Home Internationals and he knew his stuff. Richard wanted an insight into that knowledge, to the extent that when they were a man short to go out on the four that evening, he made up the crew. Frank, meanwhile, was the best-dressed cox the club had ever seen, still wearing his navy suit, white shirt and tie from work.

They rowed between the bridge by the West Cork Hotel in the town to the stone bridge closer to Deelish. It was getting dark. The heavens opened. It was rough and the boat was taking on water. They managed to get in close to the bank, hopped out, took out the oars, turned the boat upside down to empty it and got back in the water. Just as they arrived back at Deelish it happened again. This time there was a hole in the stern of the boat. It was sinking but they made it to land just in time.

Frank's suit was soaked right through. As Richard examined the boat, Frank presumed that was that. He had planned on coming back the next morning but the boat didn't look fit to take out again. However, Richard and the lads promised that they'd have it repaired by then.

'Let's meet at ten so,' Frank said, before plodding up the road towards his car.

When he was out of earshot, Denis McCarthy quipped to Richard that it was probably the last they'd see of him. As first impressions go there had been better ones. But Richard was determined not to let this opportunity pass. They needed the rowing doctor.

The stern of the boat was damaged, but that was a quick fix. The boat was joined in the middle by bolts, so they split it in two and transferred it back to Hosford's yard. It was dark now and utterly miserable. It was one of those nights where an open fire was the best ticket in town.

In the shed they surrounded the timber boat with gas heaters to dry it out. They went their separate ways to have dinner but met again in a couple of hours to work on the boat. It was well past midnight when the boat was patched up, but it was still wet and it needed the gas heaters' warmth to get through the night. Like a concerned father waiting for his youngest to come home from the disco, Richard spent the remaining few hours of that night checking in on the wooden boat every so often, to make sure that the heaters didn't burn it.

Early the next morning it was completely dry and ready to row again. They brought the boat back to Deelish pier and bolted the two halves back together, all before Frank's arrival. He was togged out this time and ready to coach.

Everyone was eager to learn. Well, almost everyone was.

***

Frank pinpointed a problem in Skibbereen straightaway.

The club had a mixture of rowers. There were those who were new to the sport, with no experience, who were easier to sculpt, and there were those with a background in gig racing, who were harder to retrain. The latter were built for coastal rowing with strong upper bodies and powerful arms that would drag a gig through the water but didn't have the leg strength required for the sliding seats. As the club was going down the route of Olympic-type rowing, they needed to get up to speed and the rower's legs needed to get stronger and faster.

Frank initially met some resistance when he explained this.

'Didn't our grandfathers and their grandfathers row out to sea and fish and then race back in to see who could sell the fish first – what do you need to teach us for?'

Frank had an idea. He got some of the rowers to row a 500-metre training piece as if it were a real race. 300 metres in they blew up. Their legs weren't strong enough. Their limit came sooner than they had expected. Frank had proven his point.

Nowadays the technique, physiology and fitness of coastal rowers is at a very high standard, but that wasn't the case back then. They'd take their boats out of hibernation in the spring, tar their arses for the rigours of the fixed seat and head into regatta season before parking up the boats until the following year.

Frank had a keen eye for spotting a coastal rower in a sliding seat. They'd jerk their body too much and lie back too far, and they were armed with a violent catch. They were old habits that weren't effective for going fast in a sliding-seat boat. Change was needed.

When Frank could, he made the trip from Bantry to Skibbereen to train crews, with his own target a simple one – get them to row properly and win races.

Frank was only involved with the club for eighteen months. He moved on in early 1974, as work took him to Cork city, but in that period he certainly made his mark.

'Frank turned the whole club around,' Mairead MacEoin says. 'It probably would have stayed as just a country club if Frank didn't come and put a bit of polish on us. He had the technique and the expertise. He was technically a very good rower.'

Frank transformed the Skibbereen women into the club's first successful crew. They outshone and outperformed the men on a consistent basis. They even put it up to the dominant Dublin Commercial crew, who were the kingpins of that era – the crew that led to the creation of the Irish international women's team that they then backboned.

A four of Nuala Lupton, Deirdre O'Byrne, Mary Ann O'Neill and Mairead MacEoin, coxed by Mary Gill, beat Commercial to win an All-Ireland ladies' Junior title in July 1974 and qualified to race Senior the following year.

Frank was gone by then, but he still stayed involved with the club and its rowers as a coach from afar, on a consultancy basis. His fingerprints were all over that boat. It sat so still in the water that a cup of tea wouldn't ripple on it. Frank would keep them there, sitting in the boat until it was completely level and balanced. They couldn't move until it was still. They chased the high standards set out in his soft yet firm Tullamore tones.

'Peel back your ears and pull like a donkey,' was his phrase of choice.

But they didn't row like donkeys. They were thoroughbreds on the water. Whatever four took to the water, it was in complete rhythm. Usually it was Martina in the stroke seat, which is closest to the stern (the rower who crosses the finish line last) of the boat. Whoever sits in the stroke seat sets the rhythm and the rate.

Then it was Nuala and Mairead, and Deirdre in the bow seat which is closest to the bow (the rower who is first across the finish line), with Mary Gill as cox. They'd concentrate on the shoulder blades of the person in front of them; every single move was co-ordinated down to the pressure they put on their feet.

It was mesmerising to watch. Four rowers in unison. The oars hitting the water at the exact same moment. That was the exactness Frank wanted. The wins followed as various regattas were conquered, and they were always in contention until life started to take them in different directions.

For all their success, however, it's a gig race that Skibb's first ladies crew is best remembered for: the Battle in Bantry.

This was the Senior women's race at the Bantry Regatta, where Skibbereen and Sneem went oar to oar. Noel Casey, from the famous Caseys of Sneem clan, used one word to describe losing: disaster. And it would be a disaster if his Sneem crew lost to Skibb. They'd clashed at the opening regatta of the season in Castletownbere. Sneem maintained they won, but so did Skibb, who received the trophy. That didn't sit well with Casey or Sneem. So they had a point to prove in Bantry.

Skibbereen powered off from the start line in Bantry Bay, as Nuala, Mairead, Deirdre and Mary Ann nudged their noses in front. Sneem were second. Skibb reached the turn first but, as they rounded the buoy, Sneem arrived and crashed straight into the side of the Skibbereen boat, piercing a small hole well above the waterline, near where Nuala was sitting.

The crews locked oars. The boats were stuck together.

Skibbereen tried to push off, but the rope for the rudder was caught and they couldn't steer. As mayhem ensued, Richard Hosford, the cox, crawled to the back of the boat to free the rope. All the time the Bantry boat, which had been in third place on the way out, took advantage, taking a wide turn at the buoy and heading straight for home.

But as the regatta commentator began to herald Bantry as the winners in waiting, Danny Murphy spotted the Skibb boat coming in the distance. They'd wrestled free from Sneem and they were catching Bantry fast. And they weren't going to be denied, powering past Bantry and taking victory.

Mad with temper, Skibbereen had beaten Sneem. They'd undoubtedly come a long way from their first gig race in Castletownbere, where they had all ducked at the gun start.

***

The Eldon Hotel was home to one of the rowing club's most important fundraisers, which became a popular fixture in the local social calendar for almost two decades.

There was a function room at the back of the hotel and, starting in the 1970s, the club held a weekly dance there, getting the approval of the owners, the Murnanes, Donal and Lil, who had an interest in rowing. This was, in effect, a late bar, so after closing time around town, The Eldon was the place to be. To get around licensing laws, chicken suppers became quite popular in Skibb on Saturday nights. The food was there if you wanted it, covered in the entrance fee.

'The regular income from the disco gave the club confidence because this was an era when it was hard to find money. The history of the club is tied up with the culture of the town and the activities that were going on,' Donal O'Sullivan says.

A deal was struck. The club had almost free reign. They would charge an entrance fee at the door, but regular customers of The Eldon would get in for free and take up their usual positions in the bar on the right inside the door.

A small hatch connected the bar to the function room in the back and this is where a hand would appear clutching a pint for a paying customer. Or a chicken supper.

The club had to collect the glasses at the end of the night, clean up, sweep the floors and set the room up for breakfast the next morning.

They also ran the door. Everyone pulled together. If you weren't a worker, you fell away pretty fast. But from the start the club was blessed with dedicated volunteers, both rowers and committee members. Often rowers held committee positions. Whatever was needed to help was done.

By the end of 1974 club membership stood at thirty-five. It was growing. The following year Nuala introduced the club to the world stage.

9

the world stage

The success of the Skibbereen oarswomen opened doors and brought opportunities. Both Nuala and Mairead were invited onto the national women's elite squad. The country girls were being noticed.

The Skibb four felt they were pushing the Commercial four. That feeling wasn't necessarily reciprocated in the capital, the Dublin boat was still well out ahead, but Skibb believed they could bridge the gap. And Nuala led the charge. She had only started sculling in 1974, but had already won a Novice single sculls race at Blessington. The Irish Amateur Rowing Union was impressed. She was on their radar.

So too was Mairead.

Working in Cork city at this stage and rowing with Cork Boat Club, Mairead was selected to row in the Home Internationals that year held at Castle Semple in Scotland. It was another accolade for her family after her brother Seamus, a year earlier, had become the first to row a scull for Skibbereen when he competed in Lee Schools' Regatta.

After the various national trials held around the country – this was long before the National Rowing Centre in Inniscarra was opened in 2007 – Nuala was selected on the first Irish women's team, a coxed four, to compete at the Senior World Championships at Holme Pierrepont National Watersports Centre in Nottingham in late August 1975.

She was the only non-Commercial member on the team.

Tina Kavanagh, Olive Middleton, Gerri McCaffrey, Brigid Conway and cox Mary Hutchings had rowed together for years. They knew each other inside out. They were great friends and international-class rowers. They had already represented Ireland three times. They were so dominant in Ireland that they started travelling to regattas in the UK to test themselves. They weren't getting the competition they wanted at home.

Together the Commercial women were unbeatable. That's why they weren't keen on Nuala joining their team. They didn't open their arms to her after she earned her place on the team. In their eyes their boat wasn't broken, so why fix it?

'We did have it pretty much all to ourselves,' Gerri McCaffrey says. 'When the IARU decided that they were going to send a crew to the Worlds we were thrilled. Then there was talk that they would open it up and make a squad. That put our noses out of joint. We thought, what's wrong with us, we've been rowing together for the last four years.'

But Nuala was as good as any of them. She improved that boat. She was the only woman in Ireland who could make it go better and she did. The World Championships were beckoning. This meant a six-week training camp in Blessington that summer ahead of the event. But Nuala was in a bind. She had three young kids and nobody to mind them. Fintan, who was now the treasurer of Skibbereen Rowing Club in his spare time, couldn't get the time off work as a garda.

Her father was also dying. Nuala, the youngest of her family, looked after her parents as they got older. Solutions were found on all fronts. It took a dinner with Fintan and Frank Durkin at The Lord Edward on Westmoreland Street in Dublin to persuade her that the impossible was possible. They told Nuala she had to go, that this was a chance that she couldn't refuse and that very few ever get an opportunity like this. Nuala knew they were right.

Her siblings all came home for two weeks each to mind her father. They would all say after how much they loved their time with him. He passed away from cancer that October. That was two months after his youngest daughter became the first person from Skibbereen Rowing Club to compete at World Championship level. Better again it was Senior, the highest rank.

Nuala ended up taking her three kids with her on the training camp. There was no other option. Funds were tight in the Irish Amateur Rowing Union and they couldn't cover the cost of accommodation and board for the crew in Blessington.

The Commercial crew could head back to their Dublin homes at the end of each day. That was a luxury not available to Nuala, so she bought a caravan from an advert she spotted in a newspaper. She didn't have time to view it. Instead the deal was struck over the phone. She had to take the seller's word that it was in good shape.

Fintan towed it from Courtown in Wexford to the lakeside in Blessington. It became home for Nuala and Liam, Caroline and Fionn – eight, seven and six years old. The caravan was yellow and white, and full of fun. Where the table and seats were by day transformed into three single beds at night, while Nuala had a fully sprung mattress for her double, a surprise comfort in a field in Blessington beside the lake. They were isolated. This was just a field with a caravan and trestles that the boats were kept on overnight.

Her kids loved it. They wanted to go back the following year for their holidays. They had the lake on their doorstep. They spent hours swimming and fishing for crabs. They were never bored. It also became HQ for the crew. There was nothing better than a hot cup of tea in the caravan after a training session.

Twice a day for two hours in each session, the women's four trained.

It was gruelling stuff. The entire Irish squad for the Worlds trained at Blessington, over half an hour outside Dublin, including the Garda Boat Club eight. Seeing as Nuala is a garda's wife, there was no shortage of babysitters and helpers to keep an eye on the three when she was on the water.

Their coach was Anne Noonan, the wife of Commercial international sculler Sean Noonan, and they rowed thirty miles a day in those six weeks. The thinking was that they needed a lot of time in the boat; seeing as Nuala was new to the crew, they would need to get used to one another and get the timings exact. Practice, practice and practice was the only way. In the morning they'd row to the Poulaphouca Dam and back again. They repeated it in the evenings.

The Commercial crew already had an understanding built on years together in the boat, but there was a different feel now with Nuala in it. She had earned her place after fighting hard. Brigid was the sub. Different combinations were trialled to get the balance right. But time was against them with the Worlds closing in. The boat needed work. Fast.

Gerri, the lightest, moved from the stroke seat to the bow. Nuala and Olive sat in the middle, seats two and three, two powerhouses, the engines. Tina, ambidextrous and able to row either side, went the opposite way to Gerri, from the bow to the stroke, and she set the rhythm for others to follow.

Nuala found it all challenging, especially on the water. She'd only ever had one coach: Frank. Even after he left Bantry, to go working in Cork city, he remained her coach. She'd travel to Cork to train with Frank, using his single scull on the Lee and competing in the Cork Sculling Ladder against men as her training. She held her own there too.

***

Nuala felt sick from the intensity of the training. She was pushing herself, maybe too hard. Maybe being the only non-Commercial rower coming from a new club with no clubhouse and very little equipment in a small town in the country meant she had something to prove to everyone else, that she deserved her place and that she was good enough. Because she was.

But there were always obstacles to overcome because she was living and training in a pocket in the far south-west. Geography didn't play fair. There was the time Nuala and Mairead had to hitchhike from Skibbereen to Dublin for a press conference. The first leg of the journey ran smoothly, but after being dropped at Glanmire outside Cork city they were hours in the one spot before they got another lift, followed by a bus journey and a frantic dash to get there on time.

From the start Skibbereen rowers were used to overcoming challenges. It hardened them. But those six weeks in Blessington, juggling her kids and rowing, were especially tough on the only mother in the crew. She was also the oldest, at twenty-eight; Mary was twenty-two, the rest all twenty-one.

'It hit me more, I think, because they were used to training with each other and I was trying to put in that extra effort. Sometimes it felt like I couldn't go on,' Nuala says.

All rowers have been there, gone to the well and felt there was nothing left inside to give. Then they look again, find that bit extra and power on. It's winning the battle in the mind. Nuala did that. She earned her place in that boat and, off the back of that training camp, they travelled to Nottingham for the fifth World Rowing Championships in optimistic form.

They had competed at the Nottingham International Regatta earlier in the summer, where they finished just a fraction behind England's number one crew. That was the Irish crew's first official international outing together.

The Irish four had led for three-quarters of the race but they caught a crab – when the oar gets caught in the water – that upset their rhythm and allowed England to overtake them. Still they battled back to within inches. That showed the Irish women were good enough. It convinced the Irish Amateur Rowing Union it was worthwhile sending this boat to the World Championships. They had been under pressure ahead of the race to prove their worth. They had proven it, and then some.

The World Championships were a whole new world. The top oarswomen in Ireland were one now of many. It was overwhelming. They'd seen nothing like it before.

The experience was memorable. But the result on the water was not what they wanted. Ireland finished eleventh overall. They'd expected better. But still, they were eleventh in the world at their first attempt.

'There were nerves, lots of them, having never competed in this environment before. It was a bit intimidating for us,' Nuala recalls.

This stage was a different world to what the Irish women were used to. A Russian coach spoke with Gerri, inquisitive about the Irish crew. She stood at five foot seven, one of the best rowers in the country. He took one look at her height and presumed she was the cox. This was a different playing field entirely. This was on another level to rowing back home.

Even if the result wasn't what they wanted, they'd broken the glass ceiling and put Irish women's rowing on the international map. Afterwards, there were talks that this crew was in the running to compete at the 1976 Olympic Games in Montreal. They had a taste for it. There was nothing concrete, however, and despite their eleventh place finish at the Worlds, they were overlooked for selection.

Disaster struck in late 1975 when Gerri and Brigid were involved in an accident. Gerri drove a motorbike, and Brigid was on the back one day when they crashed. It left Brigid with a broken leg and out of action. Try as they did, they couldn't find a suitable replacement. The Olympic dream faded and so too did that crew.

Before they bowed out, though, they helped create more history for Skibbereen Rowing Club.

Nuala held her spot in a Commercial/Skibbereen coxed four for the 1976 Irish Rowing Championships. She had offers flying in to form composite crews with other clubs, but Commercial needed someone and she was the natural and sensible fit. It was the first year the Senior coxed women's four was eligible for a national title and it was no surprise Commercial and Nuala won that day in Athlone.

She'd gone from being Skibbereen's first competitor at a Senior World Championships to winning the club's first national title.

That crew also represented Ireland in the 1976 Home Internationals held at Inniscarra. She'd opened the door for others to follow and was part of a crew that made others start to take women's rowing more seriously.

In Skibbereen, men and women were equal on and off the water. The club's women thought nothing of tying a boat to the roof of a car, or towing a trailer, and travelling to a regatta.

Nuala and Mairead did exactly this in May 1976 for the first Ulster College Sprint Regatta on Craigavon Lakes in Armagh. This regatta featured the first women's sculling championship of Ireland.

Nuala and Mairead were the Skibbereen team. They teamed up together for the double. Nuala also raced in the single. They had permission from the Garda Boat Club to use their double scull. Trinity were also using the same boat and were entered in several other races.

The Skibbereen duo set off from home with two sculls and blades on the roof rack. They picked up the Trinity trailer in Dublin and drove on to Craigavon.

Powerful, they won the double but not the single. The Trinity crews didn't turn up as they were involved in a car accident in Drogheda. Nuala and Mairead, after rigging all the boats and setting them up, de-rigged them all again, loaded up the trailer and drove to Dublin. They crossed the border late that night, two women and a trailer full of boats.

Skibbereen were working hard to climb up the ladder. And it was Nuala and Mairead who gave the club more publicity than ever before. It needed that to build a profile and spread the word. The club's name was in national newspapers. It's a shame, though, that no photo exists of Nuala in her green Ireland vest or Irish blazer. None were ever taken. Still, she'd undoubtedly put the rowing club on the map.

***

In the mid-1970s, the club had nowhere to call home. Deelish pier had served its time but the club needed its own place. The boats were at the mercy of the elements, sleeping outdoors on the riverbank. Valued at almost £3,000, they'd cost up to £10,000 to replace if they were damaged. That's money the club didn't have. There were no facilities at Deelish either. The search for a home was on. They had to invest.

Out of courtesy, they approached Joe Connolly, who owned the field where the boats lay, and offered to buy the plot they were using. He was given first refusal. He said no. The club also explored the option of setting up base in Lough Hyne, outside of town. It ticked a lot of boxes, but it wasn't long enough to fit in the mileage and distance the rowers needed.

Donal O'Sullivan took it upon himself to solve the problem. 'The decision to acquire its own piece of ground was the most crucial decision in the history of the club. Once you have your own piece of ground, you have a home,' he says.

On New Year's Day in 1976 he began his search for the most suitable site. Two miles out the road, past Deelish, a field in Drishane caught his attention. He parked the car, jumped the rusty farm gate and walked the field that sloped down to the Ilen. It was big enough to fit three houses, so size wasn't a problem. It provided access to the Ilen at all states of the tide, even low water.

This was the only site that had what the club needed. They didn't waste time. A local farmer, Johnny Shanahan, was leasing the land for grazing from Mrs McCarthy, a widow who lived in a bungalow across the road. He gave the deal his seal of approval as did Mrs McCarthy. Club treasurer Fintan and Donal called to her, outlined their thoughts and project, and she agreed to sell the club the field. Skibbereen Rowing Club had a new home.

Now they planned the clubhouse. This took time. They had to get it right. Donal Hoare was the architect. The plans were drawn up. Planning permission was granted.

Two years later, in late January 1978, the club held a press conference at The Eldon Hotel to outline its proposed new clubhouse. It included a gym so they could train indoors, changing rooms for men and women, showers and toilets, two twenty-foot-high squash courts, a viewing balcony and an eighty-foot-long boathouse – everything the club needed to take the next step.

They signed a contract worth £35,750 with constructor Miah O'Driscoll. Donal was there that night, Dominic and Teddy too, Danny Murphy, Richard Hosford and Richard Roycroft. So too was Nuala, as assistant secretary. These building blocks that they were setting ensured that the generations to come would all have the opportunities and resources they needed to find success at national, international and even Olympic level.

III
THE NEXT GENERATION

10

short shrift, long levers

Grainne O'Donovan is one of the very best oarswomen the rowing club has produced. She is nearly five foot two inches tall and spent most of her competitive days being mistaken for a cox. But she was made of steel. She wasn't shy either.

Oscar-winning actor Jeremy Irons was a regular sight on the Ilen in his rib boat when he spent time at his getaway cottage that sits on the river. This was before he bought Kilcoe Castle, which you can see from Gary and Paul's kitchen in Lisheen.

It was Saturday morning and there was a cavalcade of boats on the Ilen for pieces. Irons whizzed past in his small rib boat. A fierce wash came off it. The force was strong enough to almost knock Juniors out of their singles and the water was freezing cold. Grainne had seen this before and couldn't bite her tongue any more. She shouted after Irons to slow down. He stopped. She paddled closer to him. You're going to knock us out of our boats if you keep going that fast, she told him.

Irons listened. It was a civil, polite exchange. He then reasoned that he thought the faster he went, the higher up the rib would go and the less the wash would be. Grainne retorted that the wash was coming at force and that created a bigger impact against the boats. His reply was that he would obviously come back and pick someone up if they were knocked out. Thanks, she smiled. Sound for that. She asked him to keep a wider berth of their boats. Please. He did from then on. He was a gentleman, always saluting.

Dominic could only smile when he heard about this encounter. He knew Grainne better than most. She was a perfectionist. Mentally and physically, she pushed her own boundaries. And he admired that.

She felt she had to because of her small stature. At the World Under–23 Rowing Championships in 1992 she weighed forty-eight kilogrammes. The weight limit was fifty-nine kilogrammes. At the weigh-in Grainne felt embarrassed. She packed her backpack with spanners and adjustable wrenches so she could reach over the fifty-kilogramme mark when she stepped on the scales. That was to stop the ridicule. Other rowers still asked her if she was coxing. She was only seventeen, but she finished seventh at those championships. That year she had twenty-three victories in three different boats, winning at Junior, Intermediate and Senior levels. When she was a sixteen-year-old sculler she won her first Senior race. That was a record.

Grainne was so light that her boat would sit up too high in the water. Her lightweight boat had to be cut down so it would sit better in the water and not affect her stroke. It was a light lightweight boat.

What she lacked in height and weight, however, she made up for in technique. At a national training camp, the head coach of the Irish rowing programme at the time, Thor Nilsen, told her that her technique was up there with the best in the country. She was skilful and had a great eye for the small details. Dominic saw that and liked it. Her attitude to training was what he wanted too. Because she was small, she trained harder than anyone else. She had to make sure she was noticed.

Juggling her Leaving Certificate exams with the 1993 World Junior Championships in August, she trained twice a day, cycling to the clubhouse from home out the Tragumna road. Pound for pound she had wicked strength and held her own in the gym with the club's men. The results showed.

Grainne travelled to the Coupe de la Jeunesse, the major international Junior regatta, at Vichy in the south of France in July 1993. This was the first time Ireland had competed in the Coupe, against the top European rowing nations. She knew that to guarantee her place at the World Juniors in Oslo she needed to win.

On the first day, Saturday, she won her heat. The Junior races were timed events and her time placed her second overall. On Sunday the fastest scullers were selected to race. It was in blistering thirty-degrees heat that she stormed to gold, winning by a distance. She had qualified for the World Juniors but had put in such an effort that her legs violently cramped. She couldn't walk. The next day they felt worse. She couldn't walk down a flight of stairs.

By the time the World Juniors in Oslo came she was burned out. She was run down, busted and suffering with a massive head cold that wouldn't go away. She was sent to see an acupuncturist in Oslo to help clear her head, but what she really needed was rest. Everything had caught up with her.

The Coupe in Vichy was her fifth international regatta and she had won five gold and two silver medals in those. By then she already had six national titles as well. That year, 1993, Grainne had only been rowing competitively for three years but made history by winning four Irish Rowing Championship titles at the nationals: in the Senior single and double and the Junior single and double. Margaret Berry was her regular partner in a double; together they were powerful. A rower can compete in several different boats at the nationals and Grainne was the first oarsperson to win both Junior and Senior championships during the same season. The pocket rocket was world class.

Dominic knew she was a special talent and that she loved a challenge. Looking back, it's a sculling ladder race at the Marina in Cork city that stands out. Grainne's opponent didn't turn up, so a teenage boy was asked if he would race her. He saw the size of her, barely over five foot tall, and jumped at the chance. In his defence, he didn't know what he was going up against.

Grainne gave as good as she got against men and women. Racing a boy certainly didn't bother her. Halfway down the course, as she passed by him, he started to panic and pushed into Grainne's lane to knock her off course. She didn't stand back. She moved her boat on top of his, hacking away with her blade. The young fella was shocked. He didn't stand a chance. Grainne won by six lengths. In off the water Dominic was smiling.

'Not only did you beat him, but you tried to break his boat as well,' he laughed. It was a story he reminded her of year after year.

That strength of mind was important. She learned quickly that she had to work hard to get anything in rowing. At the national Junior women's trials in Blessington, Grainne arrived with the best score on a rowing machine in the country. But she did not sit in one crew boat that day. Her diminutive size worked against her. That's the day she realised that if she was to make an impact it would have to be in a single scull. So that's what she did.

And Dominic was keeping a constant lookout to add to the exciting pool of young talent coming through in the 1990s.

***

The instructions came from Dominic: go into school and find a tall guy. This was talent identification before it became popular, but Skibbereen style.

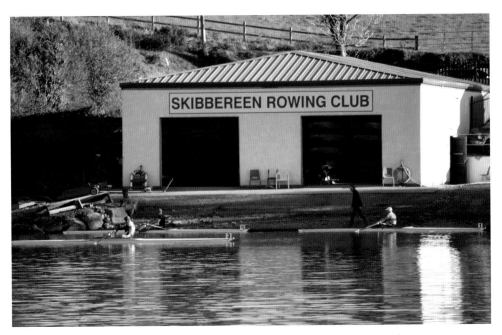

A typical busy evening at the clubhouse as a number of boats take to the Ilen River for a training spin. *Courtesy of Debbie Heaphy*

Gary (*left*) and Paul O'Donovan with their dad, Teddy (*far right*), pictured with Great British Olympic gold medallist rower Fred Scarlett when he visited Skibbereen Rowing Club in October 2002. *Courtesy of Arthur Little*

The Skibbereen Rowing Club Junior quad of, from left, Diarmuid O'Driscoll, Gary O'Donovan, Shane O'Driscoll and Paul O'Donovan that caused wreck on the Ilen River. *Courtesy of Mark Kelly*

Ireland internationals Denise Walsh and Aoife Casey (daughter of coach Dominic Casey) glued to the big screen erected at Skibbereen Credit Union, as they cheer on Gary and Paul O'Donovan in the 2016 Olympic Games. *Courtesy of Provision*

Paul and Gary O'Donovan celebrate on an open-top bus during their homecoming in Skibbereen in August 2016. *Courtesy of Anne Minihane*

Donal O'Driscoll, Tony Walsh (chairman), Richard Roycroft, Nuala Lupton (president), Fintan Lupton, Una Murray, Sean O'Brien (club captain) and Richard Hosford all raise a glass at Skibbereen Credit Union to celebrate Gary and Paul O'Donovan's silver medal at the 2016 Olympic Games. *Courtesy of Anne Minihane*

Skibbereen's first international rower and first National Championship winner Nuala Lupton pictured with Donal O'Sullivan, who served as club chairman for thirty-five years. *Courtesy of Anne Minihane*

Grainne O'Donovan, representing Ireland, receives her gold medal at the 1993 Coupe de la Jeunesse held in Vichy in the south of France. *Courtesy of Michael Heskin*

Coach Dominic Casey, third from left, with John Whooley, James Lupton and Eugene Coakley, who represented Ireland in the A final of the Junior men's quad at the 1997 World Junior Rowing Championships in Hazewinkel, Belgium.
Courtesy of John O'Donovan

The Skibbereen crew who won the Irish Rowing Championships Junior eight title for the first time in the club's history in 1997. *Back row from left:* John Whooley, Eugene Coakley, Paul O'Sullivan, Kenneth McCarthy and James Barry. *Front row from left:* Michael O'Brien, Richard Coakley (cox), Ciarán Hayes and Kevin O'Donovan.
Courtesy of Violet Hayes

John Whooley pictured with Violet Hayes' 1995 silver Toyota Corolla, with the boat on the roof, en route to the 1999 World Under–23 Championships in Hamburg. Violet's car was the Irish team transport to and from Skibbereen to Germany. *Courtesy of Violet Hayes*

The Irish lightweight men's four who qualified the boat for the 2004 Olympics in Athens. *From left:* Timmy Harnedy, Eugene Coakley, Richard Archibald and Paul Griffin. *Courtesy of Mark Kelly*

Skibbereen's Richard Coakley rowed for Ireland at the 2008 Olympics in Beijing.
Courtesy of Mark Kelly

Dominic Casey gives some advice to a Skibb ladies' crew about to hit the water.
Courtesy of Debbie Heaphy

Having won a silver medal at the 2017 European Rowing Championships, Denise Walsh is greeted with a kiss by her mother, Mary, when she arrives back in Skibbereen. *Courtesy of Anne Minihane*

Not only did Shane O'Driscoll and Mark O'Donovan dominate the world of the men's lightweight pair in 2017, but they also won the Senior men's pair title at the 2017 Irish Rowing Championships at the National Rowing Centre in Inniscarra. *Courtesy of Provision*

Established Junior rower Eugene Coakley had one fella in mind. Sixteen-year-old John Whooley, who was two days younger than Eugene. John was six foot four inches tall. He had long levers that, in theory, would move a boat faster than a shorter guy. John had played football with Castlehaven GAA Club, but now he was a free agent.

On an August evening in 1995, before they were due back to school at St Fachtna's, Eugene cycled the two miles outside of town to John's home at Lettercross. John wasn't home. He was across the way at his grandmother's. Eugene went there and outlined the plan. You're big, John, and we want you to join the rowing club.

John had zero interest. He barely knew what a rowing boat looked like. But his sister Julie came around the corner and asked Eugene what he wanted. He shared the grand plan. She said she'd love to go rowing. The next evening, John and Julie cycled to the rowing club on the opposite side of town. Not exactly sure where they were going, they kept cycling until they found the club. John was put in a double and hated every minute of it. He constantly banged the oars off his knees. He felt awkward, uncomfortable and unfit. He refused to go back.

In school, a few weeks later, Eugene promised John they'd put him in a proper boat this time, if he gave it another go. It was easier to agree than say no. He went out to the rowing club one evening after school and hopped into the quad with Eugene, James Lupton (Nuala's son) and Paul O'Sullivan. They rowed to Oldcourt, not more than ten minutes away.

John still hated it. He told himself over and over again that he wasn't coming back here any more. They came in off the water, John kept to himself and was preparing to make a quick escape. 'Never again,' he swore under his breath.

Then he met Dominic for the first time. It was 5 p.m. He was finished at the boatyard and was checking in on the club. John never forgot this initial encounter. That's when it all changed.

This was the era before the new boathouse beside the club. Back then rowing machines that were stored in the long and narrow room at the back of the clubhouse, which served as the boathouse, were pulled out into the hall inside the main door or pulled out into the open air outside the club to be used. That's where they were, four of them lined up, when Dominic landed to check out the new guy.

Dominic put John on a rowing machine. He tried to show him the technique needed and let him pull away for twenty minutes. John was dying inside. Muscles he never knew he had were revolting. He was ready to get his bag, get out of there and never look back. Three sentences changed everything.

'That's it, we have a strong four there now,' Dominic said, matter-of-factly, as if the deal had already been done. 'How would you like to win an Irish Championship this year?' And then the third sentence: 'You can't let the other three boys down now.'

Dominic saw John as tall and really strong. He was the right size for rowing. He had the big physique that Dominic liked. The plan was to surround John with more experienced rowers.

Dominic's psychological manoeuvring worked. John didn't want to let anyone down. He was young, naïve and couldn't say no. He came back and Dominic had his quad of John, Eugene, James and Paul.

In those early days John wasn't fit. In fact, he was quite stiff. When Dominic asked him to squat with a bar it was hard. He couldn't, unless there was a two-by-one piece of timber under his heel to allow him to go lower. However, this four definitely had something. Within twelve months that quartet won the men's Novice coxed four at the Irish Rowing Championships, the first of John's nine 'pots' and the title that

Dominic had predicted. (A 'pot' is the slang name given to the tankard that every member of a winning crew at the National Championships receives. Skibb rowers call them 'champs' too.)

By 10 August 1997, less than two years after he first picked up an oar, John was representing Ireland in the A final of the Junior men's quad at the World Junior Rowing Championships in Hazewinkel in Belgium, alongside Eugene and James, and Eoin Byrne of Commercial Rowing Club. Dominic was their coach.

John surprised even himself with his rise.

'I kept getting better, kept improving. I would have been delighted to make any Irish team because I never had before. I hadn't been to the Coupe de la Jeunesse or the Home Internationals because I started late enough. As the year went on, I got better. I impressed at the last trial and was picked for the Junior Worlds,' John says.

There, the Irish crew that was three-quarters from Skibb and coached by Dominic finished sixth in the A final.

The fortunes of Skibbereen rowing were firmly on the up, boosted by the success at the 1997 Irish Rowing Championships in July.

***

Ross O'Donovan dropped a couple of fucks into his pep talk for good measure, to really hit home. It was instil-the-fear-of-God stuff.

'This is your fucking chance,' he bellowed, his voice echoing off the corrugated iron walls and roof of the old, run-down University College Cork (UCC) boathouse at Inniscarra.

'Here we are, fucking bog men from Skibbereen, complete fucking underdogs and we've a lot to prove here. Give it fucking hell. Give it 120 per cent so when you cross the line you know you can't do any more.'

Skibb had never won an eight's title at the National Championships before, but they felt the Junior men's eight in 1997 could change that. They had to borrow a boat to compete, but they had still targeted this race. It was a strong crew with future Olympians and internationals spread throughout. Eugene Coakley's brother, Richard, was the cox. Kevin O'Donovan was stroke, then it was Eugene, Paul O'Sullivan, John Whooley, Ciarán Hayes, Kenneth McCarthy, Michael O'Brien with James Barry at bow.

They walked out of the boathouse, pumped up and bouncing off the ground. There was that viciousness in the eyes that Ross wanted to see. He followed a simple logic: wind up the stroke man and the number seven, and the rest will follow. He had the knack, though, of getting everyone revved up. Sometimes he trod right on the edge, but that was his style.

Dominic would draft Ross in for a rallying cry when it was needed. He knew how to get a reaction. The two didn't see eye to eye at times, but Ross was a Senior-level rower in the club who called it as it he saw it.

Ross wasn't as angry this year, giving his speech, as he had been the year before when he was banned from rowing for six months. He had been livid at that decision, insistent that the punishment didn't fit the crime. He still feels it was too harsh. At the university championships that year, he had rowed Novice with Cork Institute of Technology when he was Intermediate. An objection went in after the race when it was spotted that he shouldn't be rowing at Novice level, which is for those who are registered in their first year of rowing. He was handed a six-month suspension. During that period he had thrown himself into training with an I'll-fucking-show-them mentality.

In general, Ross was the motivator. Dominic was the expert tactician, apart from the one time he told a Junior crew to 'make their move at the cows', in reference to a herd that was in a particular field near the course. When the race came around, however, the farmer had moved the cows. They were gone.

Dominic and Ross are two very different personalities with two very different styles who share an intense love for rowing. It's hard to say no to either.

When Kenneth, only rowing a year or so and not yet hooked, told Dominic at the clubhouse one day that he was thinking of starting into running, he was quizzed.

'Why?'

'It will make me faster, definitely help my rowing and definitely make me fitter.'

'I met a man once who told me that a golfer golfs.'

'What does that mean?'

'Well, a rower should row. Just stick to the rowing.'

Kenneth still wasn't convinced. He was close to quitting. Then, after Mass one Sunday in town, Ross was waiting for him outside. Dominic had been in touch.

'Right, Kenny, are you giving up rowing or what?' delivered in a tone that only allowed one acceptable answer.

He couldn't say no to Ross. For a start, Ross was a good few years older. He was the club's top men's rower, only second to Gearoid Towey nationally, and just on the right side of madness.

Cue the sheepish reply: 'No.'

'Good. See you in the morning.'

Skibbereen won that Junior eight national title in 1997, after Ross' fiery speech, holding off the strong challenge of Neptune. It was an historic moment: the first big boat title for Skibb. That Junior win was important, because it secured the future of men's rowing in the club. That success bred more success. It lit a fuse and the club won the Junior men's eight for the next two years. Every teenager in that Junior eight rowed for Ireland at some level.

That strong group of Junior boys pushed each other on to bigger things. There were great friendships and fierce competitiveness between them, and there still is.

Those were the years when Skibb kept to themselves at the National Championships at Inniscarra, isolated from all the other clubs. There was one reason for this: to keep their focus.

Skibb never mingled. That old, rusted-brown UCC boathouse was base camp. It was a long, beaten-up old shed covered by trees and branches, a short walk down into the woods from where the National Rowing Centre now is. Boats were kept among the ferns outside, others in the shed that was falling down around them, but this was their bunker to keep the rest of the world out.

If Ross saw any of the lads with a football he'd either burst it or kick it into the lake. There was no temptation allowed for young fifteen- and sixteen-year-olds to chat to girls and boys from other clubs. No distractions. A full year's work was on the line. They were here to row and win. Nothing else. Skibb took it to the extreme, but the rowers bought into it fully. That belief in Dominic and his methods was crucial.

It was the small details too. If the weekend was hot, Dominic would hand out white T-shirts and hats, bought in Dunnes Stores, to fight off the heat. He wanted his athletes to rest, drink water and stay out of the sun so they were in the best shape for their race.

Then, like a primitive tribe emerging from the deep wilds, they'd launch their boats down at the small cove near the old boathouse and paddle up to the start line for their races. That's the first other clubs would see of Skibbereen before a race, when they appeared in the distance, from the trees and branches. They would disappear back in there afterwards. Hidden and secretive. Leaving the other clubs wondering what the hell was going on down there. That's just what Dominic wanted. There was a sense of mystery surrounding the club and its ways, tucked away on its own in every sense.

Other clubs wondered what went on in Skibbereen and if the tales really were true.

Did they really lift sheep on their backs and run up hills at training? Did they eat steak and spuds for breakfast? Did they really lower their saddles on their bikes when they were cycling to strengthen the muscles in their legs? Did they really take all the toilet seats off their toilets when their Head of the River was held in Skibbereen one year, in case any of the visitors decided to take them? Did they really jump on the body of a dead cow like it was a trampoline after it had fallen off a cliff?

Were all these tall tales true?

Each only added to the mystique.

(And yes, they did jump on a dead cow, led by Ross when he took Juniors downriver training one day. He spotted a dead cow that had fallen off a cliff into a cove, pulled the boat over, hopped out and jumped on it. It did wonders for his calf muscles, he claims.)

***

Neptune Rowing Club's Walter Maguire watched Skibbereen develop from the start. He understands better than most how the club works. He knew too that no Skibb rower would break rank.

One year around this period Walter was tasked with coaching the Ireland eight for the Home Internationals. It was a mixed eight, with rowers from his own club, Limerick, Lee and Skibbereen. They met at Neptune HQ in Dublin to train. Walter's challenge was to get these rowers from four different clubs rowing together as a cohesive unit.

'Needless to say all these clubs would have used a different starting procedure for races. All I wanted to know was what were they using so we could adapt and get a common start,' he recalls. 'I went around to all the different lads and asked them about their start. Then I asked one of the Skibbereen fellas what kind of starts they were using below. He said he couldn't tell me, that Dominic would kill him for giving away any information.'

Skibb kept their secrets safe.

***

'Ross.'

'Shut the fuck up.'

'Ross.'

'Shut up.'

'But ... Ross.'

'Shut the fuck up and concentrate, for fuck sake.'

'But we're facing the wrong way.'

Sometimes Ross' stubborn streak bit him in the arse. Like when he was the cox for Skibb Juniors and had them faced the wrong way ahead of a race.

This stubborn streak runs through his family. Grainne is his older sister. Tough as nails. Ross followed her into rowing. He never emulated her success on the water or came close to matching her thirteen national titles. But he did finish sixteenth in the single scull at the 1997 World Rowing Championships without any coach and following his own programme.

He also followed Grainne onto the roof of the clubhouse for a valuable lesson. In the days before the new boathouse, and when the boats were kept in the clubhouse, rowers were often either locked out or just forgot their keys. Grainne taught Ross another route in. Climb up on top of the lean-to roof at the back of the clubhouse, then shimmy carefully across the top. Move up along the ridge but watch each step as the roof is fragile. Then go to a window leading into the upstairs bar. Rattle it until the latch comes loose. Push open. Squeeze in. That trick was passed on to each generation.

Grainne also taught Ross not to pick the skin off blood blisters. Popping, draining and ripping the skin off will only make them worse and it will be sorer when you grip the oar. Leave them alone, she said. Let the blisters sort themselves out. Forget the discomfort and drive on. Ross listened.

Younger guys in the club looked up to him. He trained every day of the year. This was someone who sold the Ford Escort left to him by his uncle who had passed away so he could buy his first single scull. He didn't want the car. He wanted the single.

'Sculls are like your children – you mind them and you don't give them away to anyone,' he says.

His stubbornness served him well in the single, where he was on his own. The skills he learned while rowing also carried over into life. It's a sport that teaches discipline and encourages rowers to have a positive outlook. There's the well-being, fitness and health benefits too. Work hard and be confident in yourself and the results will follow.

And that was, in part, why Ross and that 1997 Junior eight marked a turning point for the club. This new generation were building up to big things.

dirty water bottle

Violet Hayes missed her son Ciarán's Junior men's quad sculls' gold medal win at the 1999 Home International Regatta held at Inniscarra. Instead, she was 1,700 kilometres away in Hamburg, rooting through a bin to find a water bottle for John Whooley.

John had thrown his away, but he needed one ahead of his B final of the men's heavyweight single sculls at the World Under–23 Championships. Violet couldn't find any water bottles for sale, but there were taps. Rifling in a bin she found a cast-off empty bottle, washed it out, filled it up and handed it to John, who was unaware of what she'd done. The bottle looked new and the water tasted grand.

Violet's job as team manager for the Irish team for the 1999 Nations Cup in Hamburg, which were the World Under–23s, was to make sure all the rowers had to worry about were their races. She looked after everything else.

This had already been an unusual trip. The Irish team consisted of just two Skibbereen rowers, John Whooley and Ross O'Donovan. They had travelled from Skibb to Hamburg in Violet's 1995 silver Toyota Corolla with their twenty-seven-foot-long single sculls strapped to the roof, sitting on a quickly pieced-together timber cradle Dominic made, painted black more for aesthetics than anything else.

She'd never driven on the other side of the road before. She'd never rowed either. But when her two kids, Ciarán and Orla, started with the club, she followed the same path hundreds of parents have followed, first ferrying them to and from training, and then rolling up her sleeves and getting stuck in.

So when Violet was asked the Saturday before the World Under–23 Championships if she'd look after the two-man Irish team in Hamburg the following weekend, she agreed. Working as a public health nurse, on Monday she put in for a week off. At 6 p.m. on Tuesday morning, with the car loaded, the trio took off.

You need to do one dangerous thing in your life, Violet maintains. This was her first.

She had no mobile phone. No credit card. There was no satnav or Google Maps to rely on, but she knew the end point was Hamburg. The route would take them through England, France, Belgium, The Netherlands and into the top half of Germany, not too far from Denmark.

Driving across England, on the Tuesday night they found a hotel to rest their heads. The three shared an executive room; that's the best they could manage. John and Ross took the bed. Violet slept on a couch. The cross-continent trek continued on Wednesday, as they inched across mainland Europe, the boats bobbing on top of the Corolla on the motorway.

Violet didn't learn until after the trip that it's actually illegal to drive on German roads with a large overhang, like the two sculls on top of her car. The fear held by some members of the club was that if she was told before they left Skibbereen, she would pull the plug on the whole trip.

John took on the role as her navigator. He sat in the passenger's seat with the map. Violet headed towards Essen in western Germany and its spaghetti network of roads. John had the air of a man who had it all under control as they neared Essen, but he was secretly sweating, as one wrong exit would slingshot them miles in the wrong direction. At one stage Violet swears she saw a signpost with Moscow on it.

Every time they stopped at a service station between Skibb and Hamburg, John and Ross would stretch their legs. They'd count five telephone poles up the road and spend ten minutes sprinting between them, just to get the blood pumping.

Well after midnight, after a second full day crammed in the car, they found their hotel in Hamburg just off the motorway. They'd arrived.

Long car journeys didn't usually faze Skibb rowers because they were used to them. Being loaded into the back of Dominic's grey Mitsubishi Isuzu jeep, with just cushions to sit on or maybe even his toolbox if you were last in, for trips from Skibbereen to Enniskillen in Fermanagh or Blessington in Wicklow, with no stop along the way, often pulling a boat trailer, toughened them up. While the car ride to Hamburg was on another level, at least they had a seat to sit on for the entirety of the journey. Small comforts.

The next day, eyes hanging from the two days of travelling, John and Ross went back to bed after breakfast, but it was out to the course that evening, where the disparity between the Irish team and the larger nations couldn't have been any greater. The country boys from Skibbereen were up against the best in the world, on and off the water. The Irish team rolled up to the boat enclosure in a Toyota Corolla. They were on a similar level to the Latvians, who pulled in at the same time with two old eights clinging onto a rickety bus from the 1970s. But this was in sharp contrast to the bigger countries.

'The Americans were there. Australia, Great Britain, France and

Germany too, all the big countries. They had their coaches, trailers, everything else, and other smaller countries had old buses, but there we were with a Corolla with two boats on top,' Violet says.

It wasn't just in transport that the Irish team came up short. They had no coach either. Dominic was their club coach, of course, but they had no international coach. John and Ross had to fend for themselves and were learning on the hoof.

They missed two days on the water, Tuesday and Wednesday, travelling, but they had to get on the water on Thursday evening to fill their lungs. It was bullishly rough. A gale was blowing and only the two Irish boats and a Romanian eight were out on the course. Paddling up to the start line, however, John and Ross realised they had no choice but to come in. It was too dangerous. Three days now and no proper row. They got out for two spins on Friday, ahead of the action that was crammed into two days that weekend.

On the water John went well, just missing out on a place in the A final, but then winning the B final on the last day of the regatta, using that second-hand water bottle and driven on by his annoyance with his performance in the A/B semi-final where he had finished fifth. By the Sunday evening he was seventh in the world overall.

It didn't go as smoothly for Ross. As a lightweight, the two-day journey in the car and trying to manage his weight took too much out of him. He missed out on the A/B semi-finals, but did finish thirteenth overall.

That same weekend, back in Inniscarra, at the Home Internationals, five Skibb oarsmen won gold, including Violet's son Ciarán in a quad alongside Dermot O'Sullivan, Mike O'Brien and Paul O'Sullivan on the Saturday. Ciarán and Mike also won silver in the Junior men's double sculls. Skibb's Cormac McCarthy took gold in the Junior men's coxed four and there were medals too for Timmy Harnedy and Emily Dulohery.

Violet learned of Ciarán's success when she rang the landline at home in Skibbereen that Saturday night from a phone box outside their hotel in Hamburg.

They left Hamburg at 5 p.m. on the Sunday evening and the destination was Calais for the early-morning ferry. Violet had to drive hard and deep into the night. They couldn't miss the boat. She knew she was crossing over and back between borders, from Germany to The Netherlands into Belgium, but at one stage she didn't know where she was.

She pulled in for coffee, a Black Booster energy drink, Red Bull and chewing gum, anything to keep her awake. Violet rang home again. Her husband, Pat, was there, and Orla too. They dug out an atlas. Violet gave them the name of the town they were in. Orla found it on the map. They told her she had just crossed into The Netherlands. They were still on track.

The Irish team Corolla drove through the night, all three awake twenty-four hours by the time they reached Calais, suffering the Red Bull sweats. They then raced across England and Wales to catch the afternoon ferry from Fishguard back to Rosslare. By the time they landed back in Skibb at 10 p.m. on the Monday night, none of the three had slept in thirty-six hours.

The difference between the Hamburg trip and the journey to Hazewinkel in Belgium for an international Junior regatta two months earlier, where Violet had also been team manager, was that she knew exactly where John and Ross were at all times in Germany. That wasn't the case in Belgium, which she only found out years later.

That trip sticks out in the memories of the seven Skibbereen rowers who travelled to Hazewinkel, and Violet, as the eight shared two bedrooms in a Dublin hotel the night before they flew out, and all watched Manchester United beat Bayern Munich with those two late goals in the 1999 Champions League final at the Camp Nou.

After their races in Hazewinkel, the Skibb seven of Violet's son Ciarán, Kenneth McCarthy, Timmy Harnedy, Kevin O'Donovan, Dermot O'Sullivan, Michael O'Brien and David O'Brien decided to seek out some late-night drama of their own.

The Skibb contingent were the only Irish Juniors at this regatta, which coincided with a World Cup regatta. They rubbed shoulders with some legends there. They met Great British rowing great Sir Steve Redgrave. Kenneth got his singlet signed by Redgrave, James Cracknell and Ed Coode. He never wore it again. It's a treasured possession. A memory.

The Sunday night before they flew home, and with their racing finished, Violet set them a curfew as they went for a walk around the suburbs where the hotel was situated. She warned them not to go into Brussels city centre on their own. But they were sixteen and seventeen years old. For some, it was their first time outside of Ireland. Everything was new: the language, the food, the accents, the sights, sounds and smells. The Belgian girls too. And the lure of late-night Brussels was too strong. Violet's words fell on deaf ears.

Piling into a subway for the first time, eyes wide open, they jumped off in the city centre and walked around the Grand-Place, the central square. Too young to get into any bar, they eventually found their way back to the hotel, almost an hour past the time Violet had set them. She was waiting in the hotel bar, reading a book, when they landed back, but remained unaware of their adventure until almost a decade later when it slipped out in conversation.

Looking back, Violet does recall how when herself, Ciarán, Kenneth and Dermot decided to take the subway to the Grand-Place the following morning for a look around, the three knew their way around better than any first-time tourist should. Years later, it all clicked into place.

***

When Grainne O'Donovan was finishing up in the late 1990s, Orla Hayes was just starting. Watching Grainne train had left a lasting impression on her. It was beyond human.

Orla followed her older brother, Ciarán, into the club when his Junior crew needed a training cox. She was twelve years old when she filled in for Richard Coakley, who had been the cox. She didn't know what she was getting herself into but was soon out on the water too.

What struck her first was the fun. That got her hooked. Training was demanding, but there was great craic in the club. That was important, as it punctured the seriousness of it all.

That's why she enjoyed their soccer games so much, even if Dominic didn't. Orla was in goal the day he landed back to the club as they were right in the middle of a game on the grass patch beside the clubhouse. They were caught red-handed. They had thought the coast was clear, but it's an impossible task to stay one step ahead of him.

The evidence was kicked into the next field. The jumpers for goalposts were quickly gathered up. Timmy, John, Richard, Kenneth, Mike O'Brien, Dermot O'Sullivan, David O'Brien, Timmy Enright, Orla, everyone there dropped to their knees and started looking closely at the grass, doing their best not to make direct eye contact with Dominic.

'We're looking for Timmy's watch,' was the party line.

Dominic smelled the bullshit. He hauled them into the squash court and, not for the first time, stressed that they weren't to play soccer. His reason was simple: he didn't want anyone to get injured before the championships and waste an entire year's work. They all saw the logic and sense behind this, but that never stopped them.

Even the squash court they stood in during this lecture was sometimes used for soccer when Dominic wasn't there. A nail had been driven into two of the walls, around six feet up, and a rope tied between them, splitting the court in half. This was football tennis. Two teams of two or three either side, one bounce allowed, tennis rules applied. These games were timed to end just before five, when Dominic finished work. But he knew what was going on and would land early some evenings to try and catch them in the act. That was why a look-out was important. This evening, however, the look-out had failed at their job.

When not playing football, Orla was working hard on her rowing. Orla graduated from cox to rower at a time when the club's women wanted in on the action as they watched the men's Junior rowers flying high in the late 1990s. Skibb hadn't won a Junior women's national title since 1994. In 2000 they wanted to change that.

'We had a complex about being girls and wanting to prove ourselves,' Orla says.

And they did prove themselves. She was stroke as Skibb won the women's Junior quad at the 2000 championships in a crew alongside Caroline Leonard, Emily Dulohery and Eileen Whooley.

Even then, at only fourteen years old, Orla could see how Dominic worked. He never told them how well they were going that year and they surprised themselves when they landed at regattas and beat everyone else. They won the national title by clear water. Shy by nature, Orla had found her calling and was addicted now. She wanted that winning feeling again and again, as well as that sense of togetherness that Dominic harnessed within the club, where they felt that the sum of themselves was stronger than anyone else.

Dominic was her coach from the start and he liked what he saw in Orla. She was focused, dedicated and trained hard. Here was a genuine talent who, in her Leaving Cert year at Mercy Heights, went on to become the Irish Junior Oarswoman of the Year after winning two gold medals at the Coupe de la Jeunesse in Italy. It's why Dominic never made it easy for her when she wanted to walk away from it all. He would always do his utmost to keep his talented rowers on-board.

***

In 2007 Orla had her flights booked to New York for the summer on a J-1 visa. She had her mind made up. She wanted a break and was sick of it all. All the training. All the commitment. Missing out on time with her friends.

The problem was Dominic wasn't entertaining this. He turned Orla's moaning back on her: 'Did you ever think that your friends might want to do what you're doing?'

She had no answer. It was his subtle use of psychology again, his ability to tap into what every crew or person needs. It's only afterwards that the rowers realise what he's done.

Orla was a tougher nut to crack. She was studying to be an educational psychologist and was wise to his ways, though Dominic always told her that while she thought she could read his mind, he could read hers too. He kept her on her toes. When she did try and step back from rowing, Dominic kept after her to come back. He called to her house and wouldn't take no for an answer. He saw the potential and felt that it was a crime not to realise it. Those who didn't have the same potential and work ethic, he wouldn't chase after. That was the difference.

Orla didn't go to New York that summer. She relented. Instead she was selected to row for Ireland in the lightweight single sculls at World Rowing Cup II in Amsterdam that June, where she finished eighth overall. In July she placed eighth at the World Under–23 Rowing Championships in Glasgow, despite being ill the week beforehand. It turns out that Dominic was right after all.

The following year was her best. There was her fifth-place finish in the lightweight single at the World Under–23s in Brandenburg. It was a week notable for Dominic hijacking the Swiss team bus after one race to take Orla and himself back to their hotel, instead of waiting for the shuttle bus. He didn't want Orla standing around and waiting when she could be resting and recovering.

Then, at the World University Rowing Championships that September, under the sweltering sun in Serbia, Orla was the youngest athlete in the A final and won bronze in the lightweight single.

Although Orla did represent Ireland at four Rowing World Cups, she never pushed on to the next stage and joined the elite ranks at international level. She felt she wasn't knocking at the door enough.

But she kept going with Skibbereen. She has a strong attachment to the club. It's the same for all its rowers. Dominic has instilled a sense of pride in all of them, to never forget where they're from and the club and community they are representing. Orla calls this their 'Skibbereenness'.

In January 2019, Cork GAA chiefs released their five-year plan to resurrect falling football standards in the county. The document made reference to Corkness and described it as 'that air of confidence just on the right side of arrogance – an unparalleled pride and our insatiable desire for Cork to be the best at absolutely everything'. But Skibbereenness existed long before Corkness hit the headlines.

Orla later rowed for Molesey Boat Club, London Rowing Club and the University of London when she studied for her psychology PhD in

England, but you couldn't peel the red and white off her to race for any club other than her own when she was in Ireland – this despite the fact that she was asked at different times by different Irish clubs to row for them.

She is a Skibb woman. It's her club, her home and her family. It's a different feeling when you put on the Skibbereen one-piece. Rowing for other clubs and colleges doesn't mean as much. They're not Skibbereen. And never will be.

12

the first olympian

Dominic wasn't entertaining Eugene Coakley today.

'Dominic, I've had enough. I'm going to pull away from this,' Eugene said, still nursing a hangover from the night out before in Cork city.

College life was good, especially in Cork. Thursday nights were worth waiting for. Eugene was enjoying his freedom and independence.

He started in UCC in 1997 on a rowing scholarship while studying civil engineering. His first year there, his discipline to train hard and regularly had been admirable, considering what college life offered. He hadn't been as disciplined in his second year, however, willingly giving in to the distractions. His social life was good. Nancy Spains on Barrack Street was a regular haunt. Gorby's Nightclub kept the party going late. Rearden's was another familiar stomping ground. That's why he was standing outside the boathouse on this dreary winter's Friday night, in the misty rain hanging in the air, talking about quitting. He had no time for rowing; there was another life waiting to be lived.

The jump from being a Junior rower to the loftier heights of an Under–23 and then Senior also weighed on his mind. He was nineteen years old, just after his first experience at the Senior World Rowing Championships that September in Cologne. In a lightweight double with John Armstrong, they finished twenty-first out of twenty-four boats. That next step seemed too wide to make. To make it worse, Eugene had hurt his back. All the signs were telling him to get out.

Perhaps it was the last sting of the hangover, a shot of Dutch courage, because he hadn't hesitated in telling Dominic he was finished. He didn't have the time for rowing and all the training that was needed. That was it for him.

Dominic said nothing for a moment, just looked at him. Then he spoke. Three words.

'Don't be stupid.'

With that he turned and walked away, leaving the heavy-eyed Eugene standing there on his own. He was back on the water the next morning.

It wasn't the first time Dominic stopped him walking away. The first time had been in 1994, when Eugene was fifteen years old. He'd been rowing for only one year when all his friends packed it in and so he decided to cut his losses. Dominic heard. In response, he introduced him to sculling and partnered him with James Lupton. They were both in St Fachtna's de la Salle secondary school in town. James was the model pro and knew his stuff. Together they won the men's Junior double scull at the 1996 and 1997 National Championships. And more.

Dominic knew even then that the potential was there. That's why he undercut Eugene's thoughts about leaving in 1994 and again ignored Eugene's resignation speech in 1998. Eighteen months later, Eugene won a bronze medal in the lightweight four at the 2000 World Under–23 Championships and was off to the Olympics that same year, selected as a sub for the Irish lightweight four at the Games in Sydney, ready to be called on if someone in the boat got sick or injured. No one did. But Skibbereen Rowing Club still had its first Olympian.

***

Small Euge, as the nickname suggests, had been small growing up. Home was a stone's throw from O'Donovan Rossa GAA Club's grounds, but Gaelic football wasn't for him. He knew that himself. An Under–14 game against a local rival, Tadhg MacCarthaigh, confirmed his suspicions. The opposition were short one player and Skibb had too many. They traded Eugene, as he was their worst player.

He found his calling on the water with the rowing club. He saw a poster hanging up in St Fachtna's that read, 'If you join Skibbereen Rowing Club, you have a seventy-five per cent chance of rowing for Ireland at some level', from the Home Internationals up to world and Olympic level. That grabbed his attention.

He was a sculler in his early years, starting off in 1993. The first time he rowed for Ireland was at the Home Internationals in 1995, in a double with James, where they finished third; they were sixteen-year-olds battling with eighteen-year-olds. By now Small Euge was growing, stretching into his frame.

He won a silver and bronze at the Coupe de la Jeunesse the following year. National titles followed and more internationals and more medals, but he felt he was struggling in limbo in 2001 and 2002, despite being an Olympian – albeit an unused one.

Eugene didn't mind being a sub for the Irish lightweight four at the 2000 Olympic Games in Sydney. He enjoyed the ride, from the training camp for three weeks north of Sydney, to a week spent in Penrith for the rowing and the next week in the Olympic Village. The four of Neville Maxwell, Neal Byrne, Gearoid Towey and Tony O'Connor finished eleventh overall. For the Skibb man, it was bonus territory. It was all about the experience, but it irked him that while he had transitioned from a Junior–18 to an Under–23 rower, he still hadn't taken that final step up the ladder to become an established Senior international rower.

That changed at the 2003 World Rowing Championships on the lakes of Idroscalo Park in Milan. Eugene was in the Irish men's lightweight four with Kerryman Paul Griffin, from Fossa outside Killarney, Coleraine rower Richard Archibald and another Skibbereen man, Timmy Harnedy, from Aughadown, outside of town.

Timmy was almost three years younger than Eugene and was a real talent, a two-time men's Junior single scull national champion. Because he was so good as a solo artist, he had won a place in the lightweight four that won silver at the Under–23 Worlds in 2001 in a boat with Eugene, Paul and Neil Casey from Dublin. They finished fourteenth at the Senior Worlds that year, but it was at the Worlds two years later that they announced their arrival on the big stage. Olympic qualification for the Athens Games was the prize on offer to the top eleven crews.

This was a crew that had it all. It was the best crew Timmy ever rowed with. Eugene feels the same. There was a bond. It was a boat of brothers in those early years, years that were special.

Eugene was a natural rower with great technique and great endurance. He's the type who will hop in a boat in his fifties and look like he was never out of the water. He never increased the speed of the boat as much as others could, but what he did better than anyone else was, due to his excellent technique, he didn't slow it down between strokes. His one weakness was just that: he was weak. Weights were his kryptonite. The gym was never his friend, but then his strengths lay elsewhere.

Kerryman Paul, on the other hand, was a force of nature. He was the stroke. He was also terrifying to race behind. He took his teammates to places their bodies didn't want to go. They were dark places but for new heights. He gave everything to move that boat faster. Absolutely everything. He had two speeds: flat to the mat or balls to the wall. Both were scary. He's the toughest man to ever pick up an oar for Ireland. He didn't say a lot, but there was a steely deepness to him. Then there were his eyes: intense, focused.

Richard and Timmy were the two outliers, at opposite ends of the spectrum. Richard was more conservative, technically very good and the calmest man in the tightest situations. His ability to relax the boat was the yin to Timmy's yang.

Timmy was the youngest of the four, at twenty-one. He was enthusiastic, impulsive and wild, but a leader in the boat with a brain for rowing. From the water to the rowing machine to weights, he was an all-rounder. He was an athlete.

It was Timmy who had encouraged Eugene to train harder when he was making the step from Under–23 to Senior, after the four finished fourteenth at the 2001 World Rowing Championships at Lucerne, a few weeks after winning that silver at the World Under–23s. They could tell that they were in with the big boys now.

Their heat at the 2001 Senior World Championships stood out for all the wrong reasons. Denmark were the powerhouse in the lightweight four and Ireland finished almost sixteen seconds behind them in that heat: 6:19.360 against a distant 6:03.740. The umpire's launch almost had to pass the Irish lads to keep pace with the leaders.

We'll never beat the Danes, Eugene felt. Why waste time trying? But Timmy's words stuck in his head: 'train harder'. Timmy believed he would make the Olympics and was smart enough to see it was possible. That rubbed off on Eugene. If Timmy thinks he can make an Olympics and I'm faster than him, then I can get there too, he reasoned.

Together the dynamics of their four worked. They finished second in their heat at the 2003 Worlds, less than two seconds behind the Italians, with the second fastest time of the heats. Better was to come. They won their repêchage – a last-chance qualifying heat where first-round losers are given another opportunity to advance to the next round – in 5:56.280, finishing ahead of Great Britain, Ukraine and Serbia. They were into the A/B semi-finals, the top twelve crews in the world. Olympic places were on offer, with the top eleven crews to qualify their boats for the 2004 Games in Athens. They were close.

And they won their semi-final in 6:00.820, ahead of The Netherlands, Canada, Australia, Russia and Poland. They were into the A final at the World Championships, but they had also qualified the boat for the 2004 Olympics.

There wasn't much time to celebrate. They had a job to do. They could win a world medal. But it all went wrong.

The Irish four could have medalled. The conditions were calm until just before the start, when a heavy headwind blew up, with a slight crosswind as well. This wasn't what the men in green wanted. They were rigged heavy as a crew. Heavy rigging is equivalent to high gears on a bike and it can be easier to exert maximum power, especially rowing with a tailwind.

For this four heavy rigging was Irish Rowing Head Coach Thor Nilsen's preference. Thor is a legendary figure. There was a presence about him. He was the master. And the Irish rowers believed in him and his methods, as did Dominic.

Thor's reputation preceded him. He guaranteed success. Italy, Norway and Spain blossomed under his system, and so had Ireland. There was huge respect for the revered Norwegian, a long-time mentor and guru with Irish rowing who had worked wonders. He shaped a world champion in Sam Lynch and took crews to Olympics. Thor's training was intense but effective. His great strength was his physical programme and he developed the standard club-training programme for most clubs in Ireland, one that even Dominic used as his template.

In one of his early training camps with the lightweight four, his strong Norwegian accent dominating his spoken English, he told them they'd know how it felt to train like an athlete who wanted to be an Olympian or world champion. Thor handed them their programme. The next day they had three sessions – running in the morning and two sessions of rowing.

He pushed boundaries. It was relentless. Only the strong survived those camps in Seville, Strömstad in Sweden and Hazewinkel in Belgium. Many broke down. There were hushed tales of legendary sessions on the rowing machine, fifteen sets of 500 metres with a one-minute break in between. This sort of stuff was previously unheard of, but Thor showed that it could be done by pushing to the limit and he brought out the big performances.

But this didn't happen in Milan.

In lane three, they were in the bronze medal position with 500 metres to go. The great Danes were in lane four. This was Eugene's proudest moment so far. Three years after this Denmark crew had presented an Irish lightweight four that included Eugene with bronze medals from the 2000 World Under–23s in Copenhagen, the Irish men were racing beside them in a world final. Timmy had been right after all. They could take on the Danes.

But, in this case, Ireland slipped back at the business end. They finished sixth, six seconds behind the winning Danes. It was unfortunate, but they underperformed. It was a learning experience for this young crew.

Mixed emotions. They'd qualified for the Olympics, but that final rankled. Things were about to get a lot worse for one of the Skibbereen men.

***

Timmy knew his Olympic dream was slipping away. It was almost gone. Hanging by a sliver. Thor was talking, reasoning. But Timmy had zoned out. A thousand thoughts were rushing through his head.

They were sitting in the food tent after World Rowing Cup II in Munich at the end of May in 2004. The Irish four had won silver a few hours earlier, but Timmy wasn't in the boat. In his place sat the experienced Niall O'Toole, thirty-four years old and already in Irish rowing's hall of fame. He had been a former world single scull champion back in 1991.

An Olympian in Barcelona and Atlanta, O'Toole came out of retirement in September 2002. He had unfinished business with the Olympics after missing out on Sydney. It didn't work out ahead of the 2003 World Championships in Milan. He broke down in a trial at Hazewinkel after he'd fallen ill and missed training at the wrong time. But O'Toole was in good shape in 2004. He was gunning for a place in the four for Athens, hitting all the times and targets.

Over the previous few months, trials for the seats in the boat for Athens had been whittled down to a straight shoot-out between Timmy and Niall. It was the young gun against the experienced veteran.

Eugene, Paul and Richard were locked in. The number three seat was up for grabs.

Trialling goes with the territory. Timmy knew this. But he felt he was good enough, and that the four who qualified the boat represented the best chance of winning a first Irish Olympic medal. Eugene felt the same. Thor kept his options open. Timmy was told the selection process would involve trials and ongoing performances over the season, so Thor could see the more complete picture and form an opinion from that.

At the Duisburg Regatta in Germany, shortly before the World Cup event in Munich, Thor sent out two different combinations. The plan was that the results would help him make up his mind. Eugene, Paul, Richard and Niall won gold on day one. The following day, Eugene, Paul, Richard and Timmy won gold. Honours even. The boat was marginally faster with Niall in it, but they won by more with Timmy in it. Different days, different times and impossible to compare.

Thor still didn't make a decision. He called a meeting where he announced that O'Toole would take the seat at the World Cup event in Munich and Timmy would get his chance at World Rowing Cup III in Lucerne three weeks later. After that, a final decision on the crew that would be sent to the Olympics that August would be made.

Timmy cornered Thor straight after the meeting. His fear was that if the crew went well in Munich without him, they'd stick with that for Athens. He was told not to worry. He still did. And his hunch was soon confirmed.

That four clinched silver in Munich. They finished just behind the Italians in the A final. It was this four's first-ever World Cup medal. They'd broken through and hit a new height. It was a landmark moment achieved without Timmy.

Thor approached Timmy afterwards. As they sat at the table in the food tent, the coach told him that the crew had performed really well and he was going to leave O'Toole in the boat for Lucerne and reassess after that. Timmy's heart sank.

While Thor explained that the Skibb man was only twenty-one years old and had a number of Olympic cycles left in him, Timmy's mind was racing. A bad winter had come back to haunt him. The seeds had been sown there. He hadn't maintained the momentum he'd built through the 2003 season.

He was strong that year. But he dipped after the Worlds. He didn't watch his diet as well as he should have. He was young, happy for his weight to go up and down, and he hit almost eighty kilogrammes, well over the crew average of seventy kilogrammes, before a training camp in Seville that winter. That must have put doubts in Thor's mind. Timmy didn't do enough to keep himself out of danger.

Timmy questioned himself, as Thor explained his decision. Did I do everything I could have done? Should I have trained harder? Should I have been more disciplined? He still arrived at the same conclusion: he was the better option for the boat. Thor thought differently.

The Irish four without Timmy finished fourth at the World Cup in Lucerne. That confirmed what he already knew: he was travelling to Athens as a sub. O'Toole had won his seat. He was the best man for the job in Thor's eyes. He'd seen enough.

Eugene understood Timmy's pain. He didn't agree with the decision and how it came about. He felt that Timmy was denied a fair shot that had been promised to him. He thought that the boat was faster and better with Timmy in it. It was a genuine medal prospect.

Eugene felt Thor didn't appreciate what Timmy brought to the boat. He was its leader. He knew how to get the best out of the rest. The only small comfort for Timmy was that he was back in the single. He was a sculler first and foremost. Not being in the four meant he raced in the single. That kept his spirits up. He was sixth in Munich, fourteenth in Lucerne and eighth at the Senior Worlds in Banyoles.

And Thor was right to say that age was on Timmy's side. There would be more Olympics in the future. Beijing was four years down the line.

But his bad luck wasn't finished yet. Worse was to come.

***

Blood. Sweat. Pain. Vomit. Sometimes not even in that order.

The rowers competing for a seat in the four had gone to polish their rough diamond ahead of the Olympic year.

The training camp had been scheduled for Seville in December. Thor had a base there. Before that, Timmy, Eugene, Paul and Neil Casey – Richard Archibald couldn't travel – decided to hop on a plane to Seville for an extra few weeks of training before the camp. They went up to Sierra Nevada for ten days at altitude as well. Then it was back down to Seville for the training camp proper during December.

Eugene's younger brother by three years, Richard, flew out to join the camp for the last two weeks. Thor was trying out various club rowers and keeping his options open with the four.

Richard Coakley was another up-and-coming sculler from Skibb. Tall and lean. He'd competed at the World Under–23s in 2003 in a lightweight four and finished fourth. Another Skibbereen rower, Ciarán Hayes, had also been in that boat.

Under orders from Eugene, Richard landed in Seville with Christmas lights to get the Irish men abroad in the festive spirit under the Spanish sun. But the holidays were the furthest thing from Richard's mind after his first training session left him slumped in a shower coated in his own vomit.

This was a Thor camp. He knows how to get results and how to build men who can conquer the world. It's survival of the fittest. The others had acclimatised. They were in the groove. Richard wasn't yet. Fresh meat off the plane, one of his early sessions was to do 500 metres on the rowing machine fifteen times with one minute off in between. It was stomach churning. Exhausting.

The intensity caught him off guard, punched him in the ribs and winded him. Near the end of the session the new boy went missing.

Eugene looked around. No sign of Rich. But it was every man for himself. Sink or swim. Eugene kept going.

It was only afterwards that he found him, lying in the shower, puking. He couldn't get up, spent ten minutes getting sick on himself, showered it off and then came back for the next session an hour later. No one cared. There were no hugs or a friendly arm around the shoulder. They were here for one reason: to get in the best possible shape for 2004.

They flew home on Christmas Eve. Eugene, Richard and Timmy landed in Cork Airport at midnight. They were home in Skibbereen for two days before flying back out to Seville for more on 27 December.

Come January, the four was flying it. Eugene was in the shape of his life and hit a new personal best over five kilometres. He came out of the boat and threw up on the ground, but he hadn't time to wipe away the vomit that still clung to his chin before he met Thor.

'Eugene, are you okay?'

'I'll be okay.'

'We will take a ten-minute break and we will do the test again.'

This was a test of mental strength. This was Thor weeding out those who didn't have the resolve to push on. The Skibb boys were different. Thor liked that. He had spotted it straightaway. That different mentality. They could package and sell mental fortitude. Eugene impressed Thor too. He was a natural.

Eugene was only fifteen years old when he stopped in the middle of a 2,000-metre test on the rowing machine with Dominic beside him, watching and teaching. Small Euge told Dominic they could finish it the next day. Dominic had other ideas. He told Eugene to take a five-minute break and do it again.

The lesson was that if you give in once to that voice on your shoulder who says it's okay to stop, you'll never be able to push yourself to that dark, dark place where you exceed your own limits. Stopping in a test is not tolerated in Skibb, so in Seville Eugene got back in the boat and went again.

The second five-kilometre test was ten seconds slower than the first, but still faster than his previous personal best. Thor showed again what was possible. Just like Dominic had done.

13

a greek tragedy

Madness. Absolute madness. The boat wasn't moving well. They had known that all week. It wasn't running as fast as it had at Munich and Lucerne. The diminishing effect of not having Timmy was being felt. Munich was great: silver. Lucerne was life without Timmy: fourth. By Athens he was a memory. There as a sub but not involved.

The boat had lost its leader. And they needed him right now. He would have challenged this latest decision. The Saturday before the A final of the men's lightweight four in Athens, which was to take place the next morning, the Irish four's oars were changed. The length stayed the same, but the blades were cut down. The thinking was that the surface area of the blade in the water would be smaller so the oar would come through the water quicker.

There was already a sense that the four had nothing to lose, that the end wasn't far away, so maybe it was time to think outside the box and try something different. But this was the day before an Olympic final. There were medals up for grabs and no Irish rowers had ever medalled at an Olympics. This wasn't the stage to trial a new idea and search frantically for a rabbit in a hat. Eugene wasn't happy. It was a crazy move. A get-rich-quick scheme doomed to failure.

They needed to test the oars. Under the blistering Greek August sun Thor sent the four out to row two 250-metre pieces at race pace, rating at thirty-five, thirty-six, one with the old blades and one with the new cut-down blades.

They went down the course at the Schinias Olympic Rowing Centre in the direction they would race the following morning. They were timed for each 250-metre burst. Hard. Fast. Full throttle.

After the first piece was completed, they pulled in to where the medal podium was and Thor and Assistant Coach Tony O'Connor, who acted as the buffer between the crew and Thor, stood there with the cut oars. They were switched.

'These are the oars that could help you stand here on this podium tomorrow,' they were told as they went off. They paddled up the course before turning around and repeating the drill. The time difference between the old and new blades was minimal. They were fractions faster with the new, cut-down blades.

Thor decided to go with the new blades. It was a big call. The regret for some in the boat is that this group, so focused in the lead-in, didn't shout stop. Maybe it was too late, anyway. But some felt that Timmy would have shouted stop. He'd have stood up and said what the rest were thinking: what the fuck are we doing here? His demotion was still being felt.

There had been tension in the boat ever since Timmy was replaced. Some could see the logic in the decision. Some didn't. And it didn't help that the pre-Olympic training in Zagreb had been flat. The stars weren't aligning.

***

Eugene slept soundly the night before the Olympic final. No nerves. The only concern was keeping his weight down to seventy kilogrammes, his race weight. Tough going for a long guy like him. He'd struggled all week but never tipped the scales.

On the morning of the race the crew made that regular journey from the Olympic Village in Athens to the rowing hub in Schinias. They were on the bus for 5.30 a.m. It was a forty-five minute journey at best. It was the last time they'd make this trip.

The lightweight double of Sam Lynch and Gearoid Towey were based five minutes from the Schinias centre. They were the preferred boat and pre-Olympic chatter had them as Ireland's best chance of a medal. Qualifying the four, the poor cousins of the two, was seen as a bonus, but the double finished fourth in their A/B semi-final and ended up finishing tenth overall.

It all came down to the four.

This Sunday morning followed a familiar routine, despite it being an early final. Warm-up. Weigh-in. Hydrate. Plenty of water because it was very warm. Get in the race zone.

They had their team meeting in a room upstairs at the course, where they talked tactics. Thor announced he wouldn't be around after the final because he had a flight to catch. He told them it was a pleasure to work with them all and hoped he would work with them in the future. He shook their hands. And left. His job was done. He had brought them this far. Now it was up to them. That created this weird vacuum in the room. It already felt like it was over, that the end had come before the biggest race of their lives. They never saw him after the race.

The Irish four made the decision to go out as hard as they could and see how they got on. Get into a medal position and stay there. Leave the water with no regrets. They had been left behind at the start all week. But here they were second after 500 metres. The new blades were lighter so they were rating higher, meaning they were taking a higher number of strokes per minute than they would have been with the previous oars. Just the Danes in front. To the casual observer watching on TV back in Ireland, there were whoops, hollers and cheers.

Back home in Skibbereen a big gang had invaded Dillon's Corner on Bridge Street to watch their local hero, Eugene, in action. His father, Richard, was there with his sister Anne, but his mother, Mary, couldn't watch. There was a large sprinkling of Skibbereen Rowing Club officers and members too: Dominic Casey, Seanie O'Brien, Donal O'Sullivan, Violet Hayes. Lord David Puttnam and his wife, Patsy, were there to support. Their house at Derrygereen overlooks the Ilen and the rowers on the water.

The noise levels peaked at the halfway mark. Eugene and Ireland in fourth. The chant went up. 'Ireland, Ireland, Ireland.' Shrieks and roars.

The reality in the boat was different. Ireland were struggling and being punished for their fast start. The brilliant Danish led, with Italy second, Australia third, Ireland four-tenths of a second behind them, then Canada, and a gap to the Dutch boat.

The miracle the Irish four needed wasn't going to happen. That cross-tailwind coming from their side that there had been talks about the evening before never materialised. That would have helped them in lane one. Instead it was flat calm. A level playing field. Lady Luck had looked away. No favours here.

Eugene knew what German sculler Marcel Hacker, a former world champion, meant when he had said his bones were burning during a World Championship race. Eugene's were on fire now. Every bone in his body. Lactic acid boiling. An abyss of pain so severe it spread to his mouth, gums, everywhere. It's a repugnant feeling all rowers know. It's wrong to do this to yourself, going right to the edge, the threshold where your body begs to stop this madness, yet you still keep going. But he had to. This was an Olympic final.

The early morning sun was unrelenting and each breath hurt. The boat was feeling heavy and getting heavier. The Irish four were about to blow a gasket. The end was imminent. It wasn't a shock to the four men in the boat.

They had been second in their heat to Australia, third in their semifinal behind Denmark and The Netherlands, bursting forward from fifth with 500 metres to go, but they had made it into the A final with the slowest time of all six finalists. They knew early in the week that they weren't where they wanted to be. The other five finalists were stronger, better and more experienced.

With 500 metres left, they were hanging on to fourth, only Canada and, in lane two and right next door, the fast-finishing Dutch behind them.

But the Irish four faded fast. It was all over well before the finish. The Canadians and Dutch powered past. There was no response. The bodies weren't able. They were resigned to their fate.

Timmy watched on from the bank. He had felt like an impostor these past two weeks. There at the Olympics but as a sub and not really part of it. Still, he hoped the four would produce something special, but he'd seen the signs too. It wasn't a surprise that it unravelled.

They crawled over the line in sixth place. A distant last. Eight and a half seconds behind the gold winners Denmark and nearly four seconds behind Canada in fifth.

The Irish four paddled in to the slip. The boat was in silence. Eugene, still in his white peak cap, was physically exhausted. His legs like jelly. Still gasping for air. It was all over. And nothing to show for it but broken bodies and shattered souls.

Back home in Skibb the buzz in Dillon's Corner had faded. But the Irish four still received a huge ovation when they crossed the line. They were proud of them, particularly their two Olympians.

Dominic offered his thoughts to the local newspaper: 'It will take more mileage, more training.'

No surprise there.

Mileage makes champions, he always says. The same wisdom is offered to beginners and the world's best. Mileage makes champions. Get back out on the water.

Eugene's sister Anne received a text message from another sister, Karen. She was at the course in Athens, along with their brother Richard, who was there to support the four he had trained with. He had flown to Athens from Poznań with Ciarán Hayes, where they'd raced at the World Under–23 Championships. The text sent home to Skibb read that the crew were in shock and that nobody was talking. They were gutted.

Twelve years before the O'Donovan brothers won Ireland's first Olympic rowing medals, the lightweight four boat could have reached that milestone. That boat was good enough to bring home a bronze or silver. Eugene felt Timmy could have made the difference.

At least time was still on their side, they felt. Eugene was twenty-five; Paul was twenty-four. Richard was twenty-six. Timmy had just turned twenty-two. Stick together and by Beijing in 2008 they'd be right in the mix. Good times did follow soon after, but by the next Olympics Eugene and Timmy weren't in the boat.

***

Thor was gone, but 2005 saw the arrival of Harald Jährling, the tough East German coach who had won gold in the coxed pair at the 1976 and

1980 Olympics. Technically and tactically, he improved the four. The results and medals show that, but Jährling's headmaster style wasn't a good fit for the more laid-back Irish.

The coach admitted to being a control freak. He said he didn't believe in sport as a democracy, he felt it was a dictatorship and someone needed to be the dictator.

Jährling wanted to lay down a marker early. He moved Richard Archibald to the stroke seat. The crew argued this was a crazy move. It made the boat slower. Timmy was back in by now, hell-bent on making up for his Athens heartbreak, now targeting the World Championships later that year. Jährling told Eugene, Paul, Richard and Timmy to discuss the change as a crew. Three disagreed with the change. One was content to follow the coach's order. It wasn't unanimous but majority ruled; they wanted to return to the old, familiar order: Paul as stroke, Eugene and Timmy in two and three and Richard as the bow. Eugene was the appointed spokesman. He went to Jährling with their decision. The change was made and they reverted back to how they had lined up before Jährling had come on-board. The coach wasn't happy. But it worked.

Their new coach was more hands-on than Thor. For a start, he lived in Ireland whereas Thor had not. The authoritative East German imposed a different style. They weren't allowed to go hard at the start and explode from the blocks. They had seen that as their strength, but he felt they faded before the finish. Instead he was keen for a more controlled middle section. They worked hard to build a consistent pace throughout the race. The results followed.

They won bronze at World Rowing Cup II in Munich that June, coming in just behind France and Germany. History was soon made in Lucerne, the luxurious and grand home of rowing, when the same four won gold. It was the first time Ireland had won the top prize in an Olympic-class boat at a World Cup regatta.

They did it in style too, with their best performance yet. Tactically they were spot on. They led all the way, trap-to-line, finishing in 6:01.010, two and a half seconds ahead of Germany in second, with Poland another second further back. That marked them out as serious contenders for the 2005 World Rowing Championships in Gifu, Japan, where they would be Ireland's leading medal prospect.

The chance to medal was promising, particularly as the Danes weren't competing. France were the big stumbling block, as they'd won the other World Cup regattas at Munich and Eton.

Ireland won their heat on the Nagaragawa International Course, moving straight into the A/B semi-final where, again, they won. Second all the way through, they moved past the Germans in the final 500 metres. Ireland had the quickest time of all six finalists.

Dominic rang Eugene. His calls are always short and to the point. No time for wasted words. No bullshit.

'The French look good. What are yer chances? Are ye going to win?'

One of Dominic's catchphrases bounced around in Eugene and Timmy's heads the day of the A final. Often his last words when pushing a boat off the slipway: 'You need to take these fellas on.'

The word had travelled from Skibbereen to Gifu: take on the French. That was the plan. Wait, then strike.

Belief in the boat was high the day of the final. Gold was within their grasp. But the French exploded from the start, making the most of the strong tailwind and the quick conditions. They held a two-and-a-half second lead over Ireland, who were in third after 500 metres. It was down to less than one-and-a-half seconds, however, at the halfway mark, with the Germans in second.

Ireland were strong and steady. But so were the French. The plan was to build a strong rhythm down the middle and then attack from 1,000 metres, move in for the kill. They did. But the gap never closed.

Inside the final 500 metres Ireland passed the Germans. The fast-finishing Italians squeezed up on Ireland. The attacks were coming from all sides. The Australians were still there. It was frantic stuff across the lanes. Down the stretch there were three boats vying for the silver and bronze medals, the French always in command of gold.

In the race for silver, Ireland pushed hard to hold off the Italians by four-hundredths of a second. Small margins again but a better colour medal. Silver, and a place on the podium.

When Eugene got back to his tiny, cramped hotel room, he tossed his medal on the bed, lay down beside it and just cried. Pure, raw, unfiltered emotion. Relief too. After all these years he had finally something tangible and real to show for his efforts. If he stopped now at least he had achieved something. He wasn't a world champion, but this was the next best thing. That night they dined on sushi. The food was good.

Timmy, meanwhile, saw it as the start of something special. He'd turned twenty-three the previous month. Silver in his back pocket from the Worlds, loads more to come, the Beijing Olympics in the distance. Life was good.

***

You must be fucking joking.

Timmy sat on the wet pavement, wincing in pain. The rain was bouncing off the ground around him. His left ankle throbbed.

Fuck. That hurts.

He'd heard a loud crack. Pop.

He presumed it was his trainers smacking off the slick footpath. It wasn't; it was his ankle snapping. The sound of his ligaments tearing. He didn't know that in the moment, but the pain was piercing. Stinging. Tender. He knew something was wrong. But what he didn't know is that this was the moment that finished him as an elite rower. One fall and it was all over. One missed step.

Fuck it.

He had lost his footing on a familiar jogging route, bounding past the Garda Boat Club in Islandbridge. Fiddling with his iPod, he looked down, took his eye off the road and missed a step.

Still on the ground, trying to get his bearings, with a street light overhead fixing its spotlight on him, he noticed Eugene whizz past on his bike on his way from work. It was still lashing down. It was a dark and dreary Friday night in late November. Eugene never even saw him. They had lived together in Phibsborough since 2003. Eugene was working after qualifying from college as a civil engineer, while Timmy was studying Russian and Business in Trinity.

Timmy shouted after him. He knew he was in trouble with the ankle.

'EUGENE!'

Headphones in and listening to the radio, Eugene thought he'd heard someone call his name. He stopped further up the road. He looked around briefly but, searching through the rain and bright lights, didn't see Timmy. He motored on. He was homeward-bound. It was just gone six in the evening and his day's work was behind him.

Timmy dragged himself up. He hobbled to the nearest bus stop where he sat down and pulled off his sock. His ankle had ballooned. He hopped on one leg to the nearest shop and asked the lady behind the counter to ring for a taxi. When he was dropped home he rang for the team physio to call out. Eugene was already home. One look at Timmy and he knew it was bad.

Ankle iced and bandaged, Timmy was on crutches for a few weeks, but he never fully recovered. That ankle injury played havoc with the mechanics of his rowing stroke. His symmetry was thrown out. His right leg was stronger than the left so there was an imbalance in his leg drive. His left ankle was stiff and he couldn't transfer the power he needed when pushing off his feet. Timmy was never the same rower after this.

He shouldn't have travelled to St Moritz for a two-week high altitude training camp early in 2006. But he did. That didn't help his rehab. In trials that followed at the end of February and March, he was slow. He couldn't get up to speed. Surgery that April was successful, but a lasting stiffness would always catch him out in the boat.

Timmy lost his place in the four and was paired in the lightweight double with Richard Coakley, who was only twenty-three, just finished college in UCC and now in his first year as a Senior rower. He had an impressive body of work behind him, including fourth at the 2003 World Under–23s in a lightweight four, and was extremely quick in the single scull. He was pushing the Senior four hard by 2005, Jährling's first year with the Irish lightweights.

Richard's thinking from 2003 on was simple: I am identical to Eugene. Same body shape. Other rowers are more explosive and powerful, but we have that endurance, built for the long hauls. I'm an inch taller. If I train hard enough I can beat him. If I beat him, I'll win medals.

That's when Richard started chasing Eugene. 2006 was meant to be another step up the ladder, but the double struggled. Timmy kept breaking down in training and couldn't hit the heights of previous years. Richard was looking to him for guidance, but Timmy had his own troubles, struggling with the realisation that life as an elite international rower was over. They shuffled to fifteenth place at the World Cup in Lucerne, and later that year, they limped home twenty-first out of twenty-four boats at the World Rowing Championships at Dorney Lake, Eton.

Timmy was done with it. Richard still had his sights on the four, with the 2008 Beijing Olympics in mind. The Irish four of Eugene, Paul Griffin, Richard Archibald and Gearoid Towey won bronze at those 2006 World Championships, a slim nine-hundredths of a second behind France in silver and China in gold, but by then Eugene was going through the motions. It was robotic for him. It felt like one of those office jobs that everyone hates.

Eugene's smile hid the truth, even if the medals were a welcome distraction, like when this four won the overall title of World Cup champions in the lightweight four in 2006. It was a first for an Irish crew at this level. They won gold in Lucerne and Poznań to add to the silver in Munich.

But life under Jährling was a hard slog and Eugene was worn down. There may have been another world medal, his collection growing, but it wasn't fun any more. Timmy was on the way out too, finished at the top level.

But Richard Coakley was coming. He felt it was his time to step out of the shadows.

the third olympian

It's a rat. The little bollocks. Beady eyes and slithering long tail, it was feasting away on one of Richard's energy bars, nibble by nibble, when it was disturbed.

He was just out of the shower at Blessington in Wicklow. He was there for a month of training. The facilities were basic. But he was used to that from home. Here it was little more than a concrete shell with toilets and showers. Spartan conditions. This was April 2007, the year before the 2008 Olympics, and a world away from the shiny new National Rowing Centre at Inniscarra.

Session on the water finished, showered and fresh, Richard reached into his gearbag for his towel. He pulled out a rat instead. Richard jumped on the bench. The rat hit the ground before scurrying off, half-full.

This solved the mystery of Richard's missing food. For the previous few days his lunch in his gearbag had gone missing. He couldn't figure out who it was until now.

When Richard fell ill shortly afterwards, he was convinced it was because of the rats that had been rooting around in his gearbag. He was put on a course of antibiotics. He asked for a few days off to get himself right. He was told no.

Richard put the head down. He trained full-time through the

antibiotics, came off them but got sick again. He was prescribed another course of antibiotics, but kept training. In one month, the Skibb man went on three rounds of antibiotics back-to-back.

By the time it came to the international season in May, he was spluttering along at fifty per cent. He'd effectively missed a month of proper training. That showed at the Huegel Regatta in Essen ahead of the opening World Cup event of the season at Linz in Austria.

Richard was in the bow seat for the four, along with the familiar trio of Eugene, Richard Archibald and Paul, but they raced poorly. It was a bad day at the office. Worse was to follow for Richard.

The headline on the *Irish Times* website shouted 'Moynihan to replace Coakley'. This was news to Richard. Nobody had told him. There was no conversation, no reasons why, nothing. It was hours later before Jährling spoke to him about the switch. Richard had even been named in the crew on the official entry list. But the change was made. Kerryman Cathal Moynihan, named in the lightweight single and a reserve for the lightweight four, was taking Richard's seat.

Richard hopped into the lightweight single for the World Cups in Linz and in Lucerne but finished a disappointing fourteenth in both. He lost interest after losing his seat in the four. Beijing seemed further away than ever.

Life wasn't much better for Eugene. The lightweight four was struggling. They were world silver medallists in 2005, third in the world the following year, but tales of rifts and rows with Jährling were doing the rounds as they slumped in 2007. They failed to automatically qualify for the Beijing Olympics, finishing twelfth at the World Rowing Championships, one place outside the top eleven who went straight to the Games. It was falling apart. A possible Olympic medal contender was imploding. Drastic action was needed. John Holland came on-board as the lightweight coach as Jährling was left to concentrate on the heavyweights.

Richard didn't shed a tear when Jährling left the lightweight group. He'd felt the East German had lost confidence in him and he wanted a clean slate. There was one year to Beijing, a boat that still had to qualify and a seat to win.

***

Eugene knew what was coming. He saw the warning signs flashing in front of him before anyone else did. Ireland were building towards the final Olympic qualification regatta in Poznań in June 2008. There were two places on offer. Having to peak twice in an Olympic year isn't ideal, but they had no other choice.

The four was going better than it had in 2007, but it still wasn't what it could be, even with Gearoid Towey back in it, taking the place of Cathal Moynihan. It's like when a boy band gets back together for the reunion tour. It's never really the same. Eugene felt this too.

Fifth place at the first World Cup of the 2008 season in Munich was, at least, a return to an A final. Richard and Cathal were in the lightweight double here, but could only manage twenty-fifth overall.

World Cup II in Lucerne at the start of June saw the four finish sixth in the A final. That was Eugene's last time ever racing in the Irish lightweight four. At a training camp in Munich ahead of the Olympic qualifier he lost the bow seat to Cathal Moynihan at short notice.

That decision didn't surprise Eugene. He was still only twenty-nine years old but felt he was on the way down. His confidence was slipping. And he found that he still really missed Timmy, the leader the boat needed but didn't have.

Without Eugene on-board, the four qualified, taking second place in Poznań behind Germany, and two seconds clear of Serbia in third. They were going to the Olympics, but without Eugene, who was now in the lightweight double with Richard.

Eugene and Richard had rowed together before at the World Cup in Eton in 2005 but this was their first time in a double for Ireland.

They had an ambitious plan and just over one week to pull it together: try and qualify that double for the Olympics at the qualification regatta in Poland.

It was doomed from the start. Never going to happen. But still, they tried.

***

It was Christmas 2017. Eugene, now living and working in London, was back in Skibbereen with his family. There is nothing better than spending the festive season at home. It provides the chance to catch up with family and friends, have a few pints in the Corner Bar, lunch in The West Cork Hotel and a few spins on the river. Even better, Richard was home from Australia.

Old habits die hard and soon the brothers were out in a double on the Ilen for the first time in years. This was a leisurely row. No stress. No pain. They were enjoying the scenery, breathing it all in again. Fun and simple. At least it was until they were near Oldcourt. There they heard that familiar rev of an engine. There was something in the water. Moments later they saw Dominic on the launch, the motorised boat used by coaches to follow rowers during training sessions, shadowing them. He was also holding a video recorder.

Shit, Eugene thought. It's Dominic.

Their international rowing days were long behind them, but that competitiveness never leaves. They upped their rate. The chat stopped, the reminiscing put on hold. They were working hard now, a lot harder than they wanted to. Legs pumping. The boat arrowed towards Inishbeg.

Dominic was still there. Following. Watching arguably two of his best students.

They couldn't let him see them taking it easy. Suddenly they were racing on the Ilen again. Lungs bursting. Arms burning. They felt they had to. It was the Dominic effect.

He soon tailed off. He'd seen enough.

For Eugene and Richard, the spin back to the clubhouse took longer than normal. They were dead in the boat. It was almost the same exhausted feeling that had washed over them when they came up short at the Olympic qualification regatta in 2008.

Thrown into the double a week out, it was always going to be a tall order to pull it together. It started promisingly when they finished second in their heat. In the semi-finals the top three from each would advance to the final. They finished fifth. Game over. Dream over.

If they had been afforded a full season in the double, they felt that they would have been fast enough to qualify. Instead they'd ten days to prepare. Never enough to hit the standard needed.

The four was Beijing-bound still. Richard went as the reserve. Eugene missed out, but he didn't lose sleep over it. He knew it was all coming to an end and he wanted to close the circle on his international days.

Thirteen years after he first rowed for Ireland, as a sixteen-year-old at the Home Internationals in Cork, Eugene raced in his last regatta for Ireland, as a twenty-nine-year-old in a double with Richard, at the 2008 World Rowing Championships for non-Olympic events in Austria at the end of July. There was no fairy-tale ending and no huge fanfare. They finished ninth, third in the B final. It was a quiet exit out the side door for Eugene. It was all over for him. But not for Richard. Beijing was calling in August.

***

Eugene had been the spare man at Sydney in 2000 and treated it as a learning experience. Timmy was the sub at Athens four years later and approached it like a holiday. Neither saw any action from the sideline. The odds of Richard getting on the water in Beijing were slim.

He had been one of the fastest single scullers in the country for some time now. He nearly always came out on top in the selection trials but never won his place in the four. He was always on the outside looking in. The same as in Beijing.

Still, he kept himself ticking over during the Games and watched his weight. He was getting by doing the bare minimum. The training volume was low. Eight kilometres every day, two laps, feet up.

Richard watched on at the Shunyi Olympic Rowing-Canoeing Park on the side of the Chaobai River as the Irish lightweight four, without a Skibbereen man, finished last in their heat on the Sunday. They bounced back two days later to win their repêchage and find their way back into an A/B semi-final. That Friday, with the top three from each semi-final to advance to the Olympic A final, Ireland finished fourth.

All that was left was the B final the next day, a race where the losing semi-finalists just go through the motions. For Richard it turned out to mean a lot more.

Gearoid Towey wasn't feeling great. There was a stomach bug doing the rounds. He was ruled out for the B final. Richard was back in the apartment he was staying in with Alan Martin, the reserve for the heavyweight four, the other boat Ireland qualified for the Games. Their base was just outside the Olympic Village. Richard's phone rang. It was team manager Mike Heskin.

'Rich, Gags is out sick. You're in.'

The next day, Skibbereen Rowing Club's third Olympian sat in the number two seat. Ireland were in lane three, Italy and Australia on one side, China and the USA on the other. Egypt never took their place in the final. Ireland were fourth after 500 metres, fifth at the halfway mark and up to fourth with 500 left. Richard was gassing. He didn't have the preparation under his belt that all the others had. Each breath was a battle. Each pull of the oar was a struggle. His body was suffering more than ever before. But the roar of the grandstand near the finish lifted the siege. He enjoyed this moment of respite at what felt like death's door.

Italy, China and Australia all finished in front of the Irish four, who had to be content with tenth place overall.

Richard was only twenty-five years old, but in the months after Beijing he was drifting in rowing limbo. Most of that Irish lightweight four retired. The next generation were too far back to wait for. The noises from Skibb's young bucks had his attention. Mark O'Donovan turned twenty in November 2008, Gary O'Donovan was sixteen, the same age as Shane O'Driscoll. Paul O'Donovan was a year back. There was no one between them and Richard. Another year of juggling life on an Irish Sports Council grant of €12,000 and the dole wasn't appealing.

For a short while, he picked up a job as a stockbroker that he didn't enjoy. He was a caged athlete in a nine-to-five office job, gone from a full-time sportsman working towards and dreaming of an Olympic medal to crunching numbers behind a desk. Enough was enough. Richard made a few calls. And plans were put in place to move to Australia in October 2010. But before that, he was to bow out of Skibbereen on a high.

**

Bags packed. Passport in date. Tickets in a safe place. A coaching job lined up. Sun, sea and a fresh start was the promise on offer. Richard was Sydney-bound. But not before he raced in the 2010 Irish Rowing Championships at the National Rowing Centre that were later than normal that year, the last weekend of September.

He had been one of the country's top rowers during the past decade but had never won a Senior National Championship title. That wrong needed to be set right.

His six championship wins from 1997 to 2000 were all as a cox, including the first year Skibbereen won the Junior eight in 1997. The week before those championships, Richard was told that the minimum weight for a Junior men's cox was fifty kilogrammes. He was fifty-three. Every kilogramme counts in a boat, so he squeezed into a wetsuit, armed with a woolly hat, and ran sweat runs for a few days to shed the excess weight. Then, two days before the championships, he was told that, instead, the minimum weight is actually fifty-five kilogrammes. Now he was trying to put on weight instead of losing it. The day of the race, he was still under the fifty-five-kilogramme mark. He downed a two-litre bottle of water and his pockets were filled with spanners and a vice-grip.

Clink. Clank. Rattle.

When he hopped on the scales the plan was discovered. The Skibb Junior eight had to carry two kilogrammes in dead weight, but they still won. That was a turning point for men's rowing in the club. It was also Richard's first National Championship.

As a rower he had won National Championships in the Junior quad, Junior double, Intermediate four and Intermediate single but never a Senior championship. When he was in his prime the championships clashed with international regattas. He was an Olympian without a Senior championship. He had to win at least one.

That all changed the weekend before he left Irish shores for Sydney. With Richard, Mark O'Donovan, Justin Ryan and Gearoid Murphy, Skibbereen won the men's Senior quad scull. Richard also won the men's lightweight single scull.

That Monday morning he left for Australia with an important box ticked. But his future as a rower was up in the air.

Four years later, however, Richard was back in the headlines after he won a silver medal for Australia at the first World Cup event of 2014. He had impressed on the water in 2013, was invited to camps at the Australian Institute of Sport and was selected to represent Australia in the lightweight single at World Rowing Cup I in Sydney that March.

He was thirty years old and could still row a lot better than most. Sydney was home. Mosman Rowing Club, only two kilometres north of the Opera House, was his rowing base, Sydney Harbour his playground. It's still not a patch on the Ilen, of course. One of the big differences is the lack of sharks in Skibbereen. Early starts at 4.30 a.m. are easier here than in Skibb. Plans to fast-track his permanent residency so he could row for Australia at the 2014 World Rowing Championships didn't work, however, and he hasn't rowed internationally since.

***

One of the Skibbereen club's greatest achievements is that it teaches its rowers lessons in life that they can take forward. It's not a coincidence that so many Skibbereen rowers have become successes in their chosen fields outside of rowing. John Whooley and Kevin O'Donovan are secondary-school teachers. James Barry is a marine engineer. Timmy Harnedy is a barrister. James Lupton works as a leading software engineer at Deutsche Bank. Murray Connolly and Paddy Murphy are doctors. Kenneth McCarthy is a school principal. Richard Coakley is a coach at a private school in Sydney. Cathal O'Donoghue is the owner of Rascals Brewing Company in Dublin.

It was this generation that the likes of Gary and Paul first walked among. This generation created the platform from which Gary, Paul, Shane O'Driscoll, Mark O'Donovan and Denise Walsh all benefitted. They are the product of those years of learning and drive. The competitiveness of that earlier generation sparked win after win. Momentum built. The club consistently won at Junior level after the breakthrough of that Junior eight in 1997 and is still winning now. Expectations and standards were raised, and then continually met. And so the current crop of star rowers have this generation to thank for driving standards ever higher.

IV
THE CURRENT CROP
AND A CLUB ON TOP

15

nowhere to stay

Shane O'Driscoll and Mark O'Donovan weren't a perfect match. They always said they could never row a pair together because they both row on bow side, both oars going out to the left. That's their preference. It's where they feel most comfortable. But if they wanted to make their presence felt at international level they had to row together and they had to make it work. Their options had been whittled down. It was the pair or nothing.

Mark switched sides first. That lasted less than twenty minutes. No joy there. Shane tried then. It wasn't perfect but it was an improvement. The decision was made. Mark stayed bow side. Shane switched. Not ideal, but necessary.

There was an instant bond between the two. It's that Skibbereen connection and trust that comes with both men graduating through the same system. Both knew the other wouldn't be found wanting, that they'd never lie down and they'd always back each other.

No fighting. No nagging. No bitching. No moaning. They avoid conflict and train the Skibbereen way: push hard and keep it simple.

Their styles are similar but their personalities are different. Mark is the dominant of the two, not just because he's slightly taller. He's louder, prefers the centre stage more and doesn't shirk the spotlight. Shane's quieter and more observant. Both have huge smiles. Both needs the other too.

It was early 2015 and Mark was twenty-six, four years older than Shane. They belonged to different groups at Skibbereen Rowing Club. Shane's was Gary and Paul O'Donovan and Diarmuid O'Driscoll. Mark had his own crew: Steven McCarthy, Brian O'Mahony, Eric Newman and Eoin O'Mahony, who were all stronger and faster. Mark had always been the lightest of the gang growing up, a scrawny teenager from Poundlick. At first, he had been shoehorned into coxing. He didn't mind too much because it taught him a lot. At one championship Dominic forgot to enter Mark in his race. Instead, he spent the weekend coxing. Mark had his suspicions. Dominic doesn't forget much. But it was a good weekend for the club.

When Mark did emerge from his coxing days, he spent most of his time in a single. It took time for him to show that he was as good as he felt he could be. He had to take the long way around. But he got better with age. There was a tenth-place finish in the lightweight pair at the 2014 World Championships and a silver from the 2010 World Under–23s in the lightweight men's quad that included another Skibb rower, Justin Ryan.

But Mark was still trying to find his place on the water. So too was Shane, who had finished third in the trial in 2014 for the men's lightweight double, of which Gary and Paul were now in possession. That left Shane in a single. But he wanted an Olympic-class boat too. Initially, the Irish lightweight four was the best option. Both Mark and Shane survived the gruelling trials and, from a group of almost thirty athletes, four men were left standing by February 2015: Shane, Mark, Niall Kenny and Anthony English.

After Niall Kenny, based in London, opted out, Micheál Bailey stepped into his place. But this boat never picked up speed. At the 2015 European Rowing Championships in Poland, they finished last in their heat. They were an embarrassing thirty-one seconds behind Great Britain. In the repêchage, they were last again. That four was dropped. Back to the drawing board. That was when Shane and Mark joined forces.

Together it worked. The foundation was in place. But they needed a lot of time in the pair to make it faster, and a lot of patience.

Mark rented a room in a small apartment over Breathnach's bar and shop in the heart of Coachford village, only a few minutes from the National Rowing Centre at Inniscarra. The apartment was threadbare and old-style. Mark had one room. Two more rowers, Kerry woman Monika Dukarska and Dubliner Helen Walshe, shared the other.

In May 2015 Shane was smuggled in. They squeezed a second single bed into Mark's small room. It left barely enough room to edge sideways into the en-suite bathroom. It was claustrophobic but snug. There were no frills. There wasn't enough room to swing an oar, but it was a roof over their heads. That's all they wanted.

Straight under their room was the pub. Every Saturday night there was a sing-song downstairs. The racket would rise up through the floor deep into the early hours. They couldn't sleep. Eyes wide open staring at the ceiling. But they were in no position to complain because Shane was an extra guest who wasn't on the books.

Mark had just enough money to cover the rent. Shane had just finished college and was stuck with a bank balance that made even ATMs feel uncomfortable. But the main positive was that they spent nearly every hour of every day in each other's company, always trying to make the boat move faster.

They were trying to create an identity for themselves. Gary and Paul were already on their way in the double, racing internationally and improving. Shane and Mark wanted a piece of the action. They needed to test themselves at the highest level and the Rowing World Cup regatta in Lucerne was coming up in July.

Shane called into Morten Espersen's office at the National Rowing Centre. He asked if Mark and himself could be sent to Lucerne. Morten wrote down four times. Hit these and they could go. The main one was that they had to break 6.35 for the 2,000 metres.

The Cork Regatta was on a week later at the National Rowing Centre. There was a strong tailwind and that's just what Shane and Mark needed. They hit each time Morten had set out. Shane had his eyes on the GPS data throughout the race. He knew it looked good. They won the men's pair by clear water in six minutes and 33.2 seconds. It was hugely impressive.

Back on land Shane strode straight up to Morten and showed him the times. Book those tickets, Morten.

There was another issue, however: they had no boat. There was nothing suitable in Inniscarra. Dominic lent them a Skibbereen pair for Lucerne, but the club needed it for the National Championships. Shane and Mark needed a boat for the rest of the summer but didn't have the money to buy one, with anywhere up to €20,000 required. They scraped €1,000 together themselves, begged and borrowed, went to boat manufacturers Filippi and struck a great deal for the rent of a boat for eight weeks. Free oars from WinTech saved them reaching into their wallets again.

Rowing is an expensive sport. Deep pockets are needed. They were battling to hang onto the bottom rung of the international ladder before they ever qualified for Irish Sports Council funding. Rowers pay levies to compete internationally. It cost Shane and Mark €600 each to row in Lucerne, and €1,000 each to compete at the World Championships later that year. They paid their way.

Teddy O'Donovan travelled to Lucerne as their temporary coach for the weekend. They had no coach of their own. Teddy had coached Shane all his life back home in Skibb. That familiar face and attention to detail helped. Teddy looked after their every need as they finished sixth in the A final in the Skibbereen pair.

That performance opened the door to that year's World Rowing Championships at Aiguebelette in France. This was where Shane and Mark needed to hit an important target: a top-half finish that would earn them international-level funding of €12,000 from the Irish Sports Council for the following year.

They needed this funding to survive, so they could train in 2016 and commit again. That €12,000 would effectively be their wage for the year. They would need to live off it. It would put food on the table, pay the rent. Put petrol in their cars. Pay for levies to enter competitions and go on training camps. The pressure was on them in France. Slip up here and they'd have to use their own money again.

Kerryman Sean Casey, a former Olympian, had come on-board with Rowing Ireland on an initial short-term contract to coach the heavyweight women ahead of the Worlds. Shane asked Sean if he would help them as well. He said yes.

They had contrasting styles. The Skibb men would constantly tinker with the boat. They would change whatever they could in their search for free speed. Sean, on the other hand, sets the boat up first day and lets it be. Let it alone, Sean would tell them. They never listened. He couldn't keep count of the number of times they changed the handles of the oars. But he took them under his wing at their first World Senior Championships together, in the pair, in their rented Filippi.

At the 2015 World Championships fourth place in their heat sent them into the lottery of the repêchage. That heat was hard work. It was only the next day that they realised why. Whatever way Mark looked he saw that the fin of their boat was bent. There had been a bang with the Armenian pair in their heat. An oar that went under the Irish boat must have damaged the fin. Mark straightened it up.

Under pressure, knowing that a poor race here would mean their regatta was over – and that there would then be no funding – they won the repêchage and went into the A/B semi-final, where the top three advanced to the A final. They finished fifth.

The B final was on the Friday. Shane and Mark knew they had to win it – to finish in the top half of the race entry – to earn funding for 2016. It was a big ask.

Sean called to their hotel room the night before. He told them that he hadn't seen their best race yet that season. They listened. This was what they needed to hear. Sean told them to go out and lead as long as they could. He preferred to see them lead for the first half of the race and fall away, rather than come last all the way. He said he would be standing at the 1,500 metre mark. If Shane and Mark led then but were not able to take one more stroke, he would be happy.

That's exactly what Shane and Mark did. They led at halfway and at 1,500 metres. Sean was standing there like he said he would be.

The last 500 metres were painful. Shane couldn't believe they were leading. But they kept the head down. There was work to do. This was not the time to lose concentration. The Spanish pair crept in front but Mark took control in the last ten strokes. He moved the boat back in the lead. They won by just over one-tenth of a second, less than one foot.

This was a race that they shouldn't have won. Three of the other crews had faster times than them coming into the final. But they dug deep. It was a seventh place finish at the Worlds. But they had still won a final at the Worlds. This was something tangible to build on. More importantly, badly needed funding was on the way.

***

Shane was in Minihan's pub on the Monday night after the World Championships. He was celebrating Gary and Paul's Olympic qualification. Mark rang. Shane walked outside because he couldn't hear him. 'The apartment is gone,' Mark said, 'we've got to get all our stuff out.' The pub had run into difficulty and shut its doors unexpectedly. Coming just days after winning the B final that was a buzzkill.

All their belongings were piled into Shane's Ford Focus. It was a hand-me-down from his brother, but that's all he could afford. The next day the search for a new home began. It offered nothing.

Money was tight. The Sport Ireland funding of €12,000 each that they had triggered wouldn't come through until February 2016. Their options were limited. They had nowhere to live. But they didn't worry too much. They knew there were beds at the National Rowing Centre, so that was the stop-gap option they went for until their house search offered up a better alternative.

So home became the rowing centre. Rowing Ireland CEO Hamish Adams had no issue with the two moving in temporarily. There are five bedrooms, some smaller than others, dotted along an L-shaped hall off the boathouse on the ground floor. These sleeping quarters are packed with bunk beds that athletes use either for naps in between training or to stay in for training camps.

They took one room each and moved in all their stuff. Shane slept on top of a bunk bed in his room. Mark took a bottom bunk in his.

The kitchen was upstairs in the crew room. It was porridge for breakfast. Dinner took a little longer, as the two small hobs they used to cook on needed time to warm up. They stuck to the basics. Chicken and mince usually.

They had the run of the place, upstairs and downstairs. At night it was just the two of them. No TV. Slow Internet. There was little to amuse themselves with, apart from their own company and a shelf full of varied books in the crew room, ranging from Tom Clancy's *Clear and Present Danger* and *Debt of Honour* to *An Accidental Diplomat* by Eamon Delaney.

They became like caretakers and spent up to thirty minutes every night closing up the rowing centre, pulling down shutters, checking doors and windows.

This arrangement had its good points. After all, they only had to roll out of bed in the morning to go training. That was handier for Shane, who is not by nature an early riser. They had the gym all to themselves. The view out over the lake at sunset is one of life's free pleasures, stretching back up the lake towards the bridge. There was easy access to the coffee machine. They had a different toilet for each day of the week too. Luxuries.

They trained hard during this period. They had to. Their technique needed a lot of work. But that seventh place at the Worlds offered encouragement. They were only a couple of months into this new partnership and they had something to build on. They had found their feet as a lightweight pair.

***

11 November 2015. Moving day.

Mark tracked down a house for rent in Dripsey. It was an upgrade on their current lodgings. Perched overlooking the lake, with a view downriver, it was ideal outside and inside. Only twelve minutes from the rowing centre too. It had four bedrooms, two sitting rooms and a fine big kitchen large enough for two fridges when Gary – at a later stage – moved in as well. The house became their mansion. It ticked every box. The paupers now lived like princes.

It also became a coffee house. The rowers love their coffee. It's not just the taste but the social aspect as well. Most days they train twice, and in between sessions they retreat to the house, make coffee, sit down, relax and chat. It's the ideal break for the body and the mind after the rigours of training.

Mark is the coffee man. He believes the coffee machine is the world's greatest invention. He bought a small Sage espresso machine that had a built-in grinder on one side where he fed the beans into and the steamer was on the other side. It made all types of coffee, not just black. They used it so much that Hamish Adams then bought a coffee machine for the canteen at the rowing centre. That was taken on the long training camps and regattas abroad. On those trips they travel prepared, Paul included, all four taking some coffee beans with them so they won't run out.

Gary stepped it up a gear then. He bought a Rocket Espresso machine for the house in Dripsey. Mark sold his machine. It didn't match up to Gary's. They experimented with different blends over the years before settling on Mahers Coffee and then, later, Velo Coffee. Both have coffee shops in Cork city. From flat whites to macchiatos, these lads know their coffee.

Fuelled by coffee morning, noon and night, things were looking up. The boat was moving faster. Medals were a realistic target too.

bouncing back

Nobody from the national media at Gary and Paul's press conference at Skibbereen Rowing Club on 29 August 2016 knew who Denise Walsh was. She was just the athletic, black-haired girl dressed in the distinctively bright Gary & Paul's Crew yellow T-shirt who was handing out slices of steak and spuds pizzas, hot from the oven at Jeff's Pizzeria in town.

Denise looked after the catering that day, alongside her mother, Mary. Her dad, club chairman Tony, was around the place too, looking smart in his club blazer and red and white tie. At one point, all five of the Walshs have been involved with the club, with Denise's younger sister, Bernadette, and brother, Sean, rowing on and off.

But Denise was the first from the clan to get involved in the club, through its groundbreaking national schools' rowing programme. This is the only one of its kind in the country. It gives kids in ten national schools within a twelve-mile radius of the club – that's 200 local primary school pupils every year – the chance to learn how to row. The club buses the kids to and from the club, teaches them the basics and takes them out on the water. It's innovative and a massive success. The club is ahead of the curve, casting its net into the local schools.

Denise wasn't the sporty type at St Joseph's National School in town, but she signed up for rowing and went on to become a world-class rower whose every decision is now made with rowing in mind. On girls' weekends away, planned not to clash with trials and regattas so Denise can switch off, she gets up early to fit in a gym session. Every St Stephen's night, her friends from school always descend on her home in Munig North, a few miles outside town. It's an annual tradition. They'll have a few drinks and then take the party to Skibb. Sometimes it clashes with Denise heading to Seville for Ireland training camps, so she can't let her hair down. Instead, she'll drop her friends to town when they're ready to go out, drive back home for a few hours and then head to the airport. She lives and breathes the sport and the rowing club.

Denise drifted out of the clubhouse soon after the press conference began. Her work was done. Her bank balance was slightly better off too, after herself and Christine Fitzgerald had both decided to put a tenner each on Gary and Paul to win a medal at the Olympics. They had been convinced they'd medal.

Denise still couldn't escape the thoughts that she could have been there too. She could have been in Rio. She could have been an Olympian. It hurt.

Her mind drifted back to the departures gate at Poznań Airport in Poland on the last Sunday in May 2015 when she was ready to fly home after competing in the lightweight double at the European Rowing Championships. That was the exact moment her dreams of becoming an Olympian at Rio started to unravel.

***

Denise was one half of the Irish double, along with Claire Lambe from Dublin. The Rio Olympics were their target. In 2015 they were selected to compete for Ireland at the Piediluco International Regatta in Italy that April and the European Championships in May held in Poznań.

In lightweight women's rowing, only the double is an Olympic-class boat. The single isn't. To reach the pinnacle of the sport and compete in an Olympics as a lightweight rower, it's the double or nothing. And Denise and Claire had the two seats that mattered.

Both self-funded and training full-time, they set up a GoFundMe account to raise €3,400 to offset their costs for a ten-day training camp in Varese between both regattas, as well as help to go towards the levies they had to pay to compete. They raised over €4,300.

'Our ultimate aim is to be selected for and then qualify for the Olympic Games in Rio in 2016. We would be making history as Ireland's first female lightweight rowers at an Olympic Games,' they wrote.

In Italy the Irish double finished third and at the Europeans in Poznań they finished sixth overall. It was looking positive. The top eleven crews at the World Rowing Championships in September would qualify for Rio, so they were on track. They had been paired together the previous year, rowed at the Worlds and at a World Cup regatta, and they felt they were shaping up for Olympic qualification.

Denise and Claire were good friends and this double was working. Denise was only twenty-two, but she was the boss of the boat. She was the stronger sprinter, more suited to high-intensity interval training than to the long miles. Claire, at twenty-five, was the opposite, built for long miles and more distance. But the combination worked. They felt they were on an upward curve. A solid Europeans strengthened their belief, but neither knew that Sunday that they'd rowed their last race together in the double.

Before they boarded the flight from Poznań to Dublin, Rowing Ireland Head Coach Don McLachlan informed Denise and Claire that they'd have to trial for their places in the double.

The return of the experienced Sinead Jennings, who had finished eighth in the lightweight single scull at the Europeans, as well as Siobhán McCrohan, meant that there were now options for the double. Four into two didn't go.

A few weeks after the Europeans, the trials were held at the National Rowing Centre. This was serious business. Sinead came to Cork in the lead-up to the trials. She trained with Denise and Claire. They rotated in the single and double so they all had practice rowing with each other. The day before the trials, Siobhán arrived at the National Rowing Centre.

There was a crosswind on the day of the trials. It was decided to run it as a time trial, one boat ahead of the other without being close enough to gauge the distance. There were three races, with one hour breaks between each, when all four rested in the crew room in the main building.

All four were quiet. They knew what was at stake. In race one, it was Sinead/Claire and Siobhán/Denise. Race two saw Sinead/Denise and Siobhán/Claire. The third race was Sinead/Siobhán and the familiar pairing of Denise/Claire.

That evening they waited upstairs in the crew room, the four of them sharing the three brown-leather two-seaters. One by one they were called into the boardroom, where Don McLachlan and Morten Espersen sat behind a table facing the door, the view of the water behind them. They had the results.

Sinead was summoned first. It was good news. She had won a seat in the double. She was in for the next World Cup regatta in Lucerne.

Denise was called next. She was nervous as she left the room to walk the forty steps to the boardroom. She felt the trial had gone well and she knew what was at stake. It was everything that she'd worked for. That's what went through her mind as she went into the boardroom. Don and Morten were waiting inside.

A few minutes later, head down and walking faster, she pushed open the grey door leading into the crew room and went straight towards Claire, still sitting and waiting. Denise couldn't stop the tears streaming down her face. She apologised to Claire and left quickly, down the stairs, through the boathouse and to her car parked just around the corner. She wanted to get out of there.

Claire thought that she'd lost her seat, that Denise was consoling her. It was only when she was called into the boardroom and was told she still had her seat that she realised it was Denise who had lost her place and was out of the boat.

There were less than two seconds between the rowers in the trial. Claire and Sinead were the fastest and so they were the new double pairing.

Claire rang Denise later that evening to console her friend. She knew how she felt because she'd been there before and knew that feeling when your world falls apart. Siobhán and Claire had tried to qualify for the 2012 Olympics in London, but the double was pulled in April, one month before an Olympic qualification regatta, due to weight-management issues. Claire's Olympic dream had been crushed.

Denise's dreams had now been flattened. There were no more trials. That was it. Struggling to come to terms with the decision, Denise clung to the hope that she'd have a chance to win back her seat in the boat. She stayed training in a single at the National Rowing Centre, waiting to prove she deserved a seat in the double. But that never happened.

At the World Rowing Championships in Aiguebelette that September, where Gary and Paul booked their Rio tickets, Denise competed in the single and finished tenth overall. Claire and Sinead finished third in their B final, ninth overall, and that was enough to qualify the boat for Rio.

Donegal native Jennings was thirty-eight years old at the time, a mother of three, and she knew better than them all how cruel sport is. She had tried to qualify for the Olympics several times in the past without reaching them. But finally she had become an Olympian. When Sinead represented Ireland in a single at a World Rowing Cup regatta in Munich in June 2000, Denise had been just seven years old. Time wasn't on Sinead's side, but she had grabbed her chance.

That was no comfort to Denise. Her Olympic dream had disappeared. She was devastated. The winter of 2015 she trained hard by herself, just in case she was needed. She finished fourth at the 2016 Europeans in Brandenburg in the single, seventh at World Rowing Cup I in Varese, but by the time the third World Cup regatta in Poznań that June came along it finally hit home: no Olympics.

Denise watched on upstairs in Skibbereen Credit Union that August Friday as Claire and Sinead finished sixth in the A final at the Olympics. Then she put all her energy behind the boys as they took silver. She buried her own disappointment, but it loitered just beneath the surface. She was constantly hoping that no one would mention 'it could have been you'. That was the trigger she didn't want. The tears were just below the surface. But thankfully no one did.

Denise took some time out from rowing, from July 2016 to that November. She needed to gather her thoughts and figure out where to go next. She did. She wasn't happy with how she'd lost her seat, but she came to terms with the knockback. The silver lining was that it hardened her. She had to get back up again, fight hard and show she was good enough to be an Olympian. Sinead did. Claire did. Now it was her turn.

There is a resilience that all Skibbereen rowers have. It's a hard edge carved from their surroundings and Dominic. Nothing is handed to you. Work hard. If you don't get the result you want then work harder. Tough as nails.

It would turn for her sooner than she thought. On the Monday of Paul and Gary's homecoming in August 2016, as she was about to board the double-decker bus that would take her to the event, she heard the news that Don McLachlan's contract with Rowing Ireland hadn't been renewed. Little did she know it then, but her new coach was only a few feet away from her.

That December, Dominic joined the Rowing Ireland payroll as the high performance coach for the lightweight group that included Denise. He knows what works for her and how to get the best out of her, that her start and finish were good, but more consistency was needed through the middle. Focusing on video analysis, he identified parts of her technique that needed work, and tweaked them. He's since made her more consistent.

Denise was given the flexibility to base herself at home in Skibbereen instead of the National Rowing Centre, so she could train on the Ilen. It can be a lonely existence in a single, so being close to home helped. Being in a single meant she had more control over what she was doing and she didn't feel pressure. Rowing was enjoyable again. Everything was starting to fall into place. She felt comfortable. Tougher. Stronger.

***

Denise felt sick. She didn't know whether it was the food or the nerves, but her stomach was in knots at the wrong time. She prayed it was the food and not her nerves, again.

Ever since the Rowing Ireland team had arrived in Račice in the Czech Republic for the 2017 European Rowing Championships in late

May, she'd struggled with the local cuisine. Salty meats and plain rice in the hotel didn't sit well with her. It was too dry. No taste.

The six-strong team was made up of the familiar five Skibb rowers – Gary, Paul, Shane, Mark and Denise – and Sanita Puspure, who lives in Ballincollig. They'd flown straight to Račice from a training camp in Varese, Italy. There they had stayed at the plush Australian Institute of Sport European Training Centre, a home away from home for Australian athletes, in the town of Gavirate, and they had been spoiled by the food.

Not in Račice, though.

Then again it might have been her nerves, those butterflies in the stomach that would terrorise her before a race. She used to vomit regularly before the start. That was the past, though. She was twenty-four years old now, more confident, with more self-belief, backed up by a strict structure to her preparations that chased away any worry and left little wiggle room for doubt.

Usually she shared a room with Sanita. They had roomed together at the AIS European Training Centre but not this time at the Hotel Ludmila in Mělník, twenty minutes from the course. Sanita had an eye infection that eventually ruled her out of competing, so it was separate rooms on medical advice. This meant that there was no one to bounce her thoughts off that morning, unless she wanted to shout across the corridor. She didn't.

This was her biggest day yet. It was the A final of the women's lightweight single sculls at the Europeans. Denise was a medal prospect, a genuine contender, though that brought its own pressure.

She'd raced well all week, won her heat and finished second in her A/B semi-final, coming in behind reigning world champion and favourite Patricia Merz of Switzerland.

Three weeks before the Europeans, Denise had won her first-ever Senior international medal – silver at World Rowing Cup I in Belgrade. That gave her the confidence to know that she was good enough to medal. There had been doubts before, but they were banished under the dull grey skies of Belgrade when a strong sprint saw her surge from fourth to second in the final 500 metres, pushing Poland's Joanna Dorociak into bronze, though still a distance off impressive winner Merz.

Under the blazing sun and suffocating heat in Račice on this Sunday morning, with RTÉ beaming the Europeans live back home, Denise faced the Swiss powerhouse again, but she wasn't thinking about her. Denise was in her zone, that familiar space she retreats into before a race. She felt sharp, ready and fast. This bubbly and animated chatterbox was quiet and serious. It was time to work.

She had her lucky socks too. The previous St Patrick's Day she'd popped into Penneys on St Patrick's Street in Cork city and bought a five-pack of socks. The first pair she wore in Belgrade had worked. She medalled. She was putting the second pair to the test now.

The plan was to start strong and stay within a length of Merz, then go really hard in the middle – normally Denise's weakest section – so she'd be in contention for a medal in the last 500 metres.

Dominic's advice was, as always, simple: 'Make sure you are there and be ready, go hard at the end.'

Denise went hard from the start, though she was only fifth after the first 500 metres. Merz was leading. At the halfway point Denise was still fifth and not going as well as she had hoped. Merz still led and was five seconds ahead of the Irish sculler. By the 1,500 metre mark, with just 500 metres to go, Denise had crept up into fourth, but she was still four seconds behind the world champion, who was leading the race for gold. Sweden and Russia were still in front of her too.

It was time to uncoil that trademark Skibbereen sprint finish. Hers is particularly deadly. It's her favourite part of the race, honed by thousands of hours racing on the Ilen back home. She knows that, if she can stay in contention through the middle, her sprint can make the difference.

Her dad, Tony, was there, standing on the bank, shouting, roaring, urging, 'Go, go, go, go for it now!'

She couldn't hear him, but she knew he was there. He was always there. Always supporting. 500 metres from the finish line is his favoured spot to watch from when he travels abroad to support Denise and the Irish rowers. This is where he plays his part.

Tony was pulling every stroke with his daughter. More than anyone else, he knew what she'd been through in recent years: the pain, the heartbreak and the disappointment. He had been there to help pick up the pieces.

'Come on Denise, go, go, go!'

'NOW!'

He could see she was moving well now, making every stroke count.

Boat by boat she picked off the field. First was Russian sculler Anastasia Lebedeva. There was still 350 metres left.

Patricia Merz, who had led for 1,500 metres but had now slipped behind Swede Emma Fredh, was next. It was effortless and magnificent to watch as Denise powered past Merz.

She was up into second place, just Fredh ahead of her. It was only now, with twenty strokes left, that Denise realised where she stood. She knew she'd win a medal, the only question was what colour. She was pushing through the pain. Harder, harder, harder, she told herself. Breathing through her ears, trying to get oxygen in.

It hurt. Harder, harder, harder. She was edging closer. Closer.

'Go, Denise, go,' Tony shouted, running up beside the course.

But the Swede was travelling well too and Denise ran out of water, though she still crossed the line in second place, in 7:38.000, 1.76 seconds behind the winner. If there had been another 100 metres Denise might have reeled Fredh in.

Her first feeling: *oh fuck, the pain*. It hurts during a race but it's worse at the end. It hit her. The lactic acid in her legs. Her entire body was on fire. She wanted to get sick. She felt awful.

There was no time to cool down, however, because she was due to head straight for the medal ceremony. There would be no chance to sit down, even, or to grab a breath and gather her thoughts. There was a quick interview with David Gillick for RTÉ that was gatecrashed by hugs and congratulations from Shane and Mark.

It was onto the podium then. She was dizzy and can't remember any of it. But she left with a bright, shiny silver medal.

Afterwards, Tony jumped straight in with a hug. It was tight. He didn't want to let her go. When he did he held her medal.

There was a smile from Dominic when Denise met him on the slipway. He had known that potential was in there. He knew she could medal and he knew she was now Ireland's top women's sculler. She had the medal to prove it.

That medal hung around her neck later that night, back on home soil in Skibbereen. It had been a long day, from winning silver to rushing to the airport in Prague to catch the Aer Lingus flight to Dublin Airport, and then the Skibb rowers all travelling by minibus another four hours home.

When they had still been in the Czech Republic, Dominic had rung Damien Long – who runs a bus company in Skibbereen – and asked him could he lay on a bus home for the rowers. Damien obliged, drove to Dublin to collect them and drove the heroes home, and all for free.

Bonfires greeted them on the Cork road, just outside the town as they touched down after midnight. Denise was greeted off the bus with a hug and a kiss from her mam. Her hero was home with two medals from her travels.

Those medals got around. Tony, who was also the local postman, saw to that. The following week in Skibbereen he decided to take her two hard-won silver medals from Belgrade and Račice on tour. Tucked into his pocket, they went on his usual delivery round with him.

Whether it's sport or politics, Tony is engaging. Manchester United's ups and downs are a regular topic. The highs and lows of Cork GAA are debated too, whether it will be the hurlers' year or whether the footballers can ever get back on the right track. The weekend's sport is dissected. But this week it was about the medals. He obliged anyone who wanted a photo with the shining silvers. Anyone who didn't soon did. He repeated this all through his early morning route up through the heart of the town.

On one of those evenings, he was out in the post van for the collections, stopping off in Union Hall, Glandore, Castletownshend, villages on the outskirts of the town. The medals kept him company. He showed them off to everyone. He couldn't contain his pride and wore a permanent smile. Denise was a European silver medallist.

The European medal now hangs in her bedroom at home with the rest. Her pots from winning Irish Rowing Championships rest on a stand at the end of the hall. Each represents a win and a memory. At her eighteenth birthday party at home, a friend had drunk out of one of her tankards. She wasn't happy. 'They're not for drinking,' she'd said. 'They're hard won.'

There was the potential of more medals to come in 2017. It was only May. The World Rowing Championships at Sarasota-Bradenton in Florida were only a few months away. She and the other Skibb rowers were determined to achieve great things at those championships.

the ecstasy and the agony

Shane is not an early riser but race day is the exception. It's the only time that he gets up before Mark.

It was just before 8 a.m., the morning of the A final of the men's lightweight pair at the 2017 World Rowing Championships at Sarasota in Florida, and Shane was already wide-eyed and alert. Mark was starting to stir in his bed.

This was the day they had been waiting for. The chance to officially be recognised as the best in the world. They had won gold at every regatta this season and emerged as one of the stories of the year. They were the wild Skibbereen men with the high stroke rate and a taste for gold, but there was one more gold medal up for grabs.

Everything was geared towards twelve noon. Usually they rose four hours before the race. That was two hours before the weigh-in. It gave them enough time to get the body and mind up to speed.

Shane went straight onto the weighing scales. He was just a little over, by three-tenths of a kilogramme. Mark was moving now. The natural instinct was to hop on the scales and check what needed to be done. It was a similar story for Mark, a fraction of weight to shed. They'd tackle this down at the course. The added promptings of an early morning coffee helped to get the bowels up and running. Everything to hit that seventy kilogramme target.

Quick look in the mirror, the moustaches were coming along. They each had one. Paul O'Donovan as well. That was the result of the training camp in Banyoles, where they had been looking for a different form of entertainment to break up the days of endless training. They had ultimately settled on watching moustaches grow.

Dominic was waiting at reception. They got the bus down to the course. Shane was quiet, yet calm. This felt natural to him. Normal even. They had become used to the big occasion. Mark was chatty. He would talk to anyone. Nerves weren't an issue.

At the course they headed straight to the room full of rowing machines. It was air-conditioned. But they had weight to sweat off, so they pulled two Concept 2 machines outside the door and plonked them on some grass off the path. The big heat hadn't arrived yet, as it was still early morning, but it was already hot. And humid.

Whirrrrrr.

They were warming up, waking up the bodies.

Whirrrrrr.

Christ, it's warm, Mark said.

Whirrrrrr.

By the time they weighed-in they were under seventy kilogrammes each. Spot on. They looked around. The Russians were late. Not a good sign for them, Shane thought.

There was less than two hours to the final. They headed back to the Irish tent and sat with Paul. His music was blaring. It was his playlist. 'The Green Fields of France', Christy Moore. The usual. 'Wrap The Green Flag Around Me' sung by Luke Kelly was another favourite. Gary took the lead on that one. Their culture is important to them. They're proud Skibbereen men, proud Irishmen. They know where they're from.

Everything was under control. Relaxed. Dominic finished preparing their ice vests and getting ice for their bottles and then he began polishing their boat. Shane and Mark always felt the difference after. The boat ran under them. There was less friction and more speed.

It was closer now to the start. Time to get on the water for the warm-up. With the heat beating down they would keep it tight. It was the same warm-up they do in Inniscarra before pieces: a four-minute step-up rate, followed by a few bursts and a few starts.

Mark makes the calls. He's the boss in the boat with the better vantage point, a few feet back from Shane, who trusts each and every call.

At high noon, the six boats lined up at the start. Ireland in lane four. Brazil to their right. Russia to their left. It was time to go to work. But there's a ten-minute delay. That's a long time to sit still in a boat before the biggest race of your life. That's too much time to think. At least some cloud cover offered respite from the sun.

Shane thought back to Morten Espersen's words of wisdom after the 2016 A final at those World Championships. 'Everyone has to experience an A final once to know what happens in it.' Shane and Mark had gone through that in 2016. That experience was in the bag. Stay calm. Keep relaxed. Not long now. Still, as they waited, Shane's thoughts drifted back over their incredible year to date.

Gold I – World Rowing Cup I, Belgrade, 7 May

Balls.

They knew it was coming, but in February 2017 it was rubber-stamped. The men's lightweight four was removed from the Olympics and replaced with the women's four in the interest of gender balance.

That's the men's boat Ireland had sent four times to the Olympics.

Eugene, Timmy and Richard were Olympians because of the lightweight four. But Shane and Mark weren't going to get that chance.

At their training camp in Seville just after Christmas they had tested a four with UCD's Shane Mulvaney and David O'Malley. It was fast. The plan was to race it at one regatta, possibly the Europeans. But the next month their dream of competing in a lightweight four at an Olympics was ended by the vote of delegates at an Extraordinary Congress of FISA, the governing body of world rowing.

Shane and Mark want to become Olympians. As lightweights, with the four scrapped from the Games, the only Olympic-class boat left was the lightweight double that Gary and Paul sit in. But if Shane and Mark were to move up to heavyweight, where there are no weight restrictions, there are more Olympic-class boat options, including the pair.

The heavyweight pair became their standout route to get to the Olympics, but for the 2017 season they decided to stay in the lightweight pair. They felt they were on the brink of something special. They had two World Championships in the lightweight pair behind them. They finished seventh in 2015 and then fourth in 2016. They were getting closer to the podium.

Dominic had been their coach since January 2017, when he came on-board as Rowing Ireland's high performance coach for the lightweights. That was brilliant for Shane and Mark. It reunited them with Gary and Paul. Dominic set out his plan. It included a huge volume of work and he gave them the direction they needed. That camp in Seville went better than they could have hoped. The devilment count was high with the four lads training together, but the signs were encouraging. Dominic set them a goal: go out and win the Europeans.

Before that was World Cup I in Belgrade.

Only four boats entered their category. An exhibition race was held on the Saturday. There was nothing much at stake, just the chance to check out the opposition. The Great British pair of Joel Cassells and Sam Scrimgeour were 2015 world champions and current European champions. They had always been really dominant in the first half of the race. Until now.

Shane and Mark were aggressive from the start. They led at the halfway point. Mark called for them to ease off after 1,500 metres, to save some energy for the final. Great Britain, huffing and puffing, passed them out and won, but the Skibb pair knew now that they were in a strong position. They saw a chink in their rivals. They saw how much they had taken out of them.

The Sunday was miserable. The clouds were dark, the rain fell and there was a chill in the air. Shane felt the cold. He wasn't 100 per cent but knew if they could beat one crew he would be on a podium at international level for the first time in his life.

The water was very calm. So too were Shane and Mark. Great Britain led after 500 metres, but the Irish boat was moving well and in front at the halfway mark. With 700 metres to go, Mark said, 'Go now!' And they went.

The British couldn't live with the pace. They blew up and finished third. The Italians were pushing hard but no crew could match the Irish.

Gold. This was Shane's first for Ireland at Senior level. He'd gone through his Under-23 career with no medal to show. He was fed up with losing. He hates losing. He wanted a medal of any colour to hold in his hand to make it all worthwhile. He got his medal. So did Mark. And they got to stand on the podium.

After the medal presentation they were carrying their boat back to the trailer when they bumped into Dominic walking against them with Denise's boat. His work is done once the rowers get in the water. Where they finish then is up to them. He's busy getting the next rower ready, particularly as the lightweight races are run off close together.

'What colour?'

'Gold. We won,' Mark replied.

'Ye won? Ye beat the British?'

'Yes, Dominic. If we wanted to win, we'd have to beat the British,' Shane fires back.

'Good men.'

Dominic was impressed.

Gold 2 – European Rowing Championships, Račice, 28 May

Morten's observation stuck in Shane's mind. They were chatting at the training camp in Seville earlier that year and reflecting on the 2016 World Championships. 2016 was the year of the fourths – Shane and Mark finished fourth in the C final at the opening World Cup event in Varese, fourth at the Europeans in Brandenburg, fifth at the third World Cup in Poznań and then fourth again at the World Championships in Rotterdam.

They were sick of fourth. That was failure. It's just outside the medals. Best of the losers. It's the worst place to finish. That feeling stuck with them. The fear of fourth drove them on. Fear of coming up short, again.

They had no complaints after the 2016 world final. They didn't deserve to win a medal. France, Denmark and Great Britain were all much better. But that A final was important in their development, Morten told Shane. It's always different in an A final. You race against crews all year, but it's different in an A world final. Crews go crazy off the start and you must go crazy with them.

Shane and Mark were about to take crazy to an entire new level at the 2017 Europeans and prove that Belgrade wasn't a freak result. They wanted to show that they weren't one-hit wonders. They were approaching every race like a world final.

Six crews lined up and Ireland blitzed the other five. They led from start to finish, sprinting out of the blocks at a manic rate of fifty-three strokes per minute. They were inside world-record pace after 500 metres, even though the conditions weren't fast or at all suited to breaking the world record. This was aggressive rowing and no other crew could keep up with them. The Russians finished strong, but Shane and Mark still had two seconds to spare. They were European champions.

Twelve months earlier at the Europeans they had finished almost ten seconds behind the Great British crew that won gold. But now they were on top. This is the moment they realised that they could be world champions. This was a turning point. It showed they were good enough.

The world was starting to sit up and take notice, even the clergy. During Mark's older brother's wedding the Friday after the Europeans, as Sean married Marie Donegan from Ballydehob at her local church, the priest asked for a round of applause for Mark and Shane.

Gold 3 – World Rowing Cup II, Poznań, 17 June

Their ferocious pace from the start and their stroke rate were now a hot topic. The way they row is unique. It's not easy on the eye. It's not the standard technique. It's not how the upper class would move a rowing boat. But it works for them. It was moving the boat from A to B faster than anyone else.

They take more strokes per minute than any other crew. They opt for shorter and faster strokes over the traditional long strokes. They sit up nice and tall, and bang their oars in the water quite aggressively. There's very little wastage. It's efficient.

The previous winter they adjusted their weights programme to improve their leg speed. Lighter squatting but faster squatting. That helped up their stroke rate. And they were at it again in Poznań. Only three boats competed. They were guaranteed a medal before it even began. But they wanted gold. And that's what they got, never falling below forty strokes per minute. Great Britain was second. Brazil, third.

Gold 4 – World Rowing Cup III, Lucerne, 17 June

Another race, another gold. This time they were made work for it by both the heat and the competition, who were doing their best to get on top of Ireland's fast starts.

Great Britain took the early lead and held it until halfway. Ireland stayed in the group until Mark called, 'Go now. Ten, ten.' That meant ten hard strokes. After that ten, they went hard for another ten. Then another ten. It was a long sprint to the line.

The Irish Rowing Championships were the following weekend and then they had a break after that before a big chunk of training in Banyoles for the World Championships in Florida, so they went for it in that last kilometre. They took the lead and won.

By the time the Worlds rolled around, Shane and Mark had made the decision to move to the world of heavyweight for the 2018 season and chase their Olympic dream in the men's pair. It wasn't made public, however, until after the 2017 World Championships because they had a job to do in the lightweight pair: finish this season with a fifth international gold.

Shane and Mark could have competed against Gary and Paul for a seat in the lightweight double. That would have meant changing from sculling – where they use one oar each – in the pair to sweeping – holding an oar in each hand – like Gary and Paul do in the double.

But Shane and Mark wanted to forge their own path. They were encouraged to go for the lightweight double but they resisted. That's Gary's and Paul's story. Shane and Mark have their own. There is room for all four at the top table.

That camp went well. There was lots of short-interval work with short recovery as well. One minute on, one minute off, ten times, and repeat that three times. Plenty of mileage too, twenty kilometres every evening.

Back at the hotel the coffee was flowing. They had brought the coffee machine from the National Rowing Centre. Everything was gearing up nicely for the World Championships at Nathan Benderson Park in Sarasota, Florida, even though Hurricane Irma briefly threatened to derail it all. But the course avoided her worst.

Gold 5 – World Rowing Championships, Sarasota-Bradenton, 29 September

The ten minutes of the delay ticked by. Each second slower than the last.

Shane glanced across to the Russians. They looked anxious. The others looked settled.

Treat this like the Skibbereen regatta, Mark said. It's just another race with a different title.

They were all waiting.

One week before this race the Irish rowers had been waiting for their boats to arrive on the container from home, but they were late. It was a scramble to find replacements to train in – and possibly even race in. Hudson had nothing for Shane and Mark. Filippi did, but it was a ninety-kilogramme-plus boat, whereas they raced in seventy-kilogramme hulls. They looked like two kids sat in it.

It wasn't ideal, but they had a World Championships to win no matter what boat they were in. This different size was creating issues, though. It was rocking. Trying to balance it and keep it level, Shane felt a twinge in his lower back and hip. But they made it work after a few training pieces. They were ready to race.

Then their own Empacher finally touched down in Florida. They were back in it when they won their heat on the previous Sunday.

Now, there was a target on their back. They were the crew everyone wanted to beat in the A final.

Great Britain shot out from the start. They caught Shane and Mark unawares and the Irish pair found themselves in and out of second and third with the Italians. They began at fifty-six strokes per minute. Great Britain set off at forty-four.

Through 500 metres, Shane and Mark were in second; shortly after that mark, however, they made their move and shot into the lead.

The intense heat was a factor now. It was twenty-eight degrees. The eighty-eight per cent humidity was suffocating them. Paul O'Donovan had warned Shane the evening before that the temperature had changed a lot from their earlier race. It was a lot hotter. If you go hard off the start you will be punished by the heat, Paul said.

800 metres in, Shane's mouth was so dry it opened up. He couldn't close it. Paul popped into his head. He had been right.

Their tempo was phenomenal. Surely impossible to maintain right to the end? But they pulled out all the stops.

They were in front hitting 500 metres to go, the British duo having faded, though the Italians and Brazilians were still pushing to their right.

Mark reverted to a familiar session: fifteen strokes on. They concentrated on the next fifteen strokes like it was the last fifteen. They had to keep the Italians at bay. If they drew level the Skibb men were in trouble because they had punished and pushed themselves. They stayed in front, the pace unrelenting. Each stroke closer to that finish line.

'Yes, this is it now,' Mark said. He was getting excited. Shane fed off that. Their legs were creaking for those last ten strokes. They drove them hard. They used their upper bodies more. The pain shot down their necks, spreading into their arms.

Then they passed the line first, in 6:32.42.

They were world champions. Best. In. The. World.

Mark was first to realise, raising his hands in the air. Shane couldn't lift his. He tried to but they had seized up. Falling out of the boat, bodies twisted in pain, they sat on the slip, side by side, and hugged.

There was celebrating in the grandstand. The Skibb crowd was making noise. Nuala Lupton, Richard Roycroft and Tony Walsh were there. Albert Swanton, a former Skibb rower who was now living in Boston, was also present. So was Frank Walley, now in San Francisco. Ditto Jim Hannigan, based in Florida. All were there, celebrating Skibb's latest success.

It was just after six in the evening back in Skibbereen when Shane borrowed a phone to ring his mam, Mary, who was waiting for this call. Shane had been pulled away for drug testing after the race. That took longer than normal because he was so dehydrated. Eventually he emerged and rang home. The house was full. Neighbours, cousins, friends. The phone was passed to nearly every person in the house, including local priest Fr Cahill. Shane told him while he was there with all the neighbours to say the stations and get it out of the way. Everyone was on a high. Like Mark back in Florida. It had been a long journey.

They had been through more downs than ups. Those lean years that had seemed endless. But it was all worth it now. They stood in the centre of the stage now. All eyes were on them.

When they flew into Cork Airport they were greeted by fans. At the homecoming in Skibb, they had equal billing to world champion Paul, who had defended his crown in Florida. They had found their feet.

It's fitting that in the year Mark appeared as an extra on episode three in series seven of *Game of Thrones* – rough, ready and bearded, clad head to toe in full armour and with a mighty sword, Mark was one of four soldiers standing menacingly in the background in a scene shot with Jon Snow in Zumaia, Spain – he actually took the throne that he really wanted.

Now he was his own king, ruling alongside Shane. The world of the lightweight pair conquered. Now on to heavyweight and back to the start again.

***

Denise was another Skibb rower with medal hopes at the World Championships. The European silver earlier in the year had put her in the reckoning for a medal in the women's lightweight single in Florida. She won her heat on the Monday. That set her up well for the semi-final on the Thursday. Denise dominated. She led after the 500-metre mark, but, in hindsight, she had pushed herself too hard, racing the semi like it was a final. It took too much out of her. The final was the following day, Friday, and there was little room for recovery.

A back injury was also playing on her mind. It had gone into spasm after the heat. When she went straight into the ice bath it locked up. It was niggling at her now, ahead of the A final.

Back at the Holiday Inn Sarasota Airport that Thursday night, she relaxed. The room was plush. She had two double beds all to herself and a full-screen TV to watch the Kardashians and take her mind off the final the next morning.

On race day she felt okay. It was a fifteen-minute shuttle bus from the hotel to the course. The tent the Irish team had was air-conditioned. The facilities were top class. Weigh-in was two hours before and she likes the structure that gives ahead of a race. It was time to refuel. She swapped the bread and Nutella for smoothies full of strawberries, bananas, oats and yoghurt. She kept it simple but still wanted to get the carbs on-board. The sapping heat meant she strapped on an ice-vest to keep cool. Her nerves were under control. Everything checked and ready, she paddled to the warm-up area and still felt good. She kept her bursts short. She felt ready.

Bang. Nothing happened. The race was only 500 metres old when Denise knew she had to do something, and fast. She was in fifth place.

She went to make a move. But nothing happened. She wasn't getting faster. She glanced down at the GPS monitor showing her stroke rate, distance and time. She was looking for signs of hope. There weren't any. She went to go again. But her legs didn't come with her. The power wasn't there. That's an awful feeling.

By the halfway point she was sixth, almost five seconds off the Netherlands in the lead. She was cut adrift by the end, limping home eleven seconds behind the new world champion, South African Kirsten McCann.

It was a race she felt she could have medalled in. Not meeting her own expectations was disappointing.

Coming off the water after the finish, Denise saw Shane and Mark, who had won world gold thirty minutes earlier. There was a quick hug.

something in the water

She congratulated them but was quiet. They kept moving, being ushered to the media tent for interviews as Denise walked in the opposite direction, alone. Dominic brought her boat in. 'Hard luck,' he offered. He knew too that she could have medalled. It was an opportunity lost. That's what hurt. It had been a year of major progress on and off the water. She had lifted her levels. But the magic wasn't there when she needed it.

18

a different animal

In all his years involved in rowing, Dominic had never seen anything like this. It was incredible. He knew there and then that Paul would be world champion again. This was the training camp in Banyoles before the 2017 Worlds and Paul was just in phenomenal form. He was on a different level to everyone else. He was in beast mode. Everyone there took notice.

By now Paul knew he would be defending his lightweight single sculls title in Florida. Gary had been forced to pull out of the double due to illness.

They had kept their momentum up throughout the international season with silver at the Europeans in the Czech Republic and World Rowing Cup II in Poznań and bronze at World Cup III in Lucerne, but as the summer wore on Gary wasn't 100 per cent.

Juggling training, award events, social engagements and his new-found celebrity status all caught up with him. It wasn't managed properly. They didn't train a whole pile between Rio and Christmas 2016 and they were on the back foot then.

Gary felt the effects the next summer. He eventually got sick. He kept training but didn't get better. He took a week off, felt better, went back training and got sick again. Run down, he missed six weeks of training.

Eventually, after the Irish Rowing Championships in July, Gary called it. He was out of the double for the Worlds. That was an instant relief. It was a weight off his shoulders. He trained in a single in Banyoles and he eased back into it. He already had one eye on 2018.

Paul now knew that he was going to the Worlds in just the single. He ripped it up in Spain during that training camp. In the morning it was pieces, where he rowed a shorter distance as fast as possible to simulate a race, and repeated this many times. In the evening it was steady state, where he rowed a far longer distance at a lower rate. Paul would head out on the lake in his single at the same time in the evening as Shane and Mark did in their pair. After they came in, Paul would spend an extra hour on the lake. He rowed up and down countless times. It was non-stop. He never relinquished any power. It was the quality that impressed Dominic. Paul rowed in excess of twenty-four kilometres on the water every evening. Depending on how he felt, he tagged on a few extra kilometres at the end. It was more than anyone else. Paul and Dominic would come in off the water in the dark. Shane and Mark would already be sitting down for dinner by then.

Paul would have some fish and pasta. Then he'd go to bed, get up the next day and do the same thing over again. He was testing his own limits in the single. The thinking was that if he messed up, at least he was only affecting himself. Instead he arrived at the Worlds in fantastic shape and as the favourite to defend his world title.

Paul's mental strength is his greatest weapon. Physically, he's an animal in the boat. Mentally, he is different to the rest. This is an endurance sport. To succeed you need mental endurance. Paul has more than most.

That strength of mind allows him to push his body beyond breaking point. There have been several times he has been lifted out of a boat after a race, or carried. That happened in Aiguebelette in 2015 after Gary and himself qualified for the Olympics. Dominic and Denise had to help him walk. That's how much effort he puts in. He gives it everything.

Pain never bothered Paul. He uses brute force to push through the barriers. He knows the pain will attack. It always does. In those final 200 metres, when he is struggling to breathe and when it really hurts, he pushes it on. He pulls, hauls and drags the boat. Ignorance helped Gary and himself build a higher threshold. When they were learning to row Dominic never mentioned lactate build-up. The pain in your legs and arms is because you're not doing it right, he would say. They drove through that agony. When they discovered it was a physical thing, they were already used to it. That mentality means Paul is never fazed. Even when it turned out that he had no boat in Florida he didn't panic.

What arrived was the lightweight double that had been shipped out from home before Gary pulled out. That meant Paul had to source his own single in Florida. Paul and Dominic looked at a WinTech boat first. But it didn't suit. Then they contacted Helmut Empacher of Empacher rowing boats. He had one single left. It was similar to Paul's. It didn't come wrapped in plastic from the factory with that new boat smell he loves, but it solved the problem.

Despite a late change in plans and in a boat he had never used before, Paul wasn't ruffled. He won his heat, quarter-final and semi-final, and produced the goods again in the final. Fourth after 500 metres he made his move in the second quarter, lifting his rate, meaning he was in front by 1,000 metres. He was in control until the end, leaving New Zealand and Norway battling it out for the other podium positions behind him.

Paul was world champion. Again.

Watching back home in Ireland, Niall O'Toole was blown away by it all. Paul is the best Irish rower of all time, he said. And he's going to be better. He's only twenty-three years old. His potential is frightening. He will get stronger.

'People achieved different things at different times in the sport that were iconic – the first gold medal, the first sweep medal, the first women's medal, the first back-to-back world champions. But what Paul has done is win an Olympic medal and win back-to-back World Championships, and I think he is the greatest Irish rower of all time,' O'Toole said.

Paul pays little heed to compliments. He listens. Then he instantly brushes them off, already moving on to the next challenge. When he heard the praise heaped on him after winning gold in the single at the Worlds in 2016 he replied, 'I'd say they're only talking shite, are they? We'll have to see what Dominic says.'

Even after back-to-back world gold medals, and that Olympic silver, he still wasn't satisfied. Maybe he never will be. But that's exactly what makes him so special. Like Teddy taught and instilled in him – and Dominic reinforces – it's always about the next race. A win is a win. It's parked. And Paul moves on.

He doesn't spend any time looking at his medals or what he has achieved. That's standing still. Do that and the fear is he will fall behind. He always wants to be better. That's why he says himself and Gary lost the 2016 Olympics. He never dreamt of winning silver as a kid. It's about the gold. His reasoning is that when you end up with silver after dreaming of gold, it means you lost. Paul found it hard to watch replays of the 2016 Olympic afterwards because he sees it as a defeat. He hates losing. It has to be perfect.

Back in his national school days, when he was learning to write, if he spelled a word wrong in a sentence, he'd erase the entire sentence instead of just the incorrect word. He justified the extra work to Trish.

'It's not right, Mam.'

That pursuit of perfection is why he is Skibbereen's best-ever rower. Tough as nails.

good cop, bad cop

The success of Skibbereen's international-level rowers was fantastic for the club, and Dominic was clearly delighted for them. But he wanted more for the club than to have a few world-class rowers. He wanted the club itself to be the number one rowing club in Ireland.

Dominic had Neptune Rowing Club in his sights from very early on. It was his mission to topple them. He repeated that statement regularly to Greg Hegarty as they worked together at O'Donovan's boatyard.

Greg didn't doubt Dominic's belief but knew it was a tall order. It was hard to imagine the country boys usurping the city slickers. The clubs were at the opposite ends of the spectrum.

One was the new kid on the block. It was a poor club where rowers who couldn't afford the one-piece uniform would wrap red electrical tape around a white vest to get the desired look. The other was a mighty club in the capital with a head start in building its foundations since 1908. It was part of the rowing aristocracy in Ireland and a leading force. In boxing terms, it was a flyweight up against a heavyweight. But Dominic believed it was possible. This was the early 1980s. Skibb had only one Irish Rowing Championship title to their name: Nuala in 1976.

During the 1980s Skibb tipped away at the nationals. By the end of the decade they had won thirteen titles. Dominic had won eight of those himself, three of them with Lar Collins in the double. Before his coaching days he was the club's top oarsman for a spell. Eleanor won a Novice single scull in 1986, Mary Rose Jennings the same title the following year, Mike Cotter and David O'Donovan won the Junior double scull in 1988 and twelve months later Elizabeth McCarthy won the women's Novice single scull. Still, they were a long way off the top.

In the 1990s, as Dominic turned his hand to coaching and his influence on the club began to take hold, the National Championships started to add up. Between Nuala's maiden win in 1976 for Skibb and 1996, the club won thirty National Championship titles. They were a coming force. But still Dominic was looking for every little advantage. Enter 'Magic Mary'.

***

One knock on her front door in 1999 changed Mary Cummins' life. When she answered, Dominic was standing outside. She had never seen this silver-haired man before, didn't know who he was and initially struggled to understand what he was saying, but she quickly learned what he wanted – and that no one can say no to him.

He had seen the bed and breakfast sign for Fana, Mary's home in Farran, just off the main road into Cork city. He wanted a base close to the National Rowing Centre for his Skibbereen rowers for the National Championships; somewhere to stay in the days leading up to the regatta and throughout the weekend itself. Mary and Tony's home was four miles away from Farran Woods. Perfect, he thought.

The trouble was that the bed and breakfast sign was a nod to the previous owners of the house. Mary hadn't bothered to take it down. She wasn't running a B&B.

'Can you keep two rowers for a couple of nights? They'll be no bother, no bother.'

She tried to explain this wasn't a B&B.

'They'll be no bother,' he repeated.

Mary ultimately relented.

She loves people. Loves when her house is packed with noise and life. And Skibbereen rowers ended up filling her home for fifteen years after this.

Like Gremlins, those initial two rowers in that first week soon multiplied to four and then eight. Initially, Skibb rowers were also staying in another B&B near the start line, but as word filtered through about Mary's roast dinners and desserts, her five-bedroom bungalow with its four en suites began to fill up.

It wasn't long before Mary's became the Skibb rowers' home for the week of the championships. Everyone wanted to stay with Magic Mary, their mother for the week.

It's only Skibbereen rowers that call her 'Magic Mary'. 'Magic' was her go-to word. Nothing was ever a problem. Everything was 'magic'.

'You've to get up at five in the morning? Magic. No problem.'

'You want me to wash your gear and have it ready for the morning? Magic. Not a bother.'

Her husband Tony was then christened 'Terrific Tony', just so he wouldn't feel left out.

Other clubs were already envious that Skibbereen set up camp at the National Rowing Centre the week before the championships and trained on the course a couple of times every day, but now they had their own 'mother' to care for them too.

'I looked after them the very same way I looked after my own three boys,' Magic Mary says.

She fed Skibb's rowers, watered them, washed and dried their gear, cleaned up after them, made them feel like they were at home. She even gave up her entire home for them when the numbers staying peaked at eighteen. They were dotted all over the house, sleeping in beds and on couches and blow-up beds. On those weeks Mary and Tony stayed in her brother's caravan beside the house and her three boys slept in their insulated timber cabin at the back.

Magic Mary loved the week of the National Championships. It was her favourite time of the year. They would land to her on the Monday and stay until it was all over, the day after the final night disco at the rowing centre, when she'd watch with amazement as the girls who lived that week with no make-up and scraped-back hair transformed into glamorous young women.

Preparations for the annual invasion began two weeks beforehand, when she scrubbed the house clean from the skirting boards to the windows. Closer to the week she made the trip to Musgraves wholesale suppliers out the Airport road in Cork city to stock up: forty pounds of mince, fifteen chickens, fifty chicken breasts on the bone, enough food so there'd be plenty of lasagne, pasta bake, all their favourites. Everything was cooked in her small galley kitchen, out of one under-pressure oven and its four rings.

The Skibb rowers' appetites always amazed her. They tucked away the food. She worked around their schedule, as they were knee-deep in 'the supercomp' – that's the training programme rolled out before the big events. If they race on the Friday of the championships, the previous Friday and Saturday on the Ilen are exhausting. Two really hard days of sprint work, two sessions both days above race pace. They go to the well and beyond, and live in dread of the next session. For the next five days before the race, it's morning and evening training again, but these are low-intensity sessions, including a ten-kilometre paddle with short twenty-stroke bursts at race pace added in. As the week moves on, every day they start to feel fitter and stronger, ready to sprint out of the traps when race day arrives. Supercomp helps them peak when it's needed. Survive it and you know you're ready, mentally and physically.

Magic Mary gave them the fuel they needed. There was the early breakfast at six in the morning, maybe some cereal. Then they'd go for a spin at the rowing centre before returning back to base for a big breakfast, with scrambled eggs and brown bread being a popular choice. Lunch was homemade soup and rolls, or quiche and salads. Those who couldn't get back were sent off with packed lunches. Magic Mary thought of everything.

Dinner in the evening was rolled out with military precision and there was never any waste. They came back for seconds, thirds and fourths. Then that night, around 9 p.m., there was hot chocolate, scones, buns, whatever they wanted. Skibb rowers were spoiled. So were their parents when they popped in to visit. Magic Mary's door was always open.

She was much more than the mother that Dominic wanted to look after the rowers. His vision was for them to be together for the week of the championships, to bond, to work hard, to drive each other on, to be close to the National Rowing Centre and, importantly, to have fun too and create their own memories. Magic Mary's open house ticked every box.

She was there to congratulate them if they landed home with 'pots', there to give them a hug if they lost, and there to cover for them if they needed saving from Dominic. She was the good cop. He was the bad cop.

***

The phone rang. It was Dominic. Magic Mary couldn't hear exactly what he was saying. The phone reception in Farran could play up at times. But she gathered through the crackling that he wasn't happy.

Turns out that's an understatement. Dominic was livid. There was no sign of Gary O'Donovan and Diarmuid O'Driscoll for their Intermediate pair race that Sunday morning at the National Championships in 2011.

The night before, a group of the Seniors had decided to hit the town. Kenneth McCarthy, Justin Ryan, Andrew Hurley and Gearoid Murphy had lost their quad race on the Saturday and their regatta was over, so it was time to let off steam.

Gary and Diarmuid were mad to join them. They had a race the next morning, but the plan was to head to the city for a few quiet ones, get back to Magic Mary's early and be fresh in the morning for the race – and all without Dominic finding out. It was foolproof, or so they believed.

Out the window of their room they jumped, down to the taxi that was taking the gang to town. One pint became two and soon multiplied to many. The lure of Rearden's Bar and The Washington Inn saw a few harmless ones turn into a session. A round of shots ended any hopes of an early night.

Justin had a rented house near the city centre. Gary, Diarmuid and the gang landed back there around 4 a.m. They had to be up for 7 a.m. for their race. But they didn't surface. Diarmuid set the alarm. Hungover, he turned it off when it sounded and went back to sleep for another few hours. Gary never heard the alarm. Diarmuid never woke him. They needed sleep.

Back at Magic Mary's that morning, she checked the room and there was no sign of the two lads. But she has a soft spot for all the rowers.

'I always made sure that they didn't get into trouble because they don't deserve that. They are up there with the finest people I ever met. I would be proud to have any one of them as a son or a daughter,' Magic Mary says.

She covered for the duo, telling Dominic that their room door was closed and she assumed they were in bed and maybe they weren't feeling well.

They missed the race, of course, meaning that Skibbereen Rowing Club was fined and Dominic and more of the committee were left seething.

Gary and Diarmuid eventually landed back to Magic Mary's to face the music and got hit with community service: they had to coach the kids on Sunday mornings for eight weeks. It turns out too that it was a soft year in the pair event, so Diarmuid and Gary could have won it and added another national title to the list. It's one that got away.

Magic Mary never flinched, though. She stuck to her story. She always looked out for the rowers; her 'babies' as she called them. Most nights Dominic would ring to see if they were all in bed. She answered the phone surrounded by all of them. They would be playing cards or just chatting. The room would go quiet. Complete silence. They knew the drill. They are all in their rooms, she'd say. Off the phone she'd tell them he'll be on his way soon and they'd scatter. When he landed, the previous hyperness in the house was replaced by total silence.

'The respect they have for him is incredible. It's insane,' Magic Mary says. 'They all listened to him because they all knew what he was doing was all for them. He was there to help them. He reared so many kids in Skibbereen through the rowing club. What makes that club so special is Dominic. He's the common denominator in it all.'

His attention to detail always amazed her. He would have a physiotherapist call to her home, where one room would be designated for the physio's table and the rowers would have a massage the day of the race as well as the day before, to relax their muscles.

On the last day of their stay with her every year the rowers would club together and buy her a present, a token of their thanks, like a piece of handmade pottery made in Skibbereen that still sits proudly on a shelf in her home.

'You did well, you did well. Next year, next year,' Dominic would say, signing off after the National Championships.

The tradition of Magic Mary's eventually faded away as times changed. More and more young rowers had their own cars and could make the trip from Skibb to Farran Woods. Magic Mary's work was done. Her babies were all grown-up.

***

At the 2015 championships Skibbereen had won four titles to go joint top of the honours list for the first time. They now shared the summit with Neptune, both tied on 150 national titles each. Skibbereen were finally in sight of the sole number one spot, and of proving that Dominic wasn't mad after all.

Ping. The email landed. All the rowers knew it was coming. It was from Dominic. Even Richard in Sydney was included in the mailing list, still part of the family, even though he left Skibb in 2010.

It was early 2016, and while the championships were a long way off, they were still the big target and this email was read from start to finish by everyone. Dominic designed them as motivational tools. They gave the rowers a purpose, a belief and something to aim for. And it was also the easiest form of communication with rowers spread all over the place, between work and college.

This one was for the men after a men's meeting earlier that day. In the first line it was stressed that a women's meeting would follow asap, and then their email would be dispatched. Both emails would share a common theme.

This was where Dominic laid down the law and rallied the troops. First there was the recap of that morning's meeting and the actions:

- Follow the programme.
- Train to the best of your ability. Each day is so important. Be totally determined in everything you do.
- Please record your training each day on the Google Docs training diary.
- Have self-belief in your ability to give it all you have got in each and every training session.
- Time-keeping and be prepared. Example, for a 7.15 a.m. session arrive at 7.10. a.m. (You will get a better session.)
- Let me know via a text if you cannot make a session. This should be done as early as possible (the night before).

Then followed Dominic's words of encouragement, using the bold font to give his words greater effect:

- I suppose it is important to **realise** that we have **a great squad of men this year,** which gives everyone an opportunity to reach their full potential.
- It is important to move on and build strong units for the regatta season.
- Each training session is so **important** to try and do your best and be happy that you are putting everything into your training.

- It will definitely help to make sure you reap the rewards. **Fitter, Stronger, Faster.**
- There is no room for complacency. **The next three months are vital and will determine your boat speed during the regatta season.**

In true Dominic style, he said: 'I know people are anxious to race and so on but I would not panic. I have no doubt that all our boats have potential and are going to go fast. We should have the confidence to know that with our programme we can win. We do not need to know now that we can do it today or at the next Head of the River. We must have a strong belief in our own ability. I have no doubt whatsoever that we can have a great season ahead but it is all in your hands. Just focus on making every session count.'

The final words in the email: 'Keep positive. Train well. You can do it.'

***

The titles just kept coming and coming on a glorious July weekend at Farran Woods. It was inevitable that Skibbereen would surpass Neptune's tally at some stage and they did it in style, winning thirteen national titles at those 2016 championships, dwarfing Neptune's two.

Even without their two main men, Gary and Paul, Skibb were too good for the rest, with Denise, Shane and Mark available to race.

It was the Junior women that kicked off the weekend on Friday morning with Aoife Casey and Emily Hegarty, the latter in her last year as a Junior, winning the Junior double sculls. They came off the water angry. They had barely won. They were like two bears. It had been too close for comfort. They were determined to not let it be that close again.

They were joined by Lydia Heaphy and Aoibhinn Keating in the women's Junior coxless four, and they had that race won by the one-kilometre mark. Emily had added the Junior scull title by the time they raced the women's Junior quad on Sunday. Skibb were going for their seventh win in a row in this race, so there was a lot at stake, a proud tradition to uphold.

The Skibb Junior women were national title-winning machines all through the current decade, from Denise to Shelly Dineen, Christine Fitzgerald and Laura Connolly in 2010. The conveyor belt has been strong over the years and there was pressure on here. No one wanted to be in the crew that lost the winning run.

Aoife and Emily were the slave drivers, Lydia and Aoibhinn feeling the pressure, but it was the latter duo in the bow that produced the goods. They needed a strong start. They got it. They won.

Aoife and Denise partnered up in the women's Senior pair to win. Denise later added the women's lightweight single scull. The titles were adding up now.

Dominic was in constant contact by phone from Banyoles in Spain, where he was on a pre-Olympic training camp with Gary and Paul. It was the first time since 1980 that he missed a National Championships as either a rower or a coach. But his presence was still felt. He kept tabs on every single race that weekend from afar.

Denise, Niamh Casey and Orla Hayes formed a composite Senior women's eight with UCC that also won, beating UCD. It was Orla's fifteenth national title.

At 10.12 p.m. that Friday night, after the first day's action, the email arrived from Spain.

'To all Athletes, Coaches and Parents. Congratulations to all the Skibbereen team on a great day's rowing today. Best of luck tomorrow and for the rest of the weekend. The message remains the same. Fight even harder and fight from the very first stroke. Give it better than your best shot. I know you can do it. Best of luck. Best Regards, Dominic.'

Shane and Mark were unbeatable, winning four titles each – the men's Senior double sculls, the men's Senior pair, the men's Senior quad with Kenneth McCarthy and Fintan McCarthy, with Mark also taking home the Senior men's single scull title and Shane winning the men's lightweight scull crown. Fintan and Jake McCarthy won the men's Intermediate double too.

Skibb blew the opposition out of the water at Inniscarra. It was now officially the number one club in the country in terms of all-time national titles won. A lifelong dream for Dominic had been realised. He missed the celebrations but his handprints were all over the success.

At 11.32 a.m. that Monday morning the email arrived: 'To all Athletes and Coaches and Parents. Thanks to everyone who made it possible to have such a brilliant National Championships. Well done to each and every one. I am really proud of you all. Best Regards, Dominic.'

He was true to his word. He had driven Skibbereen rowing to the point where they had toppled Neptune. Greg Hegarty smiled to himself at work in the boatyard the following Monday morning.

***

Ping. The email arrived in the inbox of thirty-six male rowers in the club. Gary, Paul, Shane, Mark, Kenneth, Richard in Sydney, Eugene in London, Diarmuid, Justin Ryan, John, Fintan, Jake, Timmy all included.

It was sent thirty-five minutes after his congratulatory email on the weekend's 2016 National Championships. It was 12.07 p.m. on Monday afternoon. The club had been number one for less than twenty-four hours and the success was still being celebrated when Dominic pressed send from his laptop in Banyoles.

The subject line: '2017'.

'Hi to all. Looking forward to next year's 2017 rowing calendar it might be possible to have mass participation of all our athletes. I think the Irish Championships are on the week after Lucerne, which opens up the possibility to have all our national squad athletes available to row for Skibbereen. Also the World Rowing Championships are not on until late September so that will not be a problem. The possibility of a men's Senior eight is a distinct possibility as well as all the men's championships. So if you are interested, the training will start straightaway (that is running, erging, cycling, rowing, individually aerobically). So please contact me to form a training group as communication will be key with so many athletes training all over the world. Think seriously about it as only you can make it happen and it has to be an all out effort. Best Regards, Dominic.'

He was already looking to the next race. He does not stop. Relentless. The club had never won the men's Senior eight at the National Championships before. It was the missing piece of the jigsaw. That was clearly on his mind. And the following year Skibbereen would look to finally complete that jigsaw.

20

the missing piece

Gary felt in the best shape of his life. So did Paul. Shane and Mark were flying high too. Skibb's top four men were in peak form at the right time.

The 2017 Irish Rowing Championships couldn't come quickly enough. Too often in recent years their international calendar clashed with the Nationals, so they missed out, but this year it fell nicely. The championships were scheduled for the weekend after World Cup III in Lucerne.

Gary and Paul landed home with bronze in the lightweight double. Shane and Mark's dominance of the lightweight pair had yielded a fourth gold of the season.

Spirits were high as the Skibbereen four turned their attention to the nationals at Inniscarra in mid-July. This had been in their crosshairs since Dominic's email in July 2016. They wanted to win everything, including the pot that had always evaded Skibbereen's grasp: the men's Senior eight. That was the big one.

It stands above all the others as the crown jewel of the National Championships, the last race on the Sunday evening, everything building towards this crescendo. The crowds, the anticipation, the excitement. It's the highlight. It's the race that's remembered. Winning the Senior men's eight is a sign of strength in a club, that you have eight top rowers and a cox who are better than the best other clubs can offer.

Skibbereen is a small boat club that works with singles, doubles and fours. They never consider the big boats. Training is based on small boats and the thinking is that if you can row a small boat fast, the big boat should go faster.

It's easier to put small boats on the water when it's a small club in a small area. Bigger clubs have bigger numbers. For all Skibb's success, numbers are tight. It's easier to put doubles together, get singles out on the water, especially when your four best rowers are usually ruled out of club action by international duty. But the stars were aligned, so here now was a chance for the best club to win the biggest event. Gary insisted it was an opportunity too good to turn down.

In his last year as a Junior in 2010, Skibbereen planned on winning every Junior championship that was available – the single, the double, the pair, the four, the quad and the eight. Skibb had never achieved this before. Each previous attempt had fallen short. And so did this one. They won three of the six – the four, the quad and the double. Gary and Diarmuid finished second in the pair, while Shane, Paul and Gary filled second, third and fourth spots in the single.

Their attempt to win the men's Junior eight, and follow in the footsteps of the Skibb crews of the late 1990s, ended in failure too. The crew of Gary, Paul, Shane, Diarmuid, Padraig Murphy, Cormac Leonard, Paddy Hegarty and Paudie Leonard was too young and inexperienced. Gary was devastated afterwards, his last chance to win a Junior eight gone.

But now, seven years on, he had a chance to win the Senior men's eight, that mythical pot that Skibb have chased but never caught. That was the dream, to do what no other Skibbereen crew had managed before. Plans started to take shape in Rio, the night after Gary and Paul won Olympic silver.

***

'You're a mess,' Paul quipped. 'Jesus, you're in terrible shape altogether.'

Diarmuid O'Driscoll couldn't disagree.

He was standing against the bar at a Red Bull party in downtown Rio on the Saturday night, holding his vodka and Red Bull, celebrating Gary and Paul's medal on Friday, and weighing in at 122kg. Paul stood at 70kg.

'Get back rowing, will you,' Paul continued, straight to the point and dishing out some home truths.

Diarmuid conceded this one. His weight had crept up. It wasn't exactly a secret he could hide. Two weeks of partying in the Lapa nightlife in Rio and a steady supply of Caipirinha cocktails from the local street vendors had also taken its toll on Diarmuid. By the time his feet touched down on West Cork soil again he needed something to focus on. He needed to be involved in the Senior men's eight at the 2017 National Championships.

Dominic had sent the email a few weeks beforehand. Gary, Paul, Shane and Mark were half the boat. Another four were needed.

The knock-on positives from the Olympic silver were starting to take hold in Skibb rowing and beyond. The ripples started in Rio were making waves back home. Interest in rowing was being piqued. That was good news for the club. This was the Gary and Paul effect.

Diarmuid decided to dust off his oars and end his two-year hiatus. He wanted a seat in that eight and this was the target he needed. James Lupton returned too, after several years on dry land. Kenneth was in.

So were Justin Ryan, Alan Barry, Kealan Mannix, Andrew Hurley, John Whooley and Gearoid Murphy.

The top four from the club rowers would join the Irish four to make the eight. They started getting out on the Ilen that October. When they could at weekends, they'd try to get some combination out in an eight rowed by sixes so two would get a breather at various stages. It was the ideal reintroduction.

At Christmas, Gary and Paul were around, Shane and Mark too, so John Whooley organised a mini-camp. Time in the boat was crucial. Gary and Paul needed to get back sweeping. The club's twenty-year-old eight was all they had. The hull was weak, it wasn't in race condition, but it had to do. They'd row downriver, out to Sherkin Island and back. As much mileage as they could. But the rowing was rougher than the winter water.

Well into the new year, and with no trials to select the club four, there were six in the mix for the four seats and it was decided that the fastest four at the Cork City Regatta would get the nod. They divided into three pairs: Diarmuid and Gearoid, Justin and Andrew, Kenneth and James. The last two were fastest, Diarmuid and Gearoid next in line, with Justin and Andrew missing out.

Skibb had their eight, the four world-class lightweights and the four club heavyweights. Padraig Murphy was going to be the cox; he was the best man for the boat and he'd take no notice of reputations.

Now all they needed was Dominic to give it the green light, as well as a proper boat to race in.

***

Up in Dublin, Colm Dowling heard the rumours. They'd been doing the rounds for months. Skibb wanted the clean sweep at the nationals, including a first eight, and their big four meant business.

Word reached Commercial Rowing Club that Skibbereen had ordered a Filippi eight for the championships in July, adding meat to the bones of the growing chatter. This was the crown Commercial wore. They'd won the eight in 2016, for the first time in eleven years, setting a new course record of 5:36.89.

Colm was experienced, a familiar name in rowing circles having represented Ireland at the Home Internationals in the past, and he knew a good chunk of the Skibb lads. He'd been a Junior with Mark, and formed a composite quad with Kenneth, Gary and Gearoid that won a national title in 2011, so he'd a fair idea about what Commercial were up against.

But he never doubted his crew, which included Shane MacEoin, whose father Seamus is from Skibbereen and rowed for the club in its early days, as did Shane's aunts and uncles, the MacEoins of Townshend Street. Still, the fact remained that the Commercial eight was a crew of club oarsmen up against some of the best lightweight rowers in the world.

But Commercial backed themselves. They had the work done. They didn't have the big names like Skibb, but they were more familiar with each other. They wouldn't be able to match the fitness and strength of Skibb's famous four, but what Commercial had was more time together and a more cohesive unit.

Over the winter they trained in fours and pairs, and from May through to the nationals in July the majority of their work was in the eight. They even sent a four to Henley, including Colm and Shane, in late June. Everything was ticking along nicely.

***

Shane O'Driscoll knew they were up against it in the eight. They had less than one week to pull it together. It was a massive ask. But he loves a challenge. The Irish four landed home from Lucerne the Monday before the nationals and all the attention was switched to the weekend ahead.

Dominic had finally signed off on the eight competing. He had his reservations but saw that the desire was there. Tuesday was spent rigging the Filippi eight rented especially for the race. The chosen eight got out on Inniscarra for a few paddles that week, which weren't too encouraging. They were rough around the edges. But while time wasn't their friend, as everyone was also focused on their other events as well, there was a growing sense of optimism that, maybe, just maybe, Skibb could pull this off, powered by their world stars.

The clean sweep at Senior level was also on the cards. On Friday morning, day one, Gary and Paul landed the men's Senior double, their first championship win together in this class. That afternoon, the all-star cast of Gary, Paul, Shane and Mark joined forces in the men's Senior four and raced to a phenomenal course record time (5:55.33), with Commercial three seconds back in second place. Paul jumped straight into the Senior single scull afterwards and powered to another championship title with a masterful sculling display and another course record (6:48.19). Three races, three titles, two course records. Skibb's finest were showing their class.

On Saturday morning, Shane and Mark transferred their world dominance to the national scene as they added the men's Senior pair to Skibb's overall haul. Sunday morning saw Gary win the men's lightweight title. The Skibb four wanted the quad title too, but there was no opposition so that didn't go ahead. Commercial pulled out. That irked Skibb. They wanted that race.

Kenneth and James were in action in the men's Intermediate pair final that Sunday, and Diarmuid, Gearoid, Rory O'Neill and Naoise Kennedy were in action in the men's club four final that morning too.

The clock kept ticking towards 5.20 p.m. That was Skibb's date with destiny.

***

'Well how do you do young Willie McBride?
Do you mind if I sit down here by your graveside ...'

Shane O'Driscoll didn't know why, but he burst into song. It just felt like the right thing to do. It was a familiar one, 'The Green Fields of France'. Gary joined in. Mark and Paul too.

'and rest for a while 'neath the warm summer sun.'

Skibbereen's tent, sectioned off in its familiar location at the Nationals, just past the main building at Inniscarra, was alive with the noise.

Some of the younger club members didn't know what was happening, entranced by the sight and sound of Gary and Paul in full voice. They'd heard tales of the Irish tent at international regattas abroad. This was it. And they had front row seats.

It was organic. From the heart.

The club four joined in. Kenneth, James, Diarmuid and Gearoid.

'I've been walking all day and I'm nearly done.'

Together, the eight sang, each line bringing them closer together. It was electric. They'd never done this before. But it gave them a huge lift.

That was Shane's hope from the moment the eight was first proposed, that this could close the gap between the international quartet and the club rowers, similar to inter-county players going back to their clubs in Gaelic games.

If they had wanted, the big four could have formed a composite crew with others to form an eight, but their loyalty to their club and their desire to achieve this with the men they knew meant that was never an option.

In that moment, as they joined together, they were all Skibbereen rowers on the one team, sharing the same goal.

The talking was over. The boat was set up and ready. The race plan discussed. The coffee was drunk. Mark's caffeine chewing gums had done the rounds. This was Skibb's golden opportunity.

As they carried the boat the short distance from the boathouse to the slipway under the bright sunshine, a stream of people followed to get a glimpse of Gary and Paul, and a crowd was gathering to watch Skibb launch.

It was time to go looking for the missing piece of the jigsaw.

***

There are different opinions about where it went wrong.

Diarmuid's adamant it was those first three strokes that cost Skibbereen. They gave up a foot to Commercial in those early moments. The first fifteen seconds were too disjointed, he felt. On the outside lane, Skibb were playing catch-up from the off.

Paul's analysis was to the point: Commercial got the better of Skibbereen from the start because they were the better crew, not because

Skibb had a bad start. The better crew will have the better start in an eight, Paul insisted.

Bottom line, Skibb weren't good enough. They didn't have enough time in the boat together to get it right. This final was their first-ever two-kilometre race together. There was no heat or semi-final to identify the kinks and faults, and iron them out. They badly needed a blow-out.

Still, they rowed together a lot better than in their few training spins. Behind from the start, they never gave up. The hope now was that the power and fitness of the Irish quartet would drag them back into it.

There'd been plenty of discussion about who'd sit where in the days before, whether to split Gary, Paul, Shane and Mark to have two at either end. Instead, they were weighted at the front of the boat.

The dynamic had been odd in the lead-up to the race. There were too many leaders. Kenneth and James had been mentors to the rest in their younger days, but the international four had gone on to become the best in the world. That led to confusion, different schools of thinking. Who was the leader? They were all looking to each other.

In the end, they eventually settled. Shane was stroke. He'd sat here in a Junior eight and he was able to rate high; the perfect choice to set the pace for the rest to follow. He changed his style, wanting to do the rest justice, rowed nice and long, not as short as he would in the pair. Gary slotted in at number seven, again a familiar seat from his Junior days and ideal support for Shane. Paul took six, the first of four seats in the middle that are seen as the engine room, the powerhouses. Mark was next. Then Diarmuid, Gearoid and James. Kenneth, who has a feel for boat speed and rhythm, was in the bow.

At the halfway point, Skibb were in third place. Commercial in the lane beside them led, Dublin University Boat Club in second, NUIG in fourth and the two UCD crews fifth and sixth.

Kenneth took a glance across to Commercial beside them. Skibb were gaining on them. He sensed a chance, that if they made their move Commercial would crack.

But the Dubs didn't flinch.

Heading towards the final stages, and after seeing off NUIG's challenge, Colm Dowling was surprised to see Skibbereen in second after their sluggish start. The race was panning out as Commercial wanted: hit a rhythm and push from the halfway on. They did that and always stayed ahead of a coming Skibb.

Commercial's crew of club rowers were first home, Skibb's all-star cast in silver, one second behind, then came NUIG half a second back.

It was all over for Skibb. Bodies burning, heads down. It hit home. They came in off the water, carried the eight to the boatshed and very little was said. There were kids looking for autographs, but the crew needed time to themselves. Mark pulled down the shutters. They stood inside.

'We did our best. Great effort. Heads high, lads,' Gary said.

Diarmuid never felt as sick after a race as he did here. Even a few hours later, after himself and Shane popped into Tesco in Ballincollig for refreshments for the night, he threw up outside the door of the supermarket. He was shook. He had no energy and his legs were dead. And no Senior eight pot to show for it.

Skibb's women have won the Senior eight, it should be pointed out. In 2002 Áine Harnedy, Grace O'Brien, Patricia O'Sullivan, Mary McCarthy, Catriona Lane, Eileen Whooley, Karen Hickey and Triona O'Donoghue were coxed to glory by Caroline Leonard. In 2018 the all-Skibb women's crew won the title again – Denise Walsh, Orla Hayes, Aoife Casey, Niamh Casey, Natalie Long, Marie Piggot, Áine McCarthy and Lydia Heaphy, coxed by Alicia O'Neill. And they have formed composite crews that have won the big one as well.

For Skibb's men, however, the wait goes on. Olympic medals and world gold, but still no Senior men's eight at the National Champion-ships. The collection remains incomplete. That stings.

After that 2017 disappointment, however, Gary O'Donovan was determined that he would get his hands on one medal that he really wanted the following year.

joining the club

On Wednesday 5 September 2018, the Rowing Ireland team arrived in Plovdiv. There were seventeen athletes in eight boats and nine of those rowers were from Skibbereen. That's over half the team from the club.

Gary was in the best shape of his life. He felt strong and sharp. He had missed the Worlds in 2017 and was eager to make his mark now. He felt like he was in danger of being left behind.

Gary had watched on as Paul, Shane and Mark won World Championship medals. Paul was a two-time world lightweight single scull champion. Mark and Shane won gold in the lightweight pair the year before. Eugene and Timmy raced in world A finals and won medals. But Gary had never even raced in a world final or been in contention for a world medal before – not at Junior, Under–23 or Senior levels.

There's a huge wooden board that stretches across one wall of the restaurant at the National Rowing Centre that has all the names of Ireland's World Championship medallists inscribed on it with the year they won that medal, where the regatta was held and their boat type. Gary wanted his name up there. He could recite every name on the board and what medal they had won. It's the club he wanted to be part of.

He was already on the walls of the Corner Bar after ribbing owner William O'Brien one night after the Olympics that there were pictures of them up all over the town but not in the bar they always visit. The next day two large black frames with newspaper clippings saluting Gary and Paul's Olympic medal success were hung up in the back bar. They're still there. So is the caricature painted on the bar's front window during the Olympics. Gary had gotten his picture, but he still wanted the world medal.

Go back further again and Gary had watched on as Paul made all the headlines growing up. Paul had the intent. Gary didn't as much. It was only in 2012 that he decided to throw himself fully into rowing. One year later he was at the World Under–23s. Now, six years later, he was gunning for World Senior glory.

Gold at Plovdiv had been the main aim all season. They had two summers that year. The first was in New Zealand and Australia, where they spent three months training with Shane and Mark. They competed at regattas there too. Then there was the second summer back home. Gary was flying fit. Paul felt the best he ever had too.

They ticked along nicely throughout the year and won a medal at every regatta. Bronze at World Cup I in Belgrade, gold at World Cup III in Lucerne and silver at the European Championships in Glasgow. All that was left were the Worlds.

The training camp in Banyoles went well. Up at 8.30 a.m., quick bite to eat and then out on the water. In the mornings there were five 1,500-metre pieces with a three-minute break in between. The evenings were kept for the long and steady spins, twenty-four kilometres, followed by some weightlifting in the gym. That was the routine for six days of each week. It was gruelling. They were pulling hard day after day. Gary's blistered hands told a story. They were destroyed. He suffers more than Paul does in that regard. It's blister on blister. The only way to survive is to wrap his hands in medical tape with soft tissue in between. It's not as bad at regattas. The races are six minutes. Training camps are hour after hour.

Despite all the hardship, results hinted that they were peaking at just the right time. In Bulgaria they won their heat on the Sunday and quarter-final on Wednesday before finishing third in a competitive A/B semi-final on Thursday behind Italy and then Belgium. Gary was where he wanted to be. He was through to his first world final on Saturday morning.

There was a gang from home there to cheer them on. Skibbereen Rowing Club Secretary T. J. Ryan had flown back out to Plovdiv for the business end of the regatta. He had already driven the Rowing Ireland transit van that pulled the huge boat trailer all the way from Banyoles in Spain to Plovdiv in Bulgaria ahead of the championships. He'd tow the boats back to Ireland after. Nuala and Finbarr were there. Tony and Mary to cheer on Denise. It was the usual away support gang.

***

Gary did a double-take.

'Is there a headwind?'

There was. Christ, this is good, he thought.

This was the warm-up before the A final and it went better than either of them had hoped. After a race piece Gary glanced down at the speed. It was fast. And when Paul said they were going into the headwind they knew they were going really quick. It was all coming together.

All week they felt something was building. They were getting better and better. On their off days they went paddling around the venue and they both knew they were touching on something good. It was time to put that speed to good use.

Ireland were out in lane six, the Belgians beside them, European champions Norway and Italy in the middle lanes, with New Zealand and Spain completing the line-up.

With white peak caps and shades on, Gary and Paul were comfortable in third after 500 metres and were up to second by the halfway mark, just behind the Italians. They didn't panic. They were stalking the leaders. The powerful Skibb men then pulled right up on Italy and with 500 metres to go the Irish hit the front. Gary and Paul in their yellow Empacher and green blades pulled like never before. They kept the Italians at bay and, in cruise control, romped home in 6:06.810.

They were the new world champions. It was the perfect race. Their best-ever strokes. Gary had the gold he wanted. Now he was part of a unique club: Irish world rowing champions.

Gary and Paul's gold, along with Sanita Puspure's, placed Ireland second in Olympic-class boats at the 2018 Worlds.

By the end of 2019 Ireland had won twelve World Championship golds. Five of those were by Skibb men and came within a four-year window: 2015–2019. Paul is the most successful Irish rower of all time with four world golds, two in a single and two in a double. Gary, Shane and Mark all have one each. Sanita won the world women's single sculls title in 2018 and 2019, and before that, Niall O'Toole (1991), Sam Lynch (2001 and 2002), Sinead Jennings (2001) and Gearoid Towey and Tony O'Connor (2001) all won world gold medals.

**

There were mixed results for Skibb's other seven rowers at the 2018 World Championships. Denise Walsh and Aoife Casey won the C final of the women's lightweight double to finish thirteenth overall. This was a new pairing. It was a new experience for Aoife, as she made the jump from

Junior to Senior. She had left her Junior days with an historic silver from the 2017 European Junior Championships. In a double with Margaret Cremen of Lee Rowing Club, she had won Ireland's first medals at this level.

That was an intense time. Aoife was a Leaving Cert student at Skibbereen Community School and juggled study with training. Every Wednesday is a half-day in the school, so on those days she trained with Margaret at the National Rowing Centre. They slotted in two sessions on Saturdays then. Aoife's mam, Eleanor, was one of the coaches, along with Margaret's coach, Dan Buckley. Having her mam and dad coach her offers Aoife a unique perspective. Whereas Dominic can be more intense, Eleanor is more positive. They both have their different spins on the same situation. Whatever was said in Krefeld in Germany in 2017 worked. Aoife arrived home in the early hours of Sunday morning, off a flight into Dublin Airport, with a silver medal. She was back in school on Monday morning.

At the 2018 Worlds, Emily Hegarty was one half of the women's pair that came sixth in the A final. Jake and Fintan McCarthy were half of the men's lightweight quad that finished fifth in their A final.

Meanwhile, Shane and Mark finished fourth in the C final of the men's heavyweight pair for sixteenth place overall. That result came back to haunt them in 2019 when Sport Ireland announced its funding for high performance athletes. Mark and Shane lost their 'World Class' funding of €20,000 each. It left them with no money and having to use their own savings to fund themselves. They were gutted. It was a hammer blow to their hopes of making a successful transition from lightweight to heavyweight and becoming an Olympic-standard pair. The challenge was formidable as it was, but having no money for food, for rent, for petrol, or to live on was grim. It was a kick in the teeth. They were demoralised. Left struggling in a position that they felt was unfair. Still, the next day Shane and Mark went on the water and trained hard. They did the same the next day. And the next day.

There was also some disappointing news on the way for Denise.

***

Denise wanted to stay wrapped in her warm duvet but she knew she couldn't. The bone-chilling cold that January had been threatening was waiting outside for the dawn risers in early February 2019. The sky was black. Utter darkness. Not even a chink of light to offer encouragement.

Monday to Wednesday she trained at home in Skibbereen. Thursday to Sunday it was at the National Rowing Centre. On this Saturday morning Dominic wanted the lightweights out on the lake early, the first of two sessions at 8.30 a.m.

It was just gone six. She pulled herself from the bed, headed to the kitchen and forced down plain porridge with just milk as an extra. She was sick of porridge but oats power boats. She pushed the last spoonful around the bowl before taking the plunge. It wouldn't be long before her next bowl.

She hurried into her black Volkswagen Golf, now nine years old; she had a one-hour drive from home outside Skibbereen to the National Rowing Centre. Some mornings Dominic spins her up and she squeezes a little extra out of her sleep then and lands out to his jeep holding the bowl of porridge. But she was on her own today.

She turned on Baz & Andrew's House of Rugby podcast, easy listening at this hour. It was timely too, as it was the first weekend of the 2019 Six Nations and Ireland were set to take on England at the Aviva Stadium later that day. The last few years she's taken more of an interest in rugby, unashamedly hopping aboard the bandwagon. It was an interest outside of rowing.

Dunmanway's not exactly the halfway point in this seventy-kilometre drive, but it's the coffee stop and an early-morning boost. A flat white at Galvin's Centra on the way out of the town perked her up and put her in a good mood. More fuel.

As she arrived at the rowing centre that was just waking up itself, Dominic was already out and about, his red and white scarf tucked inside his zipped-up navy jacket. He felt the cold too that morning as he got the boats ready. On mornings like this, if it's slippy and icy, he carries the boats down to the pontoon for the rowers. He covered the ground quickly that morning. There was an intent to his pace. No hanging around.

Denise parked just to the side of the main building. The closer the better. Less walking. And she needed to save that energy. She changed into her rowing gear, there was a quick warm-up in the gym to loosen the body and it was down to the water and into her black Filippi single with its distinctive pink strip.

There was a cold that morning that reached into Denise's lungs. It was one of those rare mornings where she wore gloves – not to mind her hands, but to fight off the chill. Aoife was the same in her single. Shane and Mark's hands stayed bare, knuckles blue as they gripped their oars. That biting cold meant none of the high performance gang waited around; instead, it was straight to work. Pieces were welcome on a morning like this, as they got warmer faster, rather than a long, steady state spin over a longer distance but at a slower rate.

Dominic was in his launch. He followed them as they warmed up below the bridge before paddling up past it. The lightweights generally gravitate towards the water up past the bridge. It seems calmer there. The heavyweights go the opposite direction towards the dam.

This morning it was five twelve-minute pieces, four of them up past the bridge. Twelve minutes up, rating at twenty-four strokes per minute. Stop for three minutes. Twelve minutes back down, rating at twenty-six. Again, a three-minute break. And repeat. The last twelve minutes was down past the bridge, back towards the rowing centre.

There wasn't much noise there. The engine on Dominic's launch was consistent, of course, but that was tuned out after a while. There was the odd bit of traffic near the top of the course, but mostly all Denise heard was the water and the others breathing, that panting under pressure.

Like when home on the Ilen, she uses landmarks on the lake here. The one that sticks in her mind is that tree up past the bridge that they have to avoid. It juts out from the riverbank. Up by the top the lake gets shallower, especially after that hot summer of 2018 when it was quite low.

The lake is different to home. Denise remembered Shane talking about this when he first moved closer to Inniscarra, how he found the lake alien to him. Everyone likes their own water. Skibb rowers are spoiled with the Ilen. Denise has the best of both worlds these days – the beautiful unpredictability of the Ilen and the dependable consistency of Inniscarra.

There's that toughness the Ilen has that Inniscarra doesn't, because of the tide and the current. Tactics can play more of a role at home, whereas most of the time in Inniscarra it's still water, unless the wind blows up or the dam is open.

The lake was its usual self that morning. It was a good session. By the time they came back into the pontoon the rowing centre was busier. UCC Rowing Club was there in numbers, getting ready for training. One by one, the Irish internationals pulled into the pontoon, hopped out, lifted their boats out of the water and carried them towards the boatshed. Denise was first in.

Dominic parked his launch too, with an audacious flash of skill that went largely unnoticed. Generally these launches have steering wheels, but he likes the outboard motor. In one movement, he turned the corner of the pontoon, drifting, like a car skidding around a tight right bend, before it came to rest parallel to the pontoon. He jumped out and hurried straight to the boatshed.

There was one shower working in the women's changing room. Some mornings there is a queue. It wasn't too bad this morning, and at least the water was hot. Straight upstairs to the canteen afterwards and it was more plain porridge and milk for Denise. Aoife came prepared. She had fried up beans, peppers, coriander and tuna.

They had little time to rest. A team meeting was imminent. After that it was back out again for their second session of the day, this time in the double, and that would be steady state: a long row and not as intense as the morning.

Three days later, Denise flew to Seville with Aoife for a two-week training camp. There the news came through that, just like with Mark and Shane, her Sport Ireland funding was being cut from World-Class level of €20,000 to nothing.

She had been expecting it. It was a blow but not a knock-out. She got up the following morning, rolled out of bed and did the same thing all over again. And the day after. And the day after that. It was a habit now. The magnificent monotony that all Skibbereen rowers were drawn to, working on those same repetitive movements over and over and over again. Always chasing perfection. Like all Skibb rowers.

Dominic will be there too. Like always.

22

coach casey

There's not much rowing memorabilia dotted around Dominic's house. On a ledge in the kitchen rests the gold medal he was presented with after being named 2018 World Rowing Coach of the Year. It's still in its presentation box and beside it sit two mementoes from the World Rowing Awards gala night in Berlin that November – a laminated piece of paper with World Coach of the Year written on it and a booklet from the ceremony.

The medal won't stay there long. Soon it will find a resting place in the garage. It's packed to the brim with all things rowing. To the untrained eye it looks disorganised, but he has his own filing system and knows exactly where everything is. Even the awards he has collected over the years.

'I hate awards,' he says, before repeating it to make sure he's heard. 'I hate awards. I'm sure there are people more deserving than me, but they gave it to me for some reason.'

Dominic is the definition of self-effacing. He doesn't like the media glare. But when he got wind of that World Rowing Award the week before the ceremony, he had no choice but to travel to Berlin to accept it on Friday night, 23 November. He would rather have rested on the couch by the window in his sitting room, thrown his legs up on the seat beside it and, glasses on, crunched numbers on his laptop. That's where he is most comfortable and content.

It was the third year in a row that Dominic had been nominated for World Coach of the Year. That's a tell-tale sign of the terrific consistency he and his rowers have delivered over recent years, as he has overseen the rise of Irish lightweight rowing.

'For me the reward is seeing the athlete doing their best,' he says. 'I enjoy athletes being successful. That's what keeps me going. It's nice to see them improving and winning. It's good to see a young person rowing and getting better.'

Then he steps back again, away from the glare.

'People might consider me a hopeless coach.'

But they don't.

He's not just the water bottle carrier that he made himself out to be when he was at the Rio Olympics, but don't expect him to tell you that. This is a man who had to be tricked into attending the West Cork Sports Star Awards in January 2017, where he was inducted into the Hall of Fame, an honour in recognition of his contribution to Skibbereen and Irish rowing.

Organisers of the awards had a hunch that if Dominic was announced as the Hall of Fame winner in the run-up, the odds were that he wouldn't attend. Instead it was a closely guarded secret. His wife Eleanor's job was to make sure Dominic attended. That Gary and Paul were nailed on for the overall West Cork Sports Star Award helped. He travelled as a guest. On the night Dominic was unveiled as the Hall of Famer. The top button of his shirt was open as it was announced, his green tie hung looser than normal. He was caught off guard. But at least the plan had worked.

What also works are Dominic's methods. There's no great secret here. It's hard work day after day after day. It's relentless consistency. He knows this and he gets results. He breaks it down to its simplest form.

'You don't need much. You need a river, a boat, oars, and off you go,' he says.

'You don't need anything fancy to lift weights. You just have to lift them. It's not rocket science.'

This is the Thor Nilsen influence on Dominic.

***

Dominic remembers the first time he saw Thor in action. It left an impression. The Norwegian is a walking encyclopedia on rowing. He was presented with the FISA Distinguished Service to Rowing Award in 2003 and six years later he received the International Olympic Committee's highest award, the Olympic Order.

As far back as 1991 he became a consultant coach with the Irish Amateur Rowing Union and was a regular visitor to Ireland. He had Dominic's attention instantly.

There was one training session at Blessington when Thor watched twenty boats on the water. They all came in. Later that day he went through what he saw with everyone. He remembered every single person, what boat they were in and what they needed to do. That attention to detail left an impression on Dominic, who was in the early days of his own coaching career at the time. Thor was sharp.

At a rowing seminar at the University of Limerick, Thor gave a lecture. Dominic sat in the audience and listened.

'He said to keep it as simple as possible. If you are training, keep it as simple as possible,' Dominic says. Those words stuck with him.

Dominic learns from everyone. He is a sponge for rowing knowledge. He listens and learns, and then walks away wiser.

'We are always open to what other clubs are doing. In our early days

Neptune were the kingpins, so we wanted to see what they were doing and how they were doing it. We talk to coaches abroad and we talk to different people to find out what they are doing. I'm always learning,' he says.

Dominic learned from Nuala Lupton and Richard Hosford at the start. Then Frank Durkin began to shape his outlook. He takes the best tips from every coach he crosses paths with and applies them to his own way of thinking.

Take Frank for example. He told Dominic that to be able to train hard is 99.9 per cent in the head. It's mental strength that's needed. Dominic understood that and then preached it.

'The mental approach, that's where you can win it or lose it,' he says.

It's safe to say that Thor had the biggest influence on Dominic and, as a result, Skibbereen rowing. He is the main man in Dominic's eyes. Dominic bought into Thor's ideas and concepts of coaching and his training programmes. He soaked it all up. Thor didn't know it at the time, but Dominic was his apprentice.

'It's just the way he sets up the programme – the long spins, the interval training and the technique as well,' Dominic explains. 'Keep it simple, there's no need for programmes to be complicated. Keep it simple. That's what we base our set-up on. The programme that we have had in the club is the same for the last twenty, thirty years.

'It's all down to the individual then – how they read the programme and how they adapt to it. I can give a programme to you and to someone else and both can see very different things. It's how the training is carried out.'

Dominic keeps it as straightforward as possible. 'You get in the water as much as you can,' he stresses. 'We do the gym after, but it's in the water first. Mileage makes champions. It's an old saying but it's true. You need to row to the best of your ability. A good, technical row.

'The coach is a mentor. I think a coach needs to be there for the athlete, to be present, to help them out, to watch technically and advise them as best you can.'

A coach must also listen to the athletes. Dominic excels here too. He always looks for their feedback. If he writes a training programme he will get the rowers' thoughts on it. That's always been his way. He brings the athlete along with him. It's not a dictatorship, after all.

In his own days as a rower it was the hard work that appealed to him. One of his early influences, Frank, speaks of a man who didn't know when to draw the line.

'When he started sculling at the start of the '80s he would come up to Tullamore to me,' Frank explains. 'We agreed what the training was but he did fifty per cent more than we agreed, if not twice as much. He has never stopped learning. He used to bring Skibb rowers up to me at different points, but it got to the point where I had to tell him that he had enough expertise himself and he didn't need to come to me any more.'

That work ethic of his is the same today. He hasn't become distracted. He's not burned out. He's relentless.

***

Thor's first impression of Dominic in those early days was that this fast-talking man asked a lot of questions. The more they talked, the more Thor understood why. It all came back to the club. Dominic wanted to make Skibb rowers better and faster. He wanted to learn new ways to improve.

'When you talk to him, it's one thing that comes up all the time, everything is connected to how can he help the rowers in his club improve,' Thor says. 'I remember Dominic from these clinics I held. He was very interested and active, coming from a small little place, and he was very enthusiastic.'

Thor admired the passion for rowing that he saw in Dominic. It was in his blood. Every conversation he had came back to rowing.

'The reason he is such a good coach is that he works for it. He has a good eye. If you ask other people in Ireland they will say he is stubborn like hell, but to achieve what he has you must be stubborn,' Thor says. 'He doesn't do this for his own profit, he does it because he wants the club to succeed. This comes from his heart. He loves this club. There are coaches who are more interested in the position, to put themselves forward and to use the athletes to promote themselves. But Dominic is interested in the human being. Even if you are not going to be a world champion he will get a rowing machine to help you. He wants the rowers to be good. As a coach you want to win but there is still that human attention to people around him.'

Dominic's strong attachment to Skibbereen stood out for Thor. When he visited the Skibb club for the first time he was surprised by what he saw. This small town had a small rowing club that had no money and no pontoons, yet its boathouse was bigger than most and its fleet was as good as the bigger clubs. Thor learned quickly that anything was possible here, because of the mentality of the Skibb people who made up the committee and helped out as coaches and volunteers.

'Dominic is a straightforward person. He has put his mentality on the club. I have seen clubs all over the world and you find in all these successful clubs one person who is more motivated than all the others, who is interested in the people around them and who drives it,' Thor says.

However, he adds: 'This couldn't be possible if you don't have the support from the people around you. If you get that support it means that you are doing something that other people respect. Dominic has not been alone on this. Even if he is fantastic, he needs back-up from the people around him and the club. He has the support of the community. This is exceptional.'

That Skibbereen mentality has left an impression on Thor. At the top level he coached Eugene, Timmy and Richard with Ireland. Tough as nails.

'All these rowers, they were dedicated. They were not afraid to train. They wanted to do something. They were coming from a small club, but they had the right mentality. If you told them something they did it. That mentality came from the club. The club itself and the circumstances they grew up in gave them this mentality,' Thor explains.

***

Aoife doesn't mind sharing her dad. Dominic is like a father to all the athletes he coaches. He's there to help people. That's what he does better than most. Hence the awards.

Aoife knows he's always in the room next door if she's at home and needs advice. If he's not in the sitting room, she'll find him nibbling on fruit and nut mix in the kitchen, or having set up camp in the conservatory.

'He loves watching people improve. He's there to help and that's what he does so well. He's not in this for himself. The joy he gets is the results of the athletes; that's where he gets his satisfaction.'

But while he never switches off, the general consensus is that Dominic has mellowed over the years. The desire hasn't changed, but he is not as strict as before.

'Maybe I am softer,' he admits.

But the reason for this is key to it all.

'The athlete is the priority. You have to empower him or her to do the business,' he explains.

'I say very little as a coach. I tell them what to do and they soon pick it up. It's not down to the coach. It's down to the athlete. They are the important person in all of this.

'The more experienced the athlete, the less you need to say to them. They have the knowledge, so I am there to help them out.

'If you have a big group, you'd say half seven in the morning and that's it. But if you're talking about just a few, and if it's very cold in the morning, we'd push it back to nine, little things like that. I don't like being dogmatic or being on top of them, too bossy.'

That's why he accommodates the athlete. He puts them first every time. It's why he is different to other coaches, Eleanor says.

'It's all about the athlete. He facilitates what suits the athletes. He is open to negotiation. Some like to get up later and some like to get up earlier and he'll work around them to make sure everything is geared up to suit them,' she says.

It's why Denise trained at home on the Ilen in the winter of 2016 rather than at the National Rowing Centre. He knew how to get the best out of her and that meant letting her train closer to home in her single rather than trekking up and down to Inniscarra.

'Dominic doesn't have a set training schedule where I need to be here at a certain time to do a certain thing. He works it around what's flexible for you. I am able to train more to my own schedule,' she explained, before going on to her best set of results at international level in 2017 – silver at the Europeans and sixth in the world.

He knew what was best for his athlete. It's no coincidence either that when Shane and Mark came under his umbrella at international level in the winter of 2016, they went on to dominate the men's lightweight pair in 2017. He gave them direction and belief. He worked them harder than ever before. And the results followed.

Dominic's work ethic is perfectly suited to rowing. There's a direct correlation between the work you put in and what you get out of it. That appealed to him. He enjoys working hard. That ethic helped him create a dynasty in Skibbereen that has transformed Irish rowing.

'Over the years we have been committed to the national team,' he explains.

'We would have won another sixty national championships easily – but the national team is the priority for all Skibbereen athletes. When you are on the national team then you can't row in the championships unless there is a default year. But definitely, fifty or sixty more champs.

'The motto in Skibbereen is be the best you can, and to do that you have to go to the World Championships. We had the first Olympians in Eugene, Timmy and Richard and that helped build momentum over the years. When they came back then, the young lads here would be training with them and that would drive them on. That was a big incentive for the young lads.'

Success breeds success. If a system is successful it attracts more people. Winning is important to everyone in the rowing club and that symbol is the championship board that hangs in the hall of the clubhouse. It looks at you when you walk through the front door. It has the name of every Skibbereen rower who has won a National Championship.

'When people see the board, they might not say it, but they want to get their name on it,' Dominic says.

With that mindset, they're then taught how to race.

'It's all about racing, getting used to racing, being tough and mentally strong. We do a lot of pieces together and that teaches rowers how to race and how to be tough. Other clubs can do it too. We're not the only ones who can train like this.'

Still, Dominic's pursuit of excellence is relentless.

'He is always looking for some bit of an edge. People often ask if there is something in the water in Skibb. That's a myth. There is nothing other than sheer hard work consistently over a long period of time,' former Rowing Ireland Coach Education Officer Pat McInerney says.

There is no end to Dominic. People get tired. They get worn out. They are human. Not Dominic. In his own words, he's non-stop.

In 2010 Rowing Ireland launched the Grand League Regatta Series. It was new and innovative, allowing rowers at all levels the chance to develop in a fair and competitive environment. Later that year, Pat, with St Michael's Rowing Club in Limerick, and Dominic, with Skibb, travelled on the same ferry to the Ghent Regatta in Belgium. Dominic talked rowing all the way over and all the way back. He saw certain aspects of how Ghent ran their event and liked them. He talked about transferring those ideas to the new Grand League. Off the ferry they travelled their different directions home. Pat's phone rang. It was Dominic. He wanted to talk more about Ghent.

'Endurance is his middle name. He has passed those traits on to his athletes. A coach's characteristics rub off on an athlete,' Pat says.

***

Before he became Coach Casey, Dominic rowed.

Dominic worked at the BIM boatyard in Baltimore before he got his job with O'Donovan's boatyard. Teddy O'Donovan worked there too.

He heard Teddy talking about the club that he had already joined. Greg Hegarty, who also worked at the boatyard in Baltimore before moving on to O'Donovans, rowed with the club too. He told Dominic to call and check it out. On a January evening in 1977 Dominic did.

As he drove past the rowing club with Michael Hegarty after football training with Ilen Rovers, his inquisitiveness got the better of him. He pulled the car in. There was no clubhouse then and he saw Greg and a few more down by the water. They were getting ready to go out in an eight. Greg called him down and introduced him to Richard Hosford. He had Dominic's attention immediately. It was the easiest sell of his life. Dominic and Michael hopped into the eight for a spin. Dominic never went football training again. He was back at the rowing club the next night.

The Ilen became Dominic's second home. Nowhere else compares to it for him. Some of his best memories are on the river. It's a different world with its beautiful silence. All you hear are the oars going into the water. He became a familiar figure on the Ilen in all shades of weather.

'You can leave a lot out on the water. It clears the mind. You feel like a new man when you come off it,' he says.

He took to his new world quickly. Rowing suited him. In those early years there was plenty of chopping and changing, fellas coming and going, and different combinations were tried until a four was settled on in 1980. There was Teddy, recognisable by his beard, Dominic and his brother Stephen, with Lar Harrington from Baltimore the latest addition, all four boatbuilders in Baltimore. Nuala was their coach and her twelve-year-old son Liam was the cox.

Stephen was the stroke. Lar and Dominic in the middle seats, Teddy was the bow. They trained hard, especially to get the club's new carbon-craft boat sitting perfectly. It felt different. It was more delicate. They had to put the miles and long hours in. Towards the end of the year Nuala was pregnant with Emma, but she still went on the water, with a few cushions to make her more comfortable. Everyone did whatever it took to win.

In race season their routine saw them on the water nine or ten times a week. Every evening after work. On the water, weights, running. Time-keeping was important. They were strict on this. If they said nine in the morning, no one was late. It's a trait Dominic's still strict on to this day. You'll get the reward in the session.

They won the Novice four at the Cork Regatta that July, then took fourth in the Novice four at the 1980 National Championships. The following year they stepped it up. They were now competing at Senior C. They were climbing the ladder from Junior up to Intermediate. They were being noticed. And they were about to show at the 1981 Trinity Regatta just how good they were.

***

Dominic was still out of breath. He was sitting in the boat, his heart thumping in his chest and his mind struggling to comprehend what had just happened. A man on the bank helped join the dots.

'I never thought I'd see the day that Skibbereen would beat Queen's,' he shouted.

It clicked. *We won. WE WON!*

This was their highlight.

The Trinity Regatta is a special day in the calendar, an annual regatta first held in 1886 at Islandbridge, on the Liffey River. It's two-lane racing at its finest. One boat against another.

In the opening heat of the Senior C fours in May 1981 Skibbereen were two lengths down on UCD early on and by the halfway mark they were still one and a half lengths back. But they dragged themselves back into contention and came up with a stunning three-quarter-length win. In their next race, Carlow built up a one-length lead, but a powerful last 200 metres pushed Skibb over the line first.

It was a battle with the mighty Queen's University, one of the country's established powers, in the final. The aristocrats against the farmers. Skibb won by three lengths. That was a big win. Up to then they had no idea of where they stood. It showed them they were good enough. Back home in Skibb, Nuala invited them all round to her home for a celebratory dinner. This win was worth savouring.

This crew seemed to be going places. They picked up more wins and that Trinity victory should have been the catalyst for success in the Intermediate fours at the National Championships a few weeks later. But they blew it. They lost their magic. By July they were over-cooked. There was nothing left in the engine.

That four never won the national title that they threatened. And the crew broke up shortly afterwards.

It turns out they didn't know enough about training. They trained a lot, but they didn't train properly. After a regatta on a Sunday they would be back on the Ilen on Monday night rowing two-kilometre pieces. There was no rest and no recovery. They hadn't known any better and that caught up with them.

With the four finished, Dominic turned to sculling. Nuala was once again his coach. If she told him something he would practise it forever. But he was stubborn too. They never agreed on weights training. He had his own ideas. He wouldn't listen when she warned him not to practise the power clean, which involved lifting the weights from the floor and pushing them above his head. When she wasn't there to watch him, she knew he was doing it. She told him not to train every day too. But he didn't listen and trained seven days a week.

On the water he excelled. In the 1980s he was one of the top scullers in the country. Like Skibbereen rowers today, he had a slow start but a fast finish. It was those starts that caused him problems.

Seamus 'Buster' Keating of Carlow Rowing Club knew this too. That was his glimmer of hope. The two had crossed paths in the single sculls in 1982, Dominic's first year in this boat. Dominic felt more comfortable in the single. He was now the master of his own destiny.

Seamus was on a winning streak, but it soon ended. Their battles followed a familiar pattern. Seamus would lead to the 1,500-metre mark, holding Dominic off, but then the Skibbereen boat, waiting for the kill, would pounce. Dominic would glide past. It was pure power. His strength was his strong finish. He had great endurance and always backed himself in the final sprint. That's a trait he has passed on.

Seamus knew he had to put clear water between himself and his fiercest rival if he wanted to get his hands on the men's Intermediate single sculls crown at the 1983 Irish Rowing Championships at Coosan Point in Athlone.

He was lucky to be rowing at all. In 1980 Seamus fell twenty-three feet from the side of a building straight down onto concrete. He broke his elbow in seven places and shattered his pelvis. He was told he'd never row again, but he had fire in his belly. A surgeon, who was an elbow specialist, patched him up. He got a great range of movement back in his elbow, even if his coach told him his style looked a bit funny when he was back in the boat. But he was moving fast across water. That was all that mattered.

The Intermediate race was the last of the day. Seamus was the underdog, Dominic the favourite: he had finished second the year before in the Novice sculls at the Nationals in Blessington, well beaten by almost seven lengths. Lessons were learned.

Dominic headed into the 1983 Nationals off the back of impressive wins around the country. He won the Senior C sculls at Trinity, Senior B and open sculls at Lee, Senior A and Senior C at Metro and Carlow, Senior B at Cork, and Senior A and Senior B at Limerick. He was confident. His single scull was immaculate too. This always stuck in Seamus' mind. Before racing Dominic would religiously wash and polish his scull. Every time, without fail. He was controlling the controllables.

Dominic's boat was glistening, but his start in the final was particularly poor. Seamus took advantage. After the first 500 metres he was four lengths ahead. Halfway through there were three lengths between them. They hit the 1,500-metre mark and Seamus was still two lengths in front. There was a shock on the cards. The Carlow cheers grew louder.

For a few fleeting moments Seamus could smell a championship title. Then came Dominic. His boat was lifting out of the water. He made every stroke count, ignoring the terrific pain. His body was telling him to stop, but his mind told him to keep going. Go. Go. Go. Almost there. Think of winning. He squeezed out that extra few per cent that makes the difference.

Numbing the pain, Dominic caught up with Seamus and kept going. He won in the end by three lengths. He was national Intermediate sculls champion, the first Skibbereen rower since Nuala in 1976 to win a championship title. It was the first men's National Championship in the club's history.

Rivals on the water, Dominic and Seamus became great friends off it. By the early 1990s Seamus was living in London and working at

Wormwood Scrubs Prison. Dominic and Eleanor were bringing a bunch of Skibb Juniors to London for a race. Seamus and his wife, Margaret, were flying to Greece for a week and offered them their flat, which was attached to the prison. Clearance was arranged with the prison, keys were left at the prison barrier and there were instructions to let Dominic park the boat trailer in the outer grounds.

When Seamus and his wife returned home, the Skibb contingent now back in Ireland, they found their flat cleaner than when they had left it. It was spotless. A Thank You card, a bunch of flowers and a bottle of red wine were waiting for them. Again, it was Dominic and the small details. They made the difference.

Dominic never got the chance to race at the World Rowing Championships. Between 1983 and 1988 he won eight National Championships – five in the single and three in the double alongside Lar Collins. In 1987 Dominic became the first sculler to win three national Senior championships in the one year. He won the men's Senior single sculls, men's lightweight single sculls and the men's Senior double sculls. He raced at the Home Internationals in Nottingham in 1995 and again for Ireland in Wales in 1987, but never at World Championship level.

'One year I thought I was going to be sent to the Worlds, but they told me I wasn't fast enough. I was disappointed. But that was up to the selectors. I kept going.'

But already Dominic was thinking outside the box. Ahead of the 1985 Irish Rowing Championships, and the first time Dominic and Lar won the double, they left home the week before and camped out in Blessington to practise for that weekend. No one else did that. Underdogs that week, they wanted to prove a point. They won.

That's the same level of preparation he applied when he hung up his oars in 1990 and switched to the role of Coach Casey. Numbers were small in the club. Ten at most rowed throughout the year. More came on-board for the summer. Martin and Mary Rose Jennings were among the first rowers he coached. He hasn't stopped since.

***

Inscribed in the metal shed door at O'Donovan's boatyard is 'Goodbye Dom. 2/12/16.' That's the date Dominic left Donal O'Donovan's to begin life as Rowing Ireland's high performance coach for lightweight rowers.

It was a full-time, paid job. When he coached Gary and Paul to Olympic silver, as well as working his full-time job, he was a part-time rowing coach at international level and his commitment to the club never wavered. That Olympic silver is possibly the cheapest ever won in Ireland.

Leaving O'Donovan's was a wrench. He loved that job. It was Greg who marked that day on the door, after thirty-three years working with Dominic there, since 1983. Dominic helped build timber boats, from twenty-four feet up to forty feet. Then they moved into the repair and maintenance of trawlers. Better still, the yard at Oldcourt is on the edge of the Ilen. He could watch the club rowers move up and down the river every day. No one was safe. If you stirred on the Ilen, Dominic knew. One moment he'd be working on a boat with Greg, the next he'd have vanished, reappearing down by the pier, shouting instructions to whoever he saw on the river, telling them what to do.

On the days he wasn't there, Dominic asked whoever was working to keep a count of how many boats went down past the boatyard. He never switched off.

'O'Donovan's was the workshop for the club as well,' Greg laughs. 'He would bring pieces over from the club. Weld this. Tack that. Back into the car and over to the club again. We always maintained he had shares in the boatyard! His love for the river is unreal.'

Dominic and Greg were heavily involved too in a top-secret plan that saw the two of them, with a helping hand from Michael Hegarty, build a twenty-four-foot fishing boat for Donal O'Donovan, which he would then sell. It was a half decker fishing boat called *Rock Rose*. In return, Donal would sponsor a rowing boat for the club. This was an inventive way of getting their hands on a new boat the club needed. But it was kept hush-hush. Only those involved were meant to know. From start to finish, for five months, Dominic and Greg would stay on in the boatyard after work and be there on Saturday mornings in order to build this boat, labour free, which was then sold. The money covered the cost of a new four. What lengths they went to for the club.

On his tea-break, lunch and on the way home in the evening, Dominic would stop at the club and cast his eyes over who was there and what they were doing. Each day he would follow the same routine and that rubbed off on everyone else. Nobody could say no to him. They saw what he was putting in and felt compelled to do likewise. At the club's regatta every year at the National Rowing Centre, he ropes in an army of volunteers to help over the weekend. It takes 100 volunteers to run. No one declines. They leave Skibb early and come home late. Dominic leaves earlier and is home later.

***

In writing this book one moment stands out above all others. It was the last time I called to Dominic's house for the final round of questions. After we'd finished, I was chatting with Eleanor and her friend in the kitchen. Dominic had disappeared.

Then I saw him again, standing in the hall and trying to get my attention. He didn't walk into the room. I had to go to him. He was holding something in his hand. It was a framed photo of his oldest daughter, Niamh, taken when she was twelve years old, having just won her first race for Skibbereen in 2009.

She took gold in the women's Junior–12 single scull at the Ghent International Regatta that year. Just before that 500-metre sprint, Dominic was with Niamh at the start. She told him she didn't want to race. He convinced her to. And she won.

This photo means a lot to him. It makes him smile. It was a proud moment. Niamh was the first of his four kids to row and to win.

Dominic has coached Skibbereen rowers to Olympic silver, world gold and European gold, been involved in some of the greatest moments in Irish rowing, and played his role in transforming the club into a National Championship-winning juggernaut, but this is the only photo throughout the process of writing this book that he showed me.

That's the moment I discovered a truer sense of who he is, why he does what he does and what matters to him. He thrives off watching athletes improve and fulfilling their potential. That's where the glory lies for him.

It means even more when he sees one of his own kids succeed. This is Dominic the dad.

***

In the weeks after the 2016 Olympics, Dominic wrote a message in white chalk on the blackboard hanging inside the door at the rowing club. It was for all the club rowers:

Well done Gary + Paul.
Can you follow in their footsteps?
Remember it is in your hands.

The last five words were underlined for impact.

Success breeds success. The Olympic silver medallists were still being feted when he laid down the challenge to the rest of the club.

He just never stops. A father. A friend. A coach. A motivator. Always going forward. And the rest will follow him. That's how this works.

epilogue

The initial plan was to serenade President Michael D. Higgins and his wife, Sabina, with one verse of 'Dear Old Skibbereen'. Seanie O'Brien said that wouldn't work. He stuck to his guns on this one: you can't just play one verse, because you will not get to the end of the song's story.

'Dear Old Skibbereen' means a lot to the town. It's Skibbereen's anthem. It was written by a local man, Patrick Carpenter, some time after the Great Famine. It shares the conversation between a lamenting father and his son as to why they had to leave Skibbereen during the famine. It remembers how the blight left the family on its knees, how they were evicted from their home by the English, how his young son's mother died and how they had to leave Skibb to survive, before ending by vowing revenge.

The quiet grave the father speaks of in the song sits across the way from the rowing club's HQ, on the other side of the Ilen. It's in the Abbey Cemetery, where thousands of coffin-less victims from the famine are buried.

The Dubliners, The Wolfe Tones and Sinead O'Connor have all sung it. But in Skibbereen, it means more. It's their song. It belongs to them.

It's sung by winning O'Donovan Rossa teams when they capture silverware. Skibbereen Rugby Club sing it too, when they win. It's a song that crosses all codes. It's about pride of place. The townspeople all know it well. And it was sung with great gusto by Seanie when

Skibbereen Rowing Club were invited to Áras an Uachtaráin for a special reception on Saturday 4 November 2017.

This was a momentous day for the club. It was the presidential seal of approval, the day when the club's exploits at national and international level were recognised.

This little club was being honoured on the big stage. They were special guests at the Áras. The president of Ireland opened his doors to them.

Seanie wasn't nervous as he stood before the president and his wife, who is the first cousin of Ned Cleary of the famous Cleary GAA dynasty in Castlehaven, just outside Skibbereen. Seanie has sung in pubs around the town for years. Go back further, and he was involved with The Peptones, an early Skibb pop group. After that he was with the trad group Toss the Feathers. He doesn't lack confidence when standing in front of a crowd, in other words. But this was different.

As 'Dear Old Skibbereen' echoed through the State Reception Room and floated into the State Dining Room and the grand Francini Corridor, it gained momentum and volume. The room full of proud Skibbereen people joined in.

Soon everyone was in full voice. Four minutes it lasted. It felt more like Seanie was singing in the Corner Bar back home instead of for the president of Ireland. It was a magical moment. The best of his life.

His wife, Siobhan, was front row at the Áras as Seanie added just the right chord of emotion to the occasion. They had sat together in one of the two packed buses, for just €10 return, that left the rowing club in Skibb that morning at nine. No one was late. Kenneth and Christine had everything organised. Invites had been issued in the weeks before. Then follow-up emails were sent out with all the details that anyone who was invited needed. The dress code was smart casual. No tracksuits or runners. Think jeans, chinos and dark shoes. Under–18s were asked to wear their Skibbereen Rowing Club half-zip top. Richard looked after the club ties; whoever needed a spare one came to him. This was organisation on a level that Dominic would be proud of.

In the State Drawing Room the president and his wife greeted the 150 guests one by one, including the three founding members, Richard, Danny and Donie. It felt like a family reunion.

Gary, Paul, Shane and Denise were there too. Mark was missing; he was a tutor at a rowing coaching development course and his diary was so crammed he couldn't reschedule. As many rowers as possible from past and present made the trip, including all the people in the background who have made the club's success possible. These are the people whose work goes unnoticed to the outside world, which only sees the medals and success. It's people like Seanie's wife Siobhan, Richard's wife Susan, Denise's mam Mary, who fed so many over the years.

'We always say that we could never do what we do unless the doors of the rowing club were open,' Gary explains. 'I have often said it goes deeper than the people who are directly involved in the rowing club. This is one of these special days where you get to show those people what they have done is worthwhile and important.'

Michael D. Higgins touched on this as he addressed the large Skibb gathering, when he spoke of the tireless work of volunteers, so many of whom are friends and family, stating that their work is vital.

The president had just returned to Ireland from a state visit to Australia and New Zealand. While in Melbourne, a city with nearly four million, he looked out on the Yarra River, 150 miles long, which is home to six rowing clubs.

'Compare this to Skibbereen and its surrounding townlands, an area of 11,000 people, and the twenty-one-mile length of the Ilen,' he continued, before adding, 'and yet, for all their advantages, the rowing clubs of Melbourne returned the same number of medals as Skibbereen for its country in the recent Olympic Games.'

President Higgins went on to laud this 'extraordinary club' that has put Irish rowing on the international map. He hailed the club as an example 'of what can be achieved when communities work together towards a common good'.

By the end of the event, which ran well over the allotted two hours, President Higgins was presented with a club tie and told that he was now an honorary member of Skibbereen Rowing Club, the most successful rowing club in the country.

acknowledgements

I've survived my first book. The casualties were sleep, my hair colour and a car tyre punctured on the way to Nuala Lupton's house at Tralispean outside Skibbereen.

When this book was just an idea, I met Patrick O'Donoghue of Mercier Press for a coffee and a chat. We talked about this project and its possibilities. I was a newbie. He warned me that the rabbit hole of a project such as this can be a lonely place.

I was naïve. This was longer and a lot harder than I expected. But it's the people involved who made it worthwhile. This book only came about thanks to each and every person who helped, inspired, advised, listened to, talked to and tolerated me.

The first person I have to thank is my better half, Eilish. Without her support and backing, this book was a non-runner. She held the fort at home to give me the time to tackle this; she had the patience to listen to my ramblings when I was trying to piece together this huge jigsaw, and she wasn't slow in kicking me up the arse, metaphorically, when I needed a jolt during those long days when the finish line seemed so far in the distance that I couldn't see it. Thanks, Lish.

To our three children, Cian, Callum and Layla, thanks for making Mom's life that little bit easier when I was missing in action so much during this process.

To the nans, Carmel and Mary, and Granda Denis – thanks for the support and the babysitting too, and also to Grand-aunt Kathleen, who gave over a room in her home as a 'studio' to write this book. I'll get around to paying that rent at a later stage …

The people involved in Skibbereen Rowing Club are incredible. They are among the finest and most genuine I have ever met. They are the reason this book was written and their support, backing and interest were paramount to piecing this story together. Thanks to each and every club member, past and present, who took the time to meet me, let me into their homes, answered my endless calls and texts, pointed me in the right direction and helped answer the countless queries I had.

One little anecdote stands out that shows the lengths to which club members went to help. When I met then club chairman Tony Walsh, I asked him what car his daughter Denise drove. It's the small details I was looking for.

'A black Golf.'

Ideal. Thanks.

'I'll get you her number plate,' Tony added.

'Ah, no need. I've enough there.'

The following day this text message came through: 'Kieran. Denise car black vw golf' and a number plate.

Again, it just highlights how helpful each and every club member was.

There are some club members whom I hounded more than most and they deserve to be mentioned. Thanks Dominic and Eleanor for opening the door of your house and your lives and allowing me the access that I needed to do justice to the club's and Dominic's incredible story. A massive thanks too to Kenneth and Denise, whom I've had on speed dial and been in contact with more than anyone during this process. Their knowledge and insight and patience with my constant questions were a huge help.

Huge thanks also to Eugene in London, Diarmuid in Sydney, Shane in Skibb, Nuala in Tralispean, Emily in Skibb, and Gary and Paul for their assistance.

Of course, the club's three founding members, Richard, Danny and Donie, are the reason for all this, and all three shared their stories and dipped into their memories.

Also, thanks to all those in the Irish rowing family who have helped with brilliant anecdotes and nuggets of information from their own interactions with Skibbereen Rowing Club, as well as anyone else who contributed to this book.

The team at Mercier have been top-class and a joy to deal with from the very start. Patrick ensured there was always a light at the end of the rabbit hole. His patience and encouragement were a huge help. Thanks too to editor Noel for his brilliance in joining the dots and making all the pieces fall into place. Thanks also to Deirdre, Wendy, Sarah and everyone in Mercier who played their part.

Thanks to Eamonn for his words of advice and pointers in the right direction, and to all my colleagues at *The Southern Star* for their words of encouragement.

Various archives were a huge help in piecing together this jigsaw, including *The Southern Star*'s archive, irishrowingarchives.com and the Irish Newspaper Archive. They are all invaluable treasure troves that need to be minded and supported.

One book down. Older and wiser. Would I do it all again?

Where is the entrance to that rabbit hole?

about the author

Kieran McCarthy is the long-time sports editor of *The Southern Star*, West Cork's weekly newspaper. A Kerry native, he won the Local Ireland Sports Story of the Year in 2016 for his coverage of Skibbereen Rowing Club. He was also awarded the title of Ladies Gaelic Football Association Local Journalist of the Year in 2018. This is his first book.